THIS IS MY SONG

Since hitting the spotlight at the age of ten, Petula Clark has appeared in more than thirty films, cut millions of discs in a variety of languages and become an internationally acclaimed star. Yet, until now, little has been known of the real person behind the headlines. Never before has she spoken of her true relationship with her father, or of the romances which preceded her marriage to Frenchman Claude Wolff, or of the mystery illness which has led to enormous speculation about her present health. In this book and for the first time, Petula tells, with her friends, the real and often sad story behind the public smile.

THIS IS MY SONG

A Biography Of
Petula Clark

ANDREA KON

A New Portway Large Print Book

CHIVERS PRESS
BATH

First published 1983
by
W. H. Allen & Co Ltd
This Large Print edition published by
Chivers Press
by arrangement with W. H. Allen & Co Ltd
at the request of
The London & Home Counties Branch
of
The Library Association
1984

ISBN 0 85119 279 3

British Library Cataloguing in Publication Data

Kon, Andrea
   This is my song.—Large print ed.—
   (A New Portway large print book)
   1. Clark, Petula   2. Singers—England—
   Biography
   I. Title
   784.5'0092'4   ML420.C5/

   ISBN 0–85119–279–3

For Stanley, Simone and Lucie

'And what can we expect if we
haven't any dinner
But to lose our teeth and eyelashes
and keep on growing thinner.'

Edward Lear
The Akond of Swat
1888 Edition

CONTENTS

AUTHOR'S NOTE

This is not an authorised biography of Petula Clark and, since hopefully, she will continue to entertain throughout the world for many years to come, it cannot be a complete one.

Although she has made it clear that she would rather this book had been left unwritten, I am indebted to her for spending so many hours with me in her dressing room at London's Apollo Victoria Theatre during the *Sound of Music* run. I know there were days when she was tired and under the weather and times when remembering the past became painful. Nevertheless, her help in setting the record straight and our frank conversations on previously unreported facets of her life were invaluable and greatly appreciated. Thanks too must extend to her husband, Claude Wolff, for the time he spent with me in Paris and to her daughter, Katy, both of whom took time and trouble to help me.

Many people who know and admire Petula have co-operated with me in the preparation of this story of a unique British and international star, sharing with me their memories—some glad, some sad. Special gratitude must go to Cecil Madden MBE, a pioneer of British Broadcasting and the world's first TV producer, formerly Assistant Controller of Programmes

(BBC TV) who at the grand age of seventy-nine opened his home and his wonderful private archives to me, just as he opened his heart to Petula more than forty years ago.

Thanks too to Bobby Jaye, Head of BBC Light Entertainment (radio); to John Billingham, Manager, International Recordings Unit, BBC; to Stephen Williams, Seymour De Lotbiniere, Charles Chilton, Denis Main-Wilson and Yvonne Littlewood and to Jackie Kavanagh and her staff at the BBC's Written Archives at Caversham who were all so patient and helpful as were the staff of the British Film Institute and the National Film Archive. Thanks, too, to Peter Phillips and ATV Music for permission to use the lyrics for 'I Couldn't Live Without Your Love'.

So many of Petula's family, friends and colleagues took the time and trouble to see me that it is impossible to list them all. My thanks to them all—and especially to her aunt, Emma Rose in Ystrad Mynach, her cousins Clive Rose in Montreal and Shirley Vaughan in London; to Theo Cowan, Alan Freeman, Tony Hatch, Jack Fishman, Betty Box, Peter Ustinov and George Mitchell in the UK; to Sacha Distel, Charles Aznavour, Pierre Delanoe and Leon Cabat on the continent and to Leslie Bricusse, Frank Owens and Anthony Newley in the USA—for all their help and for searching back through the years and their memories.

I am also extremely grateful to Ross Taylor for all his help and for so readily volunteering to write the foreword to this book; to Barbra Paskin and Eleanor Silver for their help with research and last but by no means least my husband Stanley for his constant encouragement and advice and my daughters Simone and Lucie for manning an excellent telephone answering service and for their tolerance with an often impatient mother.

Andrea Kon
August 1982

FOREWORD

In my long and varied career in the theatre, whenever I have worked with what the general public term a 'star' I am often asked, 'What is the person like?' and I always reply, 'Which person?' There are so many dimensions that make up the complexities of a 'star': talent, ambition, kindness, single-mindedness, devotion, professionalism and humility are just a few of the ingredients.

There are many sides to Petula Clark's outstanding talents, but the one I would single out most is her utter professionalism and devotion to her audiences and fellow artists. But if I was ever asked, 'Do you know the "real" Petula Clark?' I would have to answer truthfully 'No'. In our close association over the past two years, during the creation and playing of *The Sound of Music*, whilst I have glimpsed Petula—the musical comedy star, Petula—the TV star, Petula—the actress, Petula—the mother, Petula—the friend and most certainly Petula—the star that brings audiences to their feet nightly, I have always felt that there is still an area of herself which Petula—and Petula alone—knows and understands.

I hope that between the pages of this book, you will come to love and understand this remarkable lady, and know her as I have done over the last couple of years as a survivor in this the toughest profession in the world. When the final accolades are handed out for the greatest performances in musical comedy history, alongside Ethel Merman's 'Annie', Mary Martin's 'Nellie Forbush' and Angela Lansbury's 'Mame', I know there will be placed Petula Clark's stunning portrayal of 'Maria' in *The Sound of Music* on the London stage. This is just one facet of her many talents. Long may she continue climbing her mountains and achieving the greatness she so richly deserves.

Ross Taylor
London, August 1982

THIS IS MY SONG

INTRODUCTION

The little band of children clustered anxiously round the tall, blond director in the sandbagged underground theatre that served as a wartime studio.

They had just finished a scrumptious tea in what had once been the crush bar, with real egg sandwiches, chocolate cream éclairs, jelly, ice-cream and orange squash, tastes of a peacetime few but the eldest among them could remember. Now it was time for business.

They were all obviously nervous at the thought of the messages they would be sending within the next hour to their fathers, brothers and uncles serving overseas, across the airwaves of the BBC's British Empire Service. For many of these children, the men who longed to hear their voices were not people but faces in a photo on the mantelpiece. They were fighting in deserts or on the high seas or monitoring the air-corridors of the world so that their children might look forward to a peaceful and free future.

The children chattered and giggled nervously amongst themselves. It was the job of director Stephen Williams to calm them.

'Is there anybody here who would like to do something to entertain us—recite perhaps?' he asked, using the formula he used every week. It was almost an academic question since no child had ever volunteered since the programme's inception three years before. But this time, from somewhere at the back of the group, he saw a small hand waving wildly.

Its owner was a tiny girl with blonde, shoulderlength curly hair and stunningly clear blue eyes. Williams pulled her forward. She only looked about seven although the label pinned to her hand-knitted jumper told him she was nine years and eleven months.

'What can you do?' he asked.

'Nellie Wallace,' she replied boldly and to his huge amusement, since the lady whose imitation she proffered was a well-worn, raucous comedienne; certainly not a character he would have expected a fragile-looking child to want to imitate.

Tongue-in-cheek, he told her to go ahead. To his amazement—and to the complete surprise of everyone watching in the control room—she gave a remarkably accurate and hilariously funny impersonation of the old lady. Williams sent an urgent message to the Assistant Controller of Programmes, Cecil Madden: 'Come and see this—quick.'

'I can do other imitations too,' she announced self-confidently as the gaunt, bespectacled figure of Madden emerged from his hated paperwork in his office, a converted star's

2

dressing-room.

'Vera Lynn, Sophie Tucker, Shnozzle Durante.'

'Let's have the lot then,' he ordered, a smile playing on his lips at the very idea of this mite imitating the ugly Shnozzle. 'Would you like a piano to accompany you?'

'Oh, no. I want the entire orchestra, please!' she replied politely.

The twenty-five piece orchestra, led by the famous Jack Leon, squirmed. Precocious kids, even pretty ones, were a phenomenon they could live without just half an hour before a live broadcast to troops stationed in isolated parts of the world on this wet, wartime Saturday afternoon. The child, however, appeared totally oblivious of their discomfort.

'I'll sing "Mighty Like a Rose",' she told them. Pianist Mark Dembina gave her the key. Cecil Madden nodded his approval so, unenthusiastically, they struck up, busking since no music to the famous Paul Robeson song was to hand.

To everyone's amazement, the sound which burst forth from Petula's mouth was sheer joy. She was perfectly in tune and the music she made so overwhelmingly sweet and sincere that by the time the last notes died away, the entire orchestra was on its feet.

Madden, the studio manager, Williams, numerous technicians and even the tea-boy burst into spontaneous applause and clapped until their hands were sore in appreciation of her outstanding performance.

The date was 17 October 1942. Madden, Williams and the rest of the team were preparing to send another programme in the weekly series *It's All Yours*. They had just 'discovered' Petula Clark and were about to offer her her first chance to broadcast on the international airwaves at the start of a career which would make her name a household word from Japan to the Baltic and from Australasia to the USA.

But there was one person in the makeshift studio that afternoon who was not in the least surprised by the small girl's enormous impact. 7957203 Corporal Leslie Norman Clark—Petula's father. He was a slight, handsome man with an Errol Flynn moustache, wearing battledress and sporting the unique silver badge of the Royal Armoured Corps. He was watching the proceedings with silent delight. He had, after all, known and encouraged his daughter's talent from the time she could lisp 'Baa Baa Black Sheep'. He had laid his plans carefully to engineer this chance for his little girl.

All his life, Leslie Clark had suffered the frustrations of a thwarted theatrical career—a career which he *knew* would have been successful if only he'd had the chance to prove himself. Now he could see a chance of fulfilling

4

these dreams, at least in part, through his daughter. He could picture himself basking in the reflected rays of her rise to stardom. And, unlike his own parents who had stamped so hard on his potential and crushed his youthful dreams, he was determined to push his own child just as far as she could go.

CHAPTER ONE

DOWN IN THE VALLEY

The Welsh are renowned throughout the world for their lyrical, soulful music. Petula Clark was born of a Welsh mother and the haunting tunes from the Valleys were as much a part of her life as breathing from the day she was born.

Her mother, Doris Phillips, was the second daughter of a South Wales miner, William Phillips and his wife Jane, whose families had dug the dirty treasure from beneath the deceptive green hills for generations. With her two sisters, Emma and Olwen, Doris grew up in one of a huddle of two-up, two-down, bathroomless terraced cottages which made up the small, sloping village of Abercanaid near Merthyr Tydfil.

It was a tight, close-knit community. Everyone knew everyone else's business.

William and Jane raised their girls within the confines of the strict, religious, Welsh non-conformist traditions in which they themselves had grown up. There were prayer readings two or three evenings a week, chapel three times on Sunday. Doris sang in the chapel choir and had a notably sweet and pure voice which earned her quite a reputation. In those days, there was no cinema in Abercanaid; no community hall or other recreational facilities for the young. Outside the chapel, the only respite open to the small community was the village pub, the *Colliers Arms*, owned by a second cousin of the Phillips. It was there that the menfolk could drown the sights and smells of the all-pervading dust that filled their lungs and their lives by downing pints of bitter and enjoying the music they made themselves as their only means of entertainment.

As children, Doris and her sisters were oblivious to any other kind of life even a dozen miles from their doorstep, but their parents were determined that, no matter what sacrifices they made, it was a world their daughters would be given every opportunity to explore and, to that end, they would be given a decent education.

All three became nurses. Nursing was an excellent if somewhat tough career for a girl from the Valleys in those uncertain times. When, in the Depression of the late twenties,

6

even work in that highly trained field became scarce, Doris, along with thousands of others, emigrated to London in search of a job. Eventually, she found work in a mental hospital near Epsom in Surrey and it was there that she met and fell in love with a male nurse from the Chichester area, Leslie Norman Clark.

Leslie, or Norman as he was known to his family, had both an eye for, and a way with, the ladies. He had yearned for a theatrical career but his parents had blocked him at an early age, insisting instead that he followed a career in medicine.

'My father ran away from home when he was about fourteen and joined a travelling theatre company,' Petula says. 'My grandfather chased after him and found him. He was working as a general dogsbody and was discovered halfway up a flight of stairs, hauling a great pail of bathwater to one of the dressing-rooms. My grandfather dragged him home in disgrace and he was never allowed to mention going on the stage again.' The subject was forbidden in the Clark household, but yearnings for what might have been remained with Leslie all his life.

When Doris, the innocent young Welsh girl, first met Leslie she was bowled over by the amorous attentions of the attractive and seemingly worldly young man. They were married in early 1932. Her parents could not travel to London for the wedding as Doris's sister, Olwen, was dying and they felt that their place was with her. It was Norman's father who gave the bride away. On 15 November their first child, a daughter, was born. They registered her quite simply as Sally.

Almost from the day of her birth, Leslie Clark hoped that his own thwarted ambitions might be realised at second-hand through his daughter. One of the first requirements for being noticed in show-business, he knew, was an unusual, eye-catching Christian name.

'I've always been known as Petula,' she says. 'My father used to love to tell me how, when I was born, the first girl in the family for many years, all my aunts wanted me to be named after them. But he wouldn't have it.'

Instead, with the same force of character that later activated him to push his daughter's career, he claimed that he combined the names of two old flames, Pet and Ula, and bestowed the union on his baby daughter. In reference books, she is blessed with a trio of forenames—Petula Sally Olwen. But her birth certificate confirms that, at the time of her birth, she possessed just a single, unadventurous one.

Her first home was a modest detached house in a quiet suburban cul-de-sac at 20 Salmon's Road, Ewell. Petula's aunt, Mrs Emma Rose, now a retired midwife who still lives at Ystrad Mynach only twenty or so miles from Abercanaid, remembers she was a slim, wiry

8

baby; the sort who doesn't sleep much. She closely resembles both her mother and grandmother in looks. Like most toddlers, she was extremely active and inquisitive and great pals with the family's pet mongrel dog, Bing.

When she was only about eleven months old, it was Bing who in fact saved her life. The house at Salmon's Road was one of a million such homes erected during the building boom of the early thirties. At the time the Clarks moved in, the estate was far from complete, and one day, when Doris's back was turned for a split second, little Petula toddled out of the back door and into a concrete-lined pit left by careless builders. Bing caught her by the seat of her nappy and hung on until her screams of terror alerted Doris who came running to the rescue.

Doris loved to sing as she went about her housework and Petula soon picked up the songs her mother sang and repeated them with gusto. Leslie, who was still nursing in the same hospital, loved to spend his off-duty hours reading to her and making up games which fired her imagination.

Petula was three years old when her sister Barbara was born. Doris had contracted TB during her nursing days and wasn't always well. After the birth of her second child, she found it quite a struggle to cope with an active toddler as well as the new baby so her eldest daughter was left to play on her own a great deal.

'I lived in a world of dreams,' Petula reminisces. 'I would trot on errands in the rain with my coat flapping open, usually forgetting completely what I'd been sent out for by the time I got to the shops. I'm sure that the neighbours all thought I was slightly mad. I probably was.

'In summer, I would go out into the garden to pick raspberries and while I was picking them I would sing to myself like Mummy or tell myself stories like Daddy did. Of course, there never were any raspberries left. I'd eaten them all.'

As little more than a toddler, she discovered the equally delectable taste of pickled onions. She was only about three when her mother caught her in the larder one day, harpooning pickled onions from a jar with a stolen knitting needle. She was soundly spanked for the raid, but it had no effect whatever on her passion for pickled onions. Years later, she couldn't confront a pickled onion without gobbling it greedily. And when she was working with celebrated stars like the late Sid Field and Peter O'Toole, they conceded gracefully to swallowing them too that she might enjoy her fill.

Like most small girls, she loved dressing up in her mothers' clothes with her make-up splodged somewhat haphazardly on her face, imitating the singers she heard on the radio, but she was equally happy shinning up trees which defeated many older boys and jeering at them from the top.

Best of all, she loved being taken on visits to her maternal grandparents who still lived in the small cottage in David's Square, Abercanaid, where Doris had been born. Her own memories of those visits are vivid and treasured. Among the pits and the poverty, she was showered with warmth and love; the wonderful sounds of the singing Welsh people and Grandma Phillips' mouthwatering lamb stews and delicious home-made Welsh cakes, cooked on the open range in the tiny, homely kitchen. She still drools at the thought of the hot, flat currant-spotted scones, thickly spread with butter and jam.

'My grandmother had two china Pekinese dogs which were kept on the dresser and I was frankly terrified of them. I remember thinking them odd and old-fashioned at the time. How I'd love to have them today,' she says.

She clearly adored her grandparents just as they worshipped her. By the time she was four, it was apparent that she had inherited a crystal-clear voice from the 'Welsh side' of the family and nothing pleased the old couple more than when they heard their granddaughter sing just as her mother had done as a child.

Petula also had an amazing talent for memorising tunes and mimicking lyrics and accents. It was a gift which, only half a dozen years later, would give so much heart and hope

11

to thousands of homesick soldiers stationed continents away from their own children and would bring them closer to the families they had left behind.

On those visits to the valleys, as a very small child, Pet—as the family called her—gave her first public performances. She would stand on a table at the *Colliers Arms* just a blow of coal-dust from her grandparents' home, singing her way merrily through her repertoire which included imitations of Vera Lynn's beloved tunes she had picked up from the radio. Usually, by the time her performance had ended, even the hard-boiled, pickaxe-wielding miners would be left standing, pint in hand, mesmerised by the child's magic.

Everyone in Abercanaid—and in Pontlottyn, the village in the neighbouring valley where her Aunt Emma lived with her husband Bert and their children Clive and Shirley—knew Petula as a rather shy, introverted child who would hide coyly behind her grandmother's skirts and would rarely utter a word until she was asked to 'give us a song'. Then, her entire personality would metamorphosise as, shyness forgotten, she would delight in entertaining even total strangers. Singing was so natural to her that she never considered anything odd about suddenly bursting into song wherever she happened to be. She would arrive in Wales after a train trip from London, her pockets full of pennies, and

12

explain that she'd been given them in exchange for amusing her fellow travellers. When she popped into the sweet shop next door to Uncle Bert's grocery store, she would inevitably return with handfuls of sweets—tangible appreciation of an off-the-cuff performance. And, even though her sister Barbara was little more than two at this time, she was always conscious of her role as 'big sister' and ensured that she had her share.

At the age of five, Petula was enrolled as a pupil at Moor Lane Elementary School at Hook near Chessington, just a few minutes walk from home. Today, the building serves as an Infants and Junior School but in those days it housed children of up to fourteen years in a single, turn-of-the-century building. The infants were on the top floor. Her first headmaster was Mr J. B. Loveless whose name, according to Petula, was no reflection on the general atmosphere of the place. She was never bound for academic excellence; she had other talents to compensate. But her early schooldays were exceptionally happy ones. It was the first (and as it later transpired, only) chance she ever had of mixing with children of her own age on an equal footing. Yet having been left so much to her own devices at home, Petula found it hard to be one of a crowd.

'Even at five, I couldn't seem to get myself into one of the gangs,' she says ruefully. 'They

13

weren't yobbo gangs or anything like that—just a group of kids who banded together. I did make some friends, of course. Christine Minchington and Pamela Coe were my two special pals. They couldn't break into the gangs either so the three of us used to stick together.'

But the need for approval from her contemporaries was intense, nevertheless. To get it, she resorted to the only way she knew of attracting attention; by giving imitations of the famous performers she'd heard on the wireless and on her father's collection of gramophone records.

She would stand on a desk, surrounded by a crowd of eager children and amuse them during the break periods with impersonations of their favourites, always leaving them demanding 'more'. Yet, if her special talents gained her the approval of her classmates, they did not always provoke the same kind of response from her teachers.

'In singing lessons, the tunes we had to sing were often boring,' she says. 'Occasionally, I would put in a few obligatos just to brighten things up a bit.' But her musical initiative earned her more than a few sharp raps on the knuckles and, to her dismay, she was once even banned from singing in the school choir for such an outright display of 'showing off'. For the youngest soloist in the school, this was indeed a tragedy.

14

Nevertheless, even in those early years, there were some members of staff who recognised that there was more than mere egoism in Petula's performances. When Petula appeared in *The Sound of Music* in 1982, she received a letter from the daughter of one of her ex-teachers, Mrs Westlake, reminding Petula how her mother had often told the story of the little girl who sang her way through 'Carmen Miranda' during an air-raid: 'My mother would so have loved your current success, but unfortunately she died ten years ago. She always followed your career closely and saw your TV performances. Being of the older generation, she did not approve of *all* your songs.'

Petula was just six years old when Leslie decided it was time to introduce her to the serious theatre. He took her to see Flora Robson in a production of *Mary Tudor* at a local theatre in nearby Kingston.

'I suppose the play was rather heavy-going for a child of that age,' she laughs, 'but I made up my mind then and there that I was going to be an actress; a straight actress. I wanted to be Ingrid Bergman more than anything else in the world.'

She was at an age when most parents nod tolerantly at their children's plans for the future, but, with his own crushed aspirations still smouldering beneath the surface, Leslie Clark actually took his daughter seriously.

Petula's other heroine at that time was singer Vera Lynn whom she loved to mimic. But although Leslie knew that Pet had a very sweet voice, he didn't realise just how clever she was at impersonations until early one morning when, after a hard night's shiftwork, he fell into bed exhausted. Suddenly he heard what he believed was the wireless, blaring out a Vera Lynn song.

'For Pete's sake, Doris, turn it off,' he yelled irately. 'I want to get some shut-eye.'

'That's not the radio, it's our Pet,' Doris replied as the song ceased abruptly. Leslie's tiredness disappeared. He had honestly thought it was the radio. If Petula could sing like that and fool even her father, then he *knew* she possessed a very special talent. He also knew that it was up to him to nurture such natural ability and create from it a profession—but that, without any show-biz contacts of his own, it would need some very clever scheming on his part.

He didn't have to wait long before his first opportunity arose to display her talent in public. A neighbour approached him and asked him if he would allow Petula to sing at a charity concert in the local church hall. Leslie, of course, agreed and the little girl chose to perform her favourite song of that moment: Vera Lynn's 'Alice Blue Gown'. As the diminutive figure, wearing an appropriate pale blue summer frock, stood on the platform awaiting her introductory notes, the amateur pianist struck up the wrong key. Much to Leslie's surprise, Petula ignored it and started in the right one with no prompting at all!

Leslie was encouraged by the warmth of her reception and the huge applause she received when the song was ended. He entered her for a talent contest at a local garden fête at New Malden which she won outright. It was the first round in a county competition and the finals were held in a local cinema. Again she triumphed against more than thirty other children, many of them much older than her seven years.

But the year was 1939. The world was changing. Only a year previously, Chamberlain had returned from Munich waving his infamous piece of paper claiming a promise of peace from Adolph Hitler. Yet war-rumours mounted throughout that summer. On 1 September, the Germans marched into Poland.

It was to be a war of such chaos and horror that few could conceive on that sunny, September morning. A war that would drag on for six long years and would change the face of Europe. To the Clark family this dark and horrible war was to offer Petula a unique chance she might never otherwise have had.

CHAPTER TWO

MIGHTY LIKE A ROSE

The Clark family's reaction to the news was the same as that of thousands of other London parents. Their children must be moved out of the capital, and away from the dire warnings of bombing raids, with all possible haste. But with both grandparents and an aunt in Wales, there was no need for Petula and Barbara to be billeted with strangers as evacuees. At first, they all camped as best they could at the house in David's Square. Petula vividly remembers bath nights in a tin tub in front of the open kitchen range. But space was tight in the tiny house so it was decided to move the children to Pontlottyn in the next valley where there was plenty of room for them in the four-bedroomed maisonette above Bert Rose's grocery shop.

With the resilience of the young, Petula soon settled down—and learned among other things to speak fluent Welsh. She was enrolled at the village school her cousin Clive attended, and, in Clive, she discovered a very special soul-mate.

The two were almost exactly the same age. Clive had had a twin sister who had died soon after birth and he looked on his tomboy cousin as a replacement for her. Petula remembers how he taught her to climb trees properly—and how she always managed to pull herself one branch above him. And how they would sneak tin trays from her Aunt Emma's kitchen and carry them to the top of the slag-heaps on the outskirts of the village. There, they would crouch on them and slide down the tip with all the joy of a helter-skelter ride, landing in a coal-dust-covered heap at the bottom, and then haul the trays back up to the top again to make the descent as many times as they could before supper. Pet's childish glee at the freedom Wales offered her—probably the only real freedom she was ever to know—and her delight in her relationship with Clive is still evident.

Back at home above the shop, the four children would turn on the old-fashioned, wind-up gramophone and dance and sing until the customers below complained about the noise. Then Pet's Aunt Emma would wield a broomstick, bash the ceiling and issue dire warnings of 'mind the mantle', referring to the gas mantle which was the only form of lighting in the house. Hiding from Aunt Emma and Uncle Bert was another favourite pastime when the weather prevented trips to the slag-heaps. Emma Rose has never quite forgiven Petula for the day when she jumped out at her, straight on to the sofa and a treasured pile of '78 records, smashing the lot!

But if, at seven, she was already breaking

records, Petula was also making an earnest attempt to get into films, too.

'The local cinema was a real flea-pit,' Petula says. 'We were too young to be allowed in legally—and that was the great thing. We tried every trick in the book. We dressed up in "borrowed" finery—Clive in his father's trilby and long trousers—me in my mother's feather-trimmed hat and high heels and with all her make-up on. When that didn't work, we tried climbing in through the toilet windows or walking in backwards because we thought that made it look as though we were coming out! The manager soon got to know us and we used to hear him sighing, "Look out. Here they come again!" Clive was really a very naughty boy—and I suppose I wasn't that good myself. We were a right pair.'

If she revelled in her escapades with Clive, she also much envied her little cousin Shirley's looks. 'She had the most beautiful long black curly hair. I had blonde, wispy, flyaway locks. I wanted hair like Shirley's so badly that I used to get my mother to tie mine in rags every night. It was most uncomfortable and the end result was that I looked like Topsy.'

After the first six months of what was later termed the 'phoney' war, and when the first frightening warnings of a London Blitz seemed just to have been 'panic war-talk', Leslie who had now signed up and been posted to

20

Farnborough, brought his family back to London. Petula returned to Moor Lane School—and life resumed some semblance of normality.

One of her greatest treats was to be taken to Bentalls, a large department store in Kingston, to shop. As was usual in many London stores, Bentalls had a band which played regularly in the escalator hall for the pleasure of customers who might be persuaded to take tea in the restaurant and dance their cares away for an hour or two. One day when Petula and Leslie were visiting the store, Harry Fryer and his orchestra were playing. Petula stood with her father, listening for a while, tapping her feet and humming to the melodies.

'Oh! I wish I could sing with them, Daddy,' she breathed wistfully.

'Well, let's see if we can arrange it, then,' replied Leslie, always the optimist. He approached the bandstand.

'I have a daughter who would very much like to sing with you,' he told Fryer. 'She has sung in public before at local concerts.'

'Where is the young lady?' asked kindly Harry Fryer—and was somewhat taken aback when Leslie introduced a small child. Gulping back his surprise, he put his hand out solemnly to shake hers.

'Hello, darling. So you want to sing with me, do you?'

21

'Yes please,' Petula answered, entirely at ease.

'What songs do you know,' he inquired, expecting a nursery-rhyme reply.

'Do you know "Mighty Like a Rose"?'

'I think so,' Fryer answered. 'But I don't know if we have it in your key.'

He thought the whole thing was a huge joke, but his tolerant smile rapidly changed to a gasp of amazement as the little girl launched into her song. When she'd finished, Fryer called for the booking manager and asked her to repeat her turn. The next thing she knew, she had been booked for her first professional date; a week-long engagement singing with Fryer's band in the escalator hall. Since she was only eight years old, she couldn't be paid for her appearances. Her first wages were the biggest jar of sweets she'd ever seen—and a gold wrist-watch she lost within the week.

The end of the booking was by no means the end of Petula's relationship with Harry Fryer. He played other local dates using her as his vocalist. Having a small child on the bill was a popular draw and, as Leslie was the first to see, performing with a live band was proving a useful experience. Fryer soon discovered her aptitude for mimicry, too. He had only to play a record a couple of times and she was able to reproduce it perfectly, adapting it quite naturally to a suitable key.

While Petula was learning the art of giving professional performances, Leslie, boosted by Fryer's interest and encouragement, was busy learning technical tricks. He knew that if he was to turn Petula into Britain's answer to Shirley Temple, he would need rather more advice than he could cadge from a bandleader. He made it his business to become friendly with the stage-manager of the old Kingston Empire Variety Theatre. At night, when Petula was safely tucked up in bed, he would stroll round there and chat to the man who soon acknowledged him as a friend. In this way, he scavenged as many hints as he could on how to set a stage, how to light it and how artistes performed both before and behind the footlights.

He passed on all these tips to Petula, turning the lessons into a wonderful game—although he was in deadly earnest. At the age of eight, she was no novice to the tricks of the stage.

By 1941, the predicted Blitz had at last hit London with a terrifying vengeance. Leslie was still stationed at Farnborough and, for a short while, he moved Doris, Petula and Barbara back to the safety of Wales. Then he made a vital decision. There was no outlet for his daughter's potential among the coal-tips. Everybody sang in Wales. But in and around London, troops needed a respite from their duties. One afternoon he mentioned, quite casually, to his Commanding Officer that he had a little daughter who had sung professionally. Did the CO think it might be a good idea if she gave his colleagues a concert? The CO thought it was a marvellous idea. He immediately invited Petula to come and do just that. It was a stroke of genius on Leslie's part. Of course, the men loved her and immediately decided to adopt her as their mascot. Leslie had a little uniform made for her, complete with forage cap. The Royal Armoured Corps presented her with one of the unit's unique silver badges which she wore with great pride.

Word soon spread about the remarkable child artiste. She was invited to give another troop concert—and then another. It was generally agreed among Leslie's army chiefs that Leslie was performing a useful service for other troops by encouraging Petula, and he was given leave to accompany her all over the country to these troop shows. By early 1942, she had already performed at no fewer than fifty.

It was not only the British troops who benefited from these performances. Americans who had come to Britain enjoyed them, too. Petula was invited to sing at the newly opened Rainbow Corner—so-called because of the rainbow stripes the GIs, who congregated in the Leicester Square area, wore on their uniforms. The American Red Cross had taken over and converted a theatre in Piccadilly Circus as a showpiece canteen and leisure centre for these men. The place was a wonderful haven for the GIs with theatres, cinemas, lounges and games rooms, a restaurant and even a hobbies centre.

But, for ambitious Leslie, even this was not enough. The song 'Don't Put Your Daughter on the Stage, Mrs Worthington' might have been written with him in mind. He was rapidly shaping up as the stage-father to beat all stage-mothers.

Like most other British families, the Clarks had a number of close family and friends serving in the forces overseas. The British Empire Service of the BBC ran a special weekly request programme, *It's All Yours*, for service men and women posted thousands of miles from home. It wasn't long before Leslie had the idea that this programme might, with a bit of luck be turned to his, and Petula's advantage.

Each week, the War Office, the Air Ministry and the Naval departments submitted a list of requests from the men asking for messages from specified young relatives. For some it might, indeed, be the first time they had heard the voices of children who had been newly born when they'd left home. About twenty such requests each week were channelled back to the British Empire Service and the children's families were contacted and invited to a tea-party at the Criterion Theatre, chosen as a makeshift studio because its auditorium was the deepest in London.

As soon as these invitations were accepted, the men involved were informed so that they could be excused any duties well in advance and standby to listen to the half-hour broadcast. The request to hear Petula's voice came from one Sapper Barry Leek and, since Pet herself has no recollection of a relative of that name, it must be presumed that he was a friend of Leslie's. Somehow Leslie had managed to get a message through to him, asking him to request some news from Petula.

The programme was, of course, broadcast live and since tiny tots were often involved, there was no knowing what might happen. 17 October 1942, the day Petula was invited to tea, proved to be an eventful one for the producers of *It's All Yours*.

*　　*　　*

Another of the children present on that day— when the Government had just announced that there were to be even further transport restrictions in the Midlands, German raider planes had been shot down on the British coast and British aircraft had launched a massive offensive on enemy territory—was Colin Hamilton, now a producer of BBC's World Service *Outlook* programme, but then just another three-year-old whose father was serving in Iraq.

Says the programme's producer, Stephen Williams: 'We always laid on a super tea before a broadcast. On Bank Holidays and in fine weather, this would often take the form of an outing with a picnic in Regent's Park or on Primrose Hill. I always felt that it was my job to try to do something with these youngsters that their own fathers might have done if times had been normal.'

The day of Petula and Colin's visit was, however, wet and windy. Autumn was setting in. Tea over, Williams as usual asked the volunteers to sing or recite. Petula, prompted by Leslie, raised her hand at just the right moment. The like of the events which followed had never been witnessed in a BBC studio before. When she'd finished her party-piece, Madden and Williams made a hurried decision. She would send her message in the normal way along with the other children. But, before the programme closed, she would sing, solo, a repetition of her earlier performance.

It meant, of course, that three minutes of the planned programme schedule would have to be cut. It was Cecil Madden who decreed that the chop would fall on the slot regularly occupied by Ted and Barbara Andrews. They didn't take too kindly to the news that they were to be set aside at such short notice, even though they were still to be paid under the terms of their contract. To be axed in favour of a child was to add insult to

27

injury, particularly as they had a six-year-old daughter at home who they considered to be every bit as special as Petula Clark. They made a vociferous complaint to Madden who patiently explained that while he was sure that little Julie Andrews was every bit as brilliant an artiste as her mother and stepfather assured him she was, she was four years younger. He would, he promised, find an opening for her just as soon as she was old enough.

But the Andrews were not to be placated. Neither Petula nor Leslie had done anything personally to upset them—and in fact the two children would, during the coming years, often appear in troop shows on the same bill—but the Andrews parents bore them a grudge for what they saw as direct and dangerous competition with their own child. The incident rankled in their minds for another six years until it finally exploded, shaking the foundations of the BBC in 1948. But more of this later.

The 'programme as broadcast' sheet that day is still carefully preserved in Cecil Madden's private collection. It reads:

It's All Yours with Olive Groves, Jack Leon, Gloria Kane with Robin Richmond at the organ and Let's Join the Children.
Organ/Orchestra—Gloria Kane—theme 'Yours'
Organ/Orchestra—'Before You Know It I'll be Home, Mother'

Band/Organ/Gloria—'Arthur Murray Taught Me Dancing'

Olive Groves/Band—'When I Sing'

Children/Band—'Ma I Miss Your Apple Pie'

Band/Organ/Gloria—'Little Bo-Peep'

This is followed by the names of ten children and of the relatives to whom they were sending their messages, and details of the relationship. Top of the bill was L.A.C. Vernon Gutteridge who had asked to hear his niece, Elizabeth Metcalf. Second from bottom Sapper Barry Leek who wanted a message from his 'niece' Petula Clark. Afterwards, the programme continues with a list of other songs and artistes—songs like 'Breathless' and 'When the Waters are Blue' and then: Petula Clark and the Band—'Mighty Like a Rose'. Compère, Joan Gilbert.

It was during the 'message' part of the programme that Colin Hamilton earned himself some unwelcome notice. Stephen Williams recalls: 'He started off in the usual way—"Hello Daddy, Mummy and I are fine and we miss you and we had a lovely tea and Mummy sends her love." He was getting faster and faster, the words running together with the speed of an express train—until, suddenly, he couldn't wait a moment longer.

'"Mummy," he yelled suddenly across the studio—and across the miles of hosts of waiting soldiers—"Colin wants to go po-po."'

It was a joke which remained a classic in the Hamilton family for years. When, in 1978, Petula payed a guest visit to the *Outlook* studios, Colin jogged her memory.

'We've already met, in a BBC studio,' he told her, again in a live broadcast.

'Petula wrinkled her brow, obviously mildly embarrassed,' he says.

'You'll have to forgive me, but I don't remember,' she answered.

'Remember the Criterion?' She did.

'Good heavens!' she interpolated. 'The whole thing is coming back to me. You were the "po-po" child.' Memories of childhood started flooding back.

But the BBC hierarchy were not amused at the time. Williams received a severe dressing-down for allowing such blatant 'vulgarity' on the air. After Petula's performance, however, he also received a personal telephone call from one of the Corporation's Joint Director-Generals, Robert Foot.

'Who is that child who sang tonight?' he asked. 'She was fantastic! I would like to be informed if you plan to use her again.'

But Madden and Williams had pre-empted him. They had already issued her an invitation to return a month later.

★   ★   ★

Two days before her second visit to the Criterion, Williams rang Foot's office as instructed—and nearly caused an in-house riot. To this day there are strict codes of etiquette within Broadcasting House. Forty years ago, they were even more stringent. Producers did not ring the DG without the permission of a superior, in Williams' case the Controller of Programmes, B. J. Nicholls. Nicholls was furious. He stormed into Williams' office like an irate bull.

'I've just been informed that Mr Foot is paying us a visit tonight,' he roared. 'Why wasn't I informed? How dare you contact the DG without going through the usual channels.'

Williams and Madden between them tried unsuccessfully to explain that they were only carrying out the DG's direct orders.

'I don't give a damn who gave the orders,' Nicholls fumed. 'Next time, you tell ME first. I have the right to know about such visits.'

The public reaction to Petula's first broadcast was as enthusiastic as Madden's and Foot's. The psychology of allowing her to perform on the air had struck just the right chord. The BBC was flooded by an avalanche of letters and telephone calls demanding to know more about her. One, from a Sergeant Mourk serving on the George Cross Island of Malta, was typical.

'I would be glad if you could let me know the full name and address of the little girl of ten who sang "Mighty Like a Rose" so beautifully tonight . . .'

She paid her second visit to the Criterion on 22 November, exactly one week after her tenth birthday. Cecil Madden had asked Leslie if she could please wear exactly the same outfit as she had worn for her initial visit. At his instigation, official photographers were there to capture the moments as she posed alongside the other message-senders and sang 'Ave Maria' perched on Robin Richmond's enormous organ. Leslie no doubt justifiably felt that his hard work and training were now yielding their rewards. Petula's talent was being explored to the full, just as he had prayed it would be. When Cecil Madden approached him for a further visit, this time to take part in a show which would go down in BBC history, appearing with stars like Vera Lynn, Arthur Askey and with Geraldo's orchestra to accompany her, he felt she was well on the way.

CHAPTER THREE

I KNOW WHERE
I'M GOING

Coincidentally, Petula's tenth birthday fell within a month of the celebrations planned to conclude the first decade of the British Empire Service. An enormous birthday party was to honour the event and would be broadcast in the *It's All Yours* Saturday-night spot, but from the Queensberry All-Services Club.

Today, London's Prince Edward Theatre stands on the site of that famous, wartime club which could house an audience of 2,500 British and American service men and women. It was to be a national gala and among the artistes engaged to broadcast not merely to the troops abroad but over the Home Service were Vera Lynn, Arthur Askey, Elsie and Doris Walters, Richard Murdoch, Sidney Burchell and Michael Redgrave. Geraldo's entire fifty-piece orchestra had been engaged to accompany the stars. Petula was billed quite simply as 'A soldier's child'—which, indeed, she was.

★   ★   ★

Doris at this time made all Petula's clothes

herself—as well as Barbara's and her own. Her careful upbringing had taught her thrift, a most useful quality in those austere days of clothing coupons, when people on meagre service pay had to make do as best they could. Whenever Petula was to make an appearance, Doris would sit stitching round the clock if necessary to make sure she was prettily clad, but Madden knew that if she were to appear on such a star-studded bill, she must have a gorgeous party dress to match the glittering occasion.

Sensing that there might be a financial problem, he enlisted the help of an old friend, Lady Miriam Marks, the generous and kindly wife of Marks & Spencer chief, Sir Simon. She readily agreed to finance the dressing of the potential star—and Madden happily wrote to Petula's parents informing them of her offer. He told them that it was a way of saying 'thank you' to her as she couldn't be paid for her appearances, being under twelve years of age.

In early December, Madden received a reply from Corporal Clark, saying that he and his wife would be delighted to accept the offer of the dress on Petula's behalf 'with grateful thanks' and adding the essential information that Doris had the coupons. No amount of money would have acquired the dress without them! He would, he said, be bringing Petula to the Criterion the following Saturday as planned to decide on the numbers she would sing, and suggested that they could make a mutually convenient date then for Madden and Doris to go shopping.

Leslie was acutely aware of Cecil Madden's burgeoning interest in Petula. He felt that this was the right time to test the ground for her prospects with the BBC, so he included an impassioned plea for Madden's 'advice' on how Leslie might turn her success into a means of ensuring that both his children received what he described as 'a first-class education'. Obviously, he wrote, such an education was beyond his means in ordinary circumstances. It was as nearly a begging letter as his pride would allow—as direct a hint as he dared make that, given the BBC's interest in Petula, they might like to consider taking over responsibility for educating both his daughters!

Madden duly filed in, met Leslie and Petula on the prearranged date, chose three songs for her to sing and arranged the shopping trip for a week later. He knew exactly the kind of dress he wanted her to have for the occasion so he put on a brave face and the three began the trek around the smarter London stores, ending up at Debenham and Freebody's in Wigmore Street. At that time it was in heavy competition with Harrods for the title of London's most exclusive (and expensive) store.

Cecil Madden smiles as he remembers the quest for a gown fit for the BBC's youngest performer.

'We were all getting quite weary. Petula stood with nothing on except a pair of knickers while shop-girls bobbed backwards and forwards popping frocks over her head and off again. Nothing seemed quite right until one of the girls suddenly produced the prettiest dress I'd ever seen. It was made of ice-blue silk with a pin-tucked hem and a dainty lace trim. It was the perfect complement to her fair complexion and blonde hair and I knew it would look ideal under the stage lighting.'

As promised, Lady Marks paid the bill—and insisted that she had a pair of blue-and-white shoes to complete the outfit. Petula, who had never owned a shop-bought dress before, was thrilled with her gift. On 15 December 1942, she wrote to Miriam Marks:

'Dear Fairy Godmother,

I call you this because I dislike calling people I like Mr or Mrs and it really is very much like Cinderella, isn't it? I now have a lovely dress and shoes which I am to wear at the BBC which is more important than any ball. I do thank you and Uncle Cecil Madden for your kindness. I know I shall sing ever so much better in that beautiful dress. Love, Petula'.

True to her word, Petula gave another wonderful performance that crisp December night. She was introduced by Canadian announcer Gerry Wilmott: 'We now send you, wherever you may be, a message in song and in particular, to Gunner Rees in Iraq; here's your ten-year-old niece Petula Clark, one of the sweetest children you ever saw, to sing you "Mighty Like a Rose".'

The thunderous applause she received can still be heard on a unique, crackly recording carefully preserved in the BBC's sound archives. 'Now,' says Gerry Wilmott's voice, his delight at her performance captured forever on that surviving recording, 'I'm sure that all the boys and girls in the forces in this All-Services Club in London would like to hear you in your song which quite out-Carmen's Miranda— "When I Love, I Love".' Geraldo struck up the jolly introduction and away she went. When she reached the line 'Oh when I meet a man, and he's good-looking, I look at him and say hey what's cookin'', waggling a finger and wriggling her body, the audience responded instantly with gales of laughter and the three-foot-tall child who had to stand on a box to reach the microphone broke into a blushing grin.

But the best was, as always, saved until last. Gerry Wilmott obviously had to struggle to keep a straight face as he announced, solemnly, 'And now, Petula, why don't you let us have your impression of Sophie Tucker and "Some of These Days"?' Her transformation from the high-pitched Carmen Miranda *sotto voce* to the deep American tones of the Red Hot Mama, was sensational. The pure, little-girl English accent disappeared and her voice descended two octaves as she burst forth with a powerful imitation. Now the audience exploded with delight. From beginning to end, her performance had lasted a mere six minutes, including the applause. Six minutes with a live audience of 2,500 soldiers, sailors and airmen and of millions, who had heard the broadcast at home and overseas, which launched her properly on a career of a lifetime.

Among the guests in the celebrated audience that day was the First Lord of the Admiralty in Winston Churchill's Government, Mr A. V. Alexander, who afterwards insisted on a meeting with the show's youngest star. They were pictured shaking hands and Mrs Alexander asked Cecil Madden if she might have a copy of the photograph as a keepsake. Madden duly sent her one and shortly afterwards, the First Lord himself wrote Madden a letter of thanks on Admiralty notepaper, saying how delighted his wife was to have received it.

The newspapers were full of her triumph the following morning. It made a pleasant change to read cheerful news at this sombre time.

'Petula, 10, is star in a night' was the *Daily Mail's* headline, and it went on to say how she'd stolen the show from established greats like Vera Lynn, Arthur Askey and Michael Redgrave.

The *Star* reported: 'I do not think I have ever seen an artiste at the microphone with a greater sense of self-possession than ten-year-old Petula Clark.' She made headlines across the country, from Edinburgh to the Isle of Man and from Yorkshire and Manchester to Cornwall and Devon. But despite all the publicity which thrilled Leslie and would have done credit to any major manager and his charge, anxieties were deepening within the BBC as to her future.

Before the party, Petula had been booked to broadcast the Overseas Services Christmas Pantomime, *Babes in the Wood*, which was to go out live from the Criterion on Boxing Day. The play had been scripted by theatrical historian Walter McQueen Pope and she was cast as the 'Good Fairy Twinkle', her co-actors also being children who, as message-senders, had been noted for their clear speaking voices. But the management were concerned that this was Petula's fourth broadcast within two months.

Being under twelve years old, the only recompense legally permitted was train tickets for herself and her chaperone and a fixed three-guinea fee for 'out of pocket' expenses. Now she had made her début, other programme producers were clamouring to use her. Those most concerned for her welfare, namely Cecil Madden and Stephen Williams, were frightened that over-exposure would be harmful to such a young child, no matter how eager her father might be to quicken the pace of her career which now seemed to promise endless possibilities.

Memos flew like thistledown in a hurricane. What was the legal position? And the moral one? The furore reached the heights of the Joint DGs, Sir Cecil Graves and Robert Foot. They unanimously ordered that as she was Cecil Madden's find, he should be appointed her 'BBC guardian'. It was a responsibility he gladly accepted, but one which was to cause him numerous problems over the next two years—and make him distinctly unpopular with other Variety producers. He was, however, deeply aware of the responsibility he now bore on behalf of his protégée. When ENSA approached him for permission to use her two weeks after the pantomime, he declined, convinced that over-exposure might ruin her freshness.

A directive was issued by the office of the joint DGs advising that Petula could only appear in broadcasts four times a year. Madden happily agreed. It meant that the constant refusals could now be referred back to this directive. However, he did feel that the BBC ought to show their gratitude for her performances to date in a tangible form. He had worked out that her appearances so far must have been worth about 25 guineas in terms of fees paid to performers in ordinary circumstances. As she was ineligible to receive money, he suggested that perhaps the Corporation should buy her a gift for around that value—a second-hand piano, perhaps.

Hands were raised in horror at the very idea. She might be given a party dress or some other small present as a token of appreciation—but a piano! That would be construed as a direct attempt at evading the law!

Madden was undaunted. There was no doubt in his mind that the potential Petula showed must be worth investing in. He could only control her bookings within the BBC and there was simply no way in which he could prevent her father from taking her around the country to perform at troop concerts or anywhere else for that matter. He was well aware that these performances kept her out of school and was reminded of Leslie's hints regarding his daughter's education. Armed with this letter, he requested a formal meeting between the DGs at Broadcasting House and his protégée and her father.

Foot had already shown an interest in Petula, having witnessed her performance in November and at the birthday party, but on both these occasions he had stayed in the shadows and had never spoken either to her or to Leslie. Graves had no personal knowledge of her other than through BBC memos. Madden's request for the meeting was met by shrieks of horror.

'Such things are simply not done within the BBC,' he was informed, firmly.

'Then they should be,' he retorted, but

settled on a compromise whereby the two men agreed to see her in Madden's office at the Criterion.

After she had gravely shaken hands with them both and told them how much she loved singing and going on the stage, Petula and Leslie were dismissed and Madden outlined his plan. The BBC, he suggested, might take over responsibility for her education and thus gain control over her future appearances. Payment for school fees would be in the form of a 'loan', repayable in later years from fees paid to her by the Corporation as she fulfilled the potential he believed she promised. Both men were obviously impressed by the idea, but eventually declined to go ahead with it. On 29 December 1942, an internal memo from Sir Cecil Graves to Robert Foot read:

'My view about this is that if you think that Petula Clark has in her the makings of a first-class artiste then anything more than the most occasional use of her is doing her the worst possible disservice. Already, she has had great publicity and is no doubt being sought after by all and sundry and I don't see that we have any legal grounds to prevent her being snapped up by films or anyone else. But I do think it is a great pity that we should in any way be party to anything that might have the ultimate result of spoiling her altogether.

'Personally, I don't see how we could take her

over. I believe the legal position is very difficult. If she is really a potential radio star, what one would have liked would have been to give her say half-a-dozen broadcasts a year, assessing these at a certain fee and placing that money in a fund to be made available for her education; in return for this to have had a complete hold on her until such time as she was ready to be brought out as a finished broadcaster. But I don't think we are justified in using money in this way, for how often does an infant prodigy turn out to be an adult star? Furthermore, if at the end of her incubation she turned out to be a flop might not her parents say we had ruined her chances in other fields?

'To sum up, my view is that we should use this child on the rare occasions when a broadcast by her is appropriate and for the rest that we should let whatever talents she has find their own market, if her parents should so decide. But I don't think we should apply any pressure at all.'

The decision was final. But if the BBC refused to back her, what was to be done? Madden decided to take matters into his own hands, but first he felt it would be prudent to get an outside assessment of her value as a future performer. At his own expense, he arranged some dancing, drama and singing lessons for her with the famous Gladys Day. Having spent ten years in the broadcasting media, he knew that to succeed as a variety artiste it was necessary to be talented in all three fields.

The report he received from Miss Day was not all he had hoped for. It told him that whilst she believed Petula had a fine voice and considerable dramatic talent, she had little dancing ability. Considering her petite build, this was quite surprising. However, once Cecil Madden got an idea into his head, he was not to be swayed. He was not a wealthy man although his father was a British diplomat. He lived on a BBC producer's pay—no fortune in those times—and had a wife and child to support. There was little spare cash with which to sponsor other people's children. But he had a friend within the BBC who, he felt, might be persuaded to help him.

Seymour de Lotbinière, later Head of TV Outside Broadcasts, was at that time Controller of Overseas Services and as such technically Madden's boss. He had great respect for Madden's judgment, however, and the added advantage of still being single and having a private income to supplement his BBC pittance. Madden showed Gladys Day's report to 'Lobby', as he was known, and persuaded him to set up a joint trust fund for the child's education.

'I had heard Pet but I'd never met her,' Lobby recalls. 'The first thing I insisted on was buying her a copy of *Peter Pan* and getting her to learn parts of it by heart. I was horrified when I found out that she'd never read it! The second thing we did was to buy her a second-hand, baby grand piano. We both believed it was vitally important that she should have a piano and take lessons. There was only one major condition to these gifts, and to the gift of education which followed. Petula was not to be told who her benefactors were.'

'I always believed that the BBC had bought me the piano and paid for my entire private education,' she says.

Madden now charged Leslie with the task of finding a suitable school where she might take her lessons in small classes among young ladies. He insisted, too, that her father must keep precise accounts of every penny that he was spending, detailing whether it was for uniform, books, piano and dancing lessons and other extras. This was a task which Leslie—always hopeless with money as later events proved—loathed.

Thanks to Madden and Lobby, Petula joined the ranks of brown-uniformed pupils at St Bernards—an exclusive public day-school for girls—in September 1943. She was to stay there for an all too brief two years, but these were her happiest schooldays. As soon as she had become well-known and her picture had appeared in the *Radio Times*, the children at Moor Lane had started teasing her.

'The girls at St Bernards simply accepted me as just another one of them,' she says. 'I loved my stagework and inevitably missed large chunks of school which meant that I had a very hard time trying to catch up. The school had the most beautiful grounds and I loved to wander around them, alone, dreaming. I was never an academic, but I loved the literature lessons particularly. I had a wonderful time.'

CHAPTER FOUR

MOVIE MAD

If Cecil Madden had really believed that the BBC's restrictions which permitted Petula to perform only four times a year, coupled with the excellent private education which he and Lobby were providing, would give her the chance of a normal childhood, he was sadly mistaken. For although the latter was what Leslie had declared that he and Doris both wanted most for their daughter, he had reckoned without Leslie's premier ambition—that she should be an outstanding star. Having tasted show-biz life he now showed a remarkable tenacity for hanging on to every opportunity it offered his daughter—and it did offer every opportunity.

During the period 1942/43, she performed in

at least a hundred more troop concerts in every part of Britain. Leslie made it a policy never to refuse a request—and Petula herself loved every minute of it.

At the age of eleven, and just one year after her scene-stealing act at the birthday party, she was invited to appear on the stage of London's most prestigious concert venue—the Royal Albert Hall—alongside the massed bands of the Scots and Welsh guards, pipers of the Irish and Scots guards, Ivy Benson's Ladies' Band, the Western Brothers, Ann Shelton, Renée Houston and Donald Stewart, at a charity concert in aid of the National Fire Service.

The expansive arena with its wedding-cake tiered balconies must have stretched to eternity to the tiny eleven-year-old yet, on what was to be the first of four occasions she performed there during the next forty years, she showed no signs of nerves at all.

'I remember sitting reading a comic backstage and they had to drag me away from it when it was my turn to go on,' she says. 'Then I ran up the ramp on to the stage, sang them "Ave Maria", acted out the sketch "Movie Mad" that Daddy had written for me in which I played the role of a star-struck kitchen maid called Daisy, took my bow and went straight back to reading my comic. On other occasions when I appeared there in later years, I had such stage-fright that they literally had to push me up that ramp. It got worse every time. But that first time, I wasn't really conscious of what I was doing except that it all seemed great fun.'

Ironically, among the sea of eight thousand faces who saw the 'Movie Mad' sketch was film director, Maurice Elvey. He was in the process of casting one of a number of low-budget, propaganda-type films being made at that time for the film company, Anglo-American. It was called *Medal for the General* with Godfrey Tearle in the title role of the retired general who tries to enlist and is turned down because of his age.

Jeannie de Casalis was his wife and the cast included Irene Handl, Thorley Walters, Morland Graham and Mabel Constanduros. Elvey needed children to play the minor but vital roles of the evacuee children who are billeted with the old man who has lost all interest in life.

Leslie was ecstatic when, on the apparent strength of the sketch he'd written, Elvey came backstage after the Albert Hall triumph and offered Petula the part of Irma, a horn-rimmed know-it-all evacuee child. It was a pretty run of the mill movie. When it was released in November 1944, *Picturegoer*, the British film-fans' bible, gave it a mere two-star rating. Its critic's only praise was for the children who, he said were 'amusing and lively'. Elvey was obviously impressed by Petula's professional attitude to film-making, even at that early age,

48

and immediately offered her a slightly larger part in another film, *Strawberry Roan*.

These films took, on average, about five weeks to make from start to finish. However, Pet was only needed for two or three days at a time. There was always a tutor on set, as the law demanded, to ensure that the children missed as little schooling as possible. Yet even when the shooting was over, there were still press photographs to be taken, publicity appearances to be given and press interviews to be contended with. And still the troop concerts went on. By 1944, she had scored over three hundred!

Despite this work, Leslie was determined that the image presented of Petula to the world should be that of a 'normal' child. She was pictured helping her mother to wash up and it was emphasised time and again that she was expected to take her share of the household chores. Newspapers featured her playing with her pet dog Tieko (who had replaced the beloved Bing) and her cat, Smokey. She was taught to tell reporters that her favourite occupations were horse-riding and messing about in a rowing-boat moored in the little stream which ran by the bottom of the garden of the house in Salmon's Road. In reality, there was little time to enjoy any of these pastimes, or even to play for any length of time with her younger sister Barbara. And Pet, whilst still thoroughly enjoying the life of a child-star, was beginning to realise that it had its drawbacks.

In early 1944, London was a dangerous place for a child to live with the doodlebugs hammering their hardest at the heart of the already devastated city. But Leslie knew that, if Pet's career was to continue to advance at the incredible pace it had now gathered, it was the only place to be based.

Doris and Barbara were sent back to the safety of the Welsh mountains while Pet and Leslie battled on in London, alone. And Petula really was alone. She wasn't allowed to make friends, even had there been time to enjoy their company. When she asked if she might join some schoolfriends from St Bernards who were going to the cinema, her father told her firmly that her place was making films, not watching them. It was the price one had to pay for stardom.

'I never felt like a star,' Petula says. 'I don't even now. I found it all very hard to understand why I couldn't join in and do the things that other girls of my age were allowed to.'

For some time after her first appearance at Bentalls' store, Petula had performed at concerts with Harry Fryer. Now Fryer, who had been so kind to Pet and Leslie, felt that Leslie 'owed him one'. Petula had not been used by the BBC throughout the whole of 1943, except in the Christmas panto and Leslie felt that this must be blamed on the 'ban'.

In early 1944, Fryer approached him with an idea. He had been booked for a series on the Light Programme and he would ask the BBC if he might use Petula as his soloist. Leslie thought it a grand plan and gave his permission—but then the BBC reminded him of the rules. He was furious and thought up another way to outsmart the powers-that-were at Broadcasting House. He wrote to them saying that Petula was under a five-year contract to Fryer and that if they required to use her in future, all bookings must be made through him.

It didn't take long for this new development to reach Cecil Madden's ears. After all the love, care and cash he himself had lavished on her, he was hopping mad! He sent an urgent and confidential memo to the Variety Booking Manager, Bill Streeton, which said:

'Since you know the history of this child and how Stephen Williams and I look after her interests, it is extremely galling to be told that he (Fryer) is her manager, when apart from this, private friends have done a lot for Petula in the matter of her musical and dancing education.'

He modestly omitted to mention that the 'private friends' he referred to were Lobby and himself, or that their interest in her education extended beyond music and dance.

'I am frankly going to advise them to stop this,' the memo continued, 'but can Fryer contract a child of eleven at all?'

Streeton replied at once that indeed Fryer could put the child under contract, providing it was done with the full knowledge and permission of her father who was her legal guardian, and advising that Madden could, if he chose, refuse to deal with Fryer at all until he was satisfied that Leslie Clark had indeed bestowed on Fryer the powers he claimed he had.

In fact, there was not the slightest chance that Leslie Clark would ever sign over his daughter to anybody else. He was nobody's fool and all the hard work he had personally put into launching Petula was now paying dividends. Why, then, should he now consider relinquishing his job as her manager, even to an old pal like Fryer?

Madden and Lobby continued paying the school fees. Leslie Clark went on managing his daughter entirely alone—and with even more success than before.

During 1943 and 1944, she made four films including *Medal for the General*, *Strawberry Roan*, *Trouble at Townsend* for Gaumont British Instructional Films, in which she showed children evacuated from the city how to behave in a country environment, and *I Know Where I'm Going* directed by Michael Powell.

I Know Where I'm Going told the story of a Manchester girl who travelled to the Highlands to marry a wealthy chemical manufacturer who had rented 'Scots Island' and was said to contain one of the most terrifying storm scenes ever committed to the film-can.

Petula's part as 'Cheril' was only a small one and she had had a gentle apprenticeship to the world of film studios with the softly-spoken Maurice Elvey's direction. He had always been soberly dressed and, with his goatee beard and kind, moderate manner, she had found working with hm a delightful experience. Michael Powell was a very different proposition, vivid in dress as well as character with a loud and lusty manner of direction. Petula was frankly terrified of him.

'I will never forget one particular day during the filming of *I Know Where I'm Going*,' she says. 'I had to wear very tight jodphurs for a riding scene and just as we were ready to start shooting, I found I desperately needed to spend a penny. I was too terrified to say anything so I sat it out as long as I could. Then, I couldn't wait any longer so I'm afraid I wet my pants. I was so ashamed of myself that I just stayed where I was until everybody had left the set. Then I rushed up to the dressing-room to rinse them out and hang them on a radiator to dry in time for the afternoon shooting.'

*   *   *

Petula had not been used by the BBC since the Fryer fiasco but in June, Cecil Madden decided that the time had come to include her in one of the most popular radio shows of that time, *Variety Band-Box*. Although she gave yet another of her now expectedly superb performances, her filming schedule didn't allow time for her to broadcast again until, at Madden's invitation, she appeared in the *Variety Band-Box Christmas Show* which went out from the Queensberry Club on Sunday, 24 December 1944.

'We could not give you much time as there is a very big bill,' Madden wrote to her, 'but we would like to have you if you can come.' Leslie wrote back accepting on Petula's behalf and suggesting that she could sing 'Yiddishe Momma' for which she had full band parts and 'Victory Polka' which, he said, he considered both short and topical. Again, she could receive only her train tickets and the standard expenses of three guineas.

Petula had worked almost ceaselessly throughout 1944. Christmas Day that year was to bring her a welcome respite. The Clarks had planned a simple, family Christmas for four at home. Food was of course rationed and what was available was not of the best quality. Fuel was under the same restrictions—it was more necessary to conserve it to keep the armament factories in production than to warm the deprived British public.

Doris didn't light the fire in the front room

54

until after the family's meagre Christmas dinner that day. Then, alone for once as a unit, the little group settled down to play games and sing together, just like thousands of other British families.

Suddenly, a fleet of black limousines wound their way into Salmon's Road and parked adjacent to the door of Number Twenty. Out spilled GI men and women, led by Sergeant Ernie Tassin. Petula and Barbara pulled aside the white lace curtains and peeped out in fascination as girls and boys in American uniforms began unloading crates and boxes from the cars' boots.

The task completed, each collected as much as he or she could carry from the piles on the pavement and proceeded through the gate and up the narrow pathway of the house, knocking loudly on the door.

'We've come to say thank you to Petula for giving us so much pleasure and reminding us of our kids back home,' Tassin, a member of the US Army Headquarters Band, explained. These were the men and women to whom she'd given such joy at Rainbow Corner, and along with their gifts they brought the added honour of inviting 'their' little girl to become 'Queen of Rainbow Corner'.

But it wasn't until they had gone that the full extent of their kindness was revealed. As they unpacked, the Clarks found ice-cream packed in coolers, bars of chocolate, packs of chewing gum, tins of ham and fruit, nylon stockings for Doris, cigarettes for Leslie, oranges, bananas and other treats too numerous to number.

It was a glorious end to the old year, but the new one just dawning was to prove even more promising. The newly-formed Rank Organisation were highly conscious of the box-office draw of child-stars. In America, Liz Taylor and Margaret O'Brien were at a peak of popularity. Mr J. Arthur Rank was well aware of their impact. In early 1945, he spotted Petula at one of her regular troop concerts. Her reputation as a professional had spread even though the only film of hers that had so far been released (apart from the educational film, *Trouble at Townsend*) was *Medal for the General*.

He decided to cast her in a film adaptation of Seamark's famous story *Query*, which was titled *Murder in Reverse*, playing Jill Masterick as a child; Dinah Sheridan took the adult role of the same character with Jimmy Hanley as Peter Rogers. It was released in November 1945—and between the time of its making and its release, a lot was to happen.

In March 1945, Leslie Clark let it be known that his daughter was being considered for a part in what it was announced would be the greatest British musical picture of all time, *London Town*. Petula was due to sing in *Clear the Decks* in April and in a jubilant letter to the booking manager, Leslie Clark asked if her picture might be used in *Radio Times* to give her an extra boost since her broadcasts were so limited, and added delightedly that the *Radio Times* might like to mention that Wesley Ruggles, who was to direct *London Town*, had seen her at a concert the previous week and wished to interview her for a 'big part'.

Rank had formed a subsidiary, Wesley Ruggles Productions, with J. Arthur Rank himself as President. The all-British cast of *London Town* was to be headed by the now legendary comedian, Sid Field. Tessie O'Shea was cast as herself and an eighteen-year-old starlet, Kay Kendall, had her first screen role as Sid's girlfriend. To both Leslie and Petula's huge delight, she was asked to take the part of Peggy, Sid's film daughter. It was a major breakthrough.

The film was the talk of the industry. Pre-publicity was almost as gigantic an operation as the shooting itself. Forecasts that the film would break all previous box-office records both in the United Kingdom and the USA were formally declared in every newspaper. Agnes de Mille, niece of Cecil B., was being imported especially to choreograph a stupendous 'Daffodil' ballet. A working piano, large enough for twelve chorus members to play simultaneously, was being built for the production.

Each of the stars, including Petula, was

subjected to massive pre-release build-ups. 'No less than a brilliant performance can be expected from Rank's newest contract star, twelve-year-old Petula Clark,' announced the Press Office of the august Rank Organisation, proudly.

Petula looks back on making *London Town* as one of the most enjoyable experiences she ever had in film-making. She especially loved working with Sid Field—'Uncle' Sid as she called him: 'He was an absolute darling. I can remember one day going for lunch to the canteen with Daddy and finding that the menu included corned beef and pickled onions. I told Daddy that was for me, but he said I'd better not eat pickled onions as I had to do a close-up with Sid that afternoon and it wasn't fair.

'Sid was sitting at the next table and overheard our conversation. The next thing I knew he'd ordered a whole jar of pickled onions which he proceeded to tuck into all on his own so, of course, I was allowed to have them too. Later, on the set, I asked Sid if he really liked pickled onions as much as I did. He told me that not only did he hate them but that they did dreadful things to his insides!'

The man who then held the title of Britain's greatest comedian had charmed his twelve-year-old co-star forever.

Another person who has vivid memories of the halcyon summer days on the *London Town* set was Petula's cousin Clive. 'I used to spend all my summer holidays with Uncle Leslie and Pet,' he says. 'I came down to London that year of the filming and Uncle Leslie, Pet and I set up house on a houseboat owned by an Indian called Ghangi while work was in progress. Whenever we could, Pet and I used to escape for "adventures" together. One memorable day, I borrowed a skiff and took her off down the river. We had a grand time. But when we got back, the producers were frantic and Uncle Leslie was furious. You see, at that time neither of us could swim! Not only that, but we hadn't asked permission for our outing. I got a real belting for taking one of the leading ladies off without permission on such a daring sortie.'

Petula didn't get a single note to sing in *London Town* but her dramatic talent, at least, was established. Rank put her on a seven-year-contract with a rising salary. Leslie could scarcely have wished for more, especially when he heard the details of the new distribution agreement which Rank had struck with the leading American film magnates.

That year, Rank and Universal had signed a long-term extension of the distribution agreement between General Film Distributors Ltd. and Universal Films Incorporated. It meant that GFD would continue to distribute exclusively the entire Universal studio output in Britain and Universal would do likewise for GFD in the States. The first thirty-six films in the package included two of Petula's: *I Know Where I'm Going* and *London Town*.

Despite Petula's own fond memories of *London Town*, the attempt to combine all the elements of the Sam Goldwyn and Busby Berkeley musicals in a single film flopped miserably and nearly crippled Rank. Wesley Ruggles, the director in whom Rank had put his trust, and his money, was a 'has-been', and the fact that he'd only ever made one moderately successful musical during his entire career seemed to have been totally overlooked.

When the film was released in 1946, the critics were scathing. Leonard Mosely wrote in the *Daily Express:*

'Whack whack whack—down should come the axe on hundreds and hundreds of feet of this long (two hours), lavish and expensive film. By sheer comic genius, (Sid Field) saves it from being the most expensive flop since *King of Jazz*. How dare they bring over a Hollywood director to make a film around someone so intrinsically and hearteningly English as Sid Field?'

Despite the GFD/Universal Films agreement, it was another seven years before *London Town* made it to the States. When it did arrive, it had been retitled *My Heart Goes Crazy*, was cut from its already shortened 105 minutes' running-time to a measly seventy minutes, and was run as a second feature.

Ruggles himself was said to be delighted with Petula's work, despite all the adverse criticism the film itself received, and there was now much gossip that on the strength of her performance she would be offered a Hollywood contract.

Leslie, who liked to keep all interested parties on their toes, wrote to BBC's *Children's Hour* asking whether, in view of her success in the picture, they might be interested in using her for 'reading' and in October to Cecil Madden, accepting another part in the *Christmas Variety Band-Box* and telling him that they had had a 'very attractive' offer from Hollywood which he had not yet refused.

The 'offer' was said to involve Bing Crosby— but since no more was ever heard of it, it might be assumed that Leslie, always keen to develop Petula's career, was pre-empting release of studio gossip.

CHAPTER FIVE

VICE-VERSA

8 May 1945—and the allies declared victory in Europe. Although the war still raged on in the East, peace was finally coming after six long, hard years of battle. For those whose loved ones would never return, the joy and relief they

experienced was tinged with sadness.

The first night of peacetime, Britons flooded into London to mass in their millions outside Buckingham Palace and to drink their fill in Trafalgar Square.

Petula Clark, wearing a special dress bought for her by her GI fans at Rainbow Corner, came to sing them into victory and peacetime just as she had comforted them with her songs during the war years.

But by VJ day in August, she was determined to celebrate as a private person. She travelled to London with her father and her cousin Clive and mingled with the crowds around Piccadilly Circus, for once unrecognised. The small girl whose picture had adorned the fronts of tanks as the British Army marched to battle at El Alamein and to whom the war had presented such a wealth of opportunity must now, surely, be entering a new phase of her career. As the victory-drunk crowds celebrated the end of the Second World War that night, Leslie Clark must have had other things on his mind. Would he be able to continue the momentum of his daughter's career as peace returned once more to Britain?

He need not have worried. She had been kept constantly busy with film work throughout 1945 and had made all four permitted BBC broadcasts. As her thirteenth birthday approached, bringing with it the end of the

BBC's restrictions on her use, Leslie found himself overwhelmed with requests for her services and decided that she now needed an agent as well as a manager.

On his demob, he had not returned to his job at the Longrove Mental Hospital and was now working as Petula's full-time manager. He appointed Gaby Rogers as her agent and informed the BBC that, in future, all offers of work must go through him.

But old habits died hard. He was still writing to producers such as May E. Jenkins of *Children's Hour* begging auditions for her for 'straight' parts. In October 1945, he received a terse reply from Miss Jenkins, informing him that she had not heard that his daughter had now blossomed into a straight actress but that she would 'bear her in mind'. She obviously did. On 9 November and with three years' broadcasting experience tucked comfortably beneath her belt, Petula appeared in a *Children's Hour* broadcast reading a dramatic monologue and singing just one song. For this, she received her very first fee from the BBC—fifteen guineas.

Whilst her father was delighted at her progress, Cecil Madden was becoming more and more concerned at the lack of formal education she was receiving, despite the high fees he and Seymour de Lotbinière were paying for just that purpose. He broached a new idea to Lobby which he thought might solve the problem once and for all—boarding-school. He had, he told him, heard of an excellent finishing-school in Yorkshire where he believed she might with luck get at least a couple of years' uninterrupted education and the chance of the tail-end of a normal childhood without interference, however well-meaning, from her enthusiastic father.

Lobby was by this time a married man himself. The school Madden suggested was even more expensive than St Bernards. However, he believed strongly in Madden's cause so he cabled a cousin of his, also of independent means, outlining the plan.

She telegraphed by return to say that she would go halves with him, but the scheme never came to fruition because Leslie Clark disapproved of it.

Madden, not a man to give up easily, decided the answer must lie in a crammer. There was such a school with the intriguing name of 'Rominoffs' not far from Petula's home. The staff-pupil ratio in the élite establishment was in the order of about one to six. She was packed off there, much to her disgust, after two all-too-brief years at the beloved St Bernards. Right from the start, she loathed it with the same, intense passion that she had loved the other.

However, just as she had missed out on schooling at St Bernards and Moor Lane to fulfil professional engagements, she was now quite happily missing time at the new seat of learning. Radio was no longer the sole broadcasting medium. Television, which had had a brief introduction during the immediate pre-war days, was to be reintroduced in July 1946. As luck would have it, Cecil Madden, who had been a pioneer of the medium when the world's first regular TV service had been launched ten years previously, had been moved back to Alexandra Palace in charge of Variety.

As one might have expected, Leslie was quick to seize the opportunity provided by this contact. In April he wrote to Madden, again extolling Wesley Ruggles' delight at Petula's work in *London Town* and explaining how he felt that she could be the one to break through the barrier of American child-stars.

Madden, as much under Petula's spell as ever, immediately suggested that she might like to take part in the test film which would be shown on the new televisions sets now in the shops, to boost their sales. He was, however, well aware of the far-reaching impact the film was likely to have and wrote a cautionary note to its producer, Philip Dorte, explaining his guardianship of the child and adding: 'I am officially her guardian for all BBC work, mostly to restrict her performances, not to encourage them, as her father is apt to want to overdo this.'

Petula appeared on the small screen for the

first time to help promote the sales of the new medium dressed in a frilly frock with huge puffed sleeves 'which made me look as though I had sparrow's arms', plastered with heavy make-up 'which I hated'. It was almost impossible to pass a radio shop without seeing her face. Her father was naturally delighted to have her literally in the public eye. Wherever she went, she was immediately recognised as the 'little girl on television'.

Despite his declaration that he was anxious not to encourage her performances to any degree, Cecil Madden was equally determined that she should appear on a proper TV programme as soon as possible. The service was re-launched with a variety show called *Cabaret Cartoons* during which the world-renowned artist Harry Rutherford drew the performers as they worked and presented his sketches to viewers at the end of the programme—the forerunner of Rolf Harris without the didgeridoo!

Leslie was hugely excited when Petula was invited to appear on the second *Cabaret Cartoons*, broadcast on 30 July 1946. Alongside her on the programme were Kathie Moody (now Lady Lew Grade) and the Beverley Sisters (another Madden discovery). Her first 'live' television appearances earned her a fee of ten guineas, with a further six guineas when the programme was repeated, again live, on 3 August.

Leslie was, as always, keen to promote his own technical abilities. He wrote to Madden suggesting that she might perform two songs on the programme—'Summery Summery Day' and 'Down in the Valley', both of which, he said, lent themselves to a rustic atmosphere. Not content with suggesting her material, he proposed that the scene should be set in a hayfield where she would be discovered wearing dungarees, an open-necked shirt and a straw coolie hat. And, even though he'd never before worked with television cameras (in those days, few had), he intimated that one particular line in the first song might warrant a 'close-up to head'. He had the good grace to add, in brackets, 'I should think.'

For once, his idea was accepted. The BBC's wardrobe department told him that they would provide the dungarees if they could have Petula's measurements but asking if she could please bring a checked blouse of her own.

It took fifteen engineers inside the studio and another dozen outside to beam the programme to a fantastic, fifty-mile radius around the Alexandra Palace studio. The sketch Harry Rutherford produced on that memorable occasion still hangs proudly on the wall of Cecil Madden's Chelsea flat, showing her in the orange BBC-issue dungarees!

On the basis of her performance, the petite thirteen-year-old in pigtails found herself the envy of many mature stars when she was offered a fifteen-minute Sunday afternoon programme all of her own called simply *Petula Clark*. Apart from singing, she set competitions for the younger viewers (though it was agreed as a matter of policy that no prizes might be offered, not even autographed photographs of herself, since this might 'set a precedent'). So she had to reveal all the answers at the end of the programme.

As she had already appeared in three *It's All Yours* Christmas shows, it was decided to offer her the title role in the BBC TV's first Christmas Day offering, *Alice in Wonderland*. But, although Leslie was as anxious as ever to accept the booking, he had already crammed her diary to capacity in December, 1946.

She had a booking to appear live on-stage in Dublin for ten days from the 5th to the 15th December and she was scheduled to start shooting a new Rank film, *Vice-Versa*, with Peter Ustinov and Anthony Newley on the 18th. It wasn't until he came to sign the 'Alice' contract that Leslie realised she would be needed for rehearsals from the 17th to the 20th. It meant that if she accepted the panto part, she would have to cut into her filming schedule.

There was also the small matter of her fee. As Madden had discovered, Leslie was never very good at holding on to money. But he had learned how to bargain for the highest possible remuneration for himself and his daughter. He felt that the thirty guineas which she was being offered for the four days' work was a pittance for a star of his daughter's experience. Apart from all her stage, radio and TV appearances, she had now entertained troops at no fewer than five hundred concerts. He registered his formal protest.

But, in the event, the 'Alice' offer had to be scrapped. Leslie told the programme's producers that if she appeared in the panto, she would lose the film. He appreciated that the loss of the film was no concern of the BBC—but he felt that the fee she had been offered was paltry in comparison to the £10.10s she received for her fifteen-minute afternoon shows and, anyway, the Rank Organisation would not release her to do the work.

For a fourteen-year-old who could still pass for ten on her appearance, it must have been a punishing schedule, even though she still claimed she was enjoying it all as much as ever.

But when Cecil Madden offered her a replacement spot on a Christmas Eve programme, Leslie surprisingly turned that down too. Even he now realised that the pressures on her were beginning to take their toll. He had promised her that this Christmas she would not have to work over the holiday. He hated to think that she might grow up with no childhood memories of an ordinary, family

Christmas so he was keeping three whole days, from 23 to 26 December, free for her to enjoy. He thought she deserved it, he said.

Madden, who had had strong views on the matter for a long time, could do no more than agree. He of all people, certainly didn't begrudge her her Christmas.

By this time Petula was beginning to feel the frustrations that the restrictions placed upon her by her father and her career undoubtedly invoked. She was constantly featured by newspapers and magazines who tried to glean every ounce they could from her virtually non-existent private life. The teenager they nicknamed 'Our Pet' was the basis for a cartoon character in *Radio Fun*, a popular children's comic where she was portrayed as the model child who did a good deed every day. But while she was undoubtedly growing into a pleasant and remarkably unspoiled young lady (thanks largely to Leslie's strict disciplinarian régime), part of her yearned to be the tomboy she naturally was. She longed for a little freedom and time when she could just be herself.

Pet's cousin, Shirley, remembers one occasion when she and Clive came to London to spend a week with the Clarks:

'Pet was desperate to show us how much she was growing up. Barbara and I were about eleven or twelve at this time and Pet told us that she was going to take us out for a really slap-up

meal. We all travelled into town on the tube—
and Clive lost his ticket. It was hilarious. Pet
told us not to worry, just to keep quiet. She
would sort it out. She seemed such a woman of
the world that we did as we were told.

'We got to the ticket collector. Pet approached
him and started speaking gobbley-de-gook
which she made to sound as French as she
could. She argued and gesticulated wildly at the
poor man for about a quarter of an hour. We
just stood there nodding and shaking our heads
every so often as though we were agreeing with
her. In the end, the man let us through in pure
frustration.

'She took us to this supposedly posh
restaurant for the slap-up meal we'd been
promised. It turned out to be corned beef with
lumpy mashed potatoes. It was quite horrible
but we had to pretend we were enjoying
ourselves. It was a phase she was going through,
trying to exert her own personality.'

Providing a slap-up meal for her sister and
cousins out of her own pocket must have posed
more of a problem than any of them imagined.
Despite her apparently enormous earnings, she
was still only allowed 2s 6d a week pocket-
money. Treating them would have cost her
several weeks' savings.

Whenever she could escape the clutches of her
father and the film people, Petula endeavoured
to find escapades to relieve the tedium of work.

71

'I had no friends apart from Clive,' she says. 'On one occasion a bit later, when I was shooting down in Wales I was befriended by a girl called Marion who was my stand-in and about my age. She was the first girlfriend I'd had in years. I "borrowed" a wig from the wardrobe department and pretended my name was Christina. We wandered off and met some gypsies. I don't think they were real gypsies, just hop-pickers on holiday. We spent the whole day with them and one of the boys took a liking to me and we trotted off to Woolworth's where he bought me a ring with a green glass stone. He had absolutely no idea who I really was and for once I could just be myself. I treasured that ring. It was a symbol of what I wanted to be—an ordinary girl.'

Sadly, the friendship with Marion ended when she outgrew her role as Pet's understudy. Such friendships—and such escapes—were rare.

'As far as the worlds of broadcasting and films were concerned, I was very worldly and I knew all the tricks of the trade,' she says. 'But I had very little idea of what normal life was like. And there was another problem emerging. I was very conscious of the fact that I was growing-up. I was a teenager, but everyone wanted me to stay a child. As my breasts began to develop, I wanted to be proud of my new figure and show it off. But in the studios, they bound me up to make me appear as flat as a seven-year-old. I

72

began to get extremely depressed about the whole thing.'

Undoubtedly, adolescence was a miserable period for Pet. She was suffering a major identity crisis both at home and at work, just as every young girl does. But hers was exaggerated out of all proportion by her public image and by her changing personal relationship with her father.

'I believed my father to be the handsomest, most wonderful man on earth,' she says. 'The trouble was that he couldn't separate our public and our private roles. There would be times when we were sitting round the dinner table at home and I would ask him a question as my father—but it was my manager who answered me. I longed to say to him: "Daddy, it's your daughter speaking!" But he wouldn't listen.'

The problem stemmed basically from Leslie's fear that his daughter's appeal would dramatically diminish if he allowed her to stop being the sweet little girl and to be seen as the sometimes temperamental, sometimes sad, sometimes rebellious young woman she really was, with thoughts and ideas of her own. The childhood 'act' had to go on—nurtured by the film parts in which she was cast and the programmes she was broadcasting both on radio and TV.

Rank was making the most of their youngest contract artist, too. *Vice-Versa*, the classic story based on F. Anstey's Victorian novel, was directed by Peter Ustinov who also wrote the screen-play. Roger Livesey with whom she had already worked in *I Know Where I'm Going* took the part of Paul Bultitude, the acrimonious Victorian papa who swops bodies but not personalities with his young son (Tony Newley). James Robertson Justice was boarding-school headmaster Dr Grimstone and Pet his daughter Dulcie, with whom Tony naturally falls in love. It was a brilliant film in true, if youthful, Ustinov tradition, but again Petula was cast as a little girl with an outsize bow in her hair and mid-calf Victorian child's dress and pinafore.

Working with Petula on *Vice-Versa* left a lasting impression on Peter Ustinov:

'Her father had her very much under his thumb—and he was ever present. He played the kind of role more usually filled by ambitious mothers—and it was strange to see it being taken by a man. He seemed to take a dual role, both of watching over and pushing her at the same time. I'm always suspicious of people like that, who want their children to go on to the stage.

'She gave me the impression then, although she certainly doesn't now, of someone who was wound up in the morning and put back in her box at night. She was awfully sweet with me; she had a precocious quality, not as a precocious child but as a premature adult. She seemed to be a very lonely little girl. In fact, the whole situation struck me as sad. I didn't understand why she needed such protection—or such promotion.

'While filming was in progress, she took direction in an absolutely adult way—but the sight of her father nodding or giving instruction from the pit gave one the impression of a manufactured child. It was as though there was a complicity between him and the producer; if it had been a boxing match, he would have been in her corner, occasionally having to be told by the referee not to shout instructions.

'The only time I ever saw her behave like a child was when we finished filming. She cried.'

As well as her film work, she now had a growing number of radio and TV engagements. Even while she was filming *Easy Money* at Pinewood she was rehearsing such popular radio shows as *A Cabin in the Cotton* produced by Charles Chilton and starring Edric Connor as the narrator of Uncle Remus stories. Chilton, who later wrote the blockbuster *Oh! What a Lovely War* and radio's *Journey Into Space* remembers how, on one occasion, while she was still filming Leslie had booked her for a variety performance in Brighton.

'The film had overrun so an orange-box plane had been booked to get her down to Brighton in time for the show. She had never flown before and was very excited at the prospect, if a little scared, too. She was due on-stage within half an hour of arrival so the only way for me to get her material to her was to go down to Brighton with some gramophone records myself. She was a marvellous mimic with a very quick mind so I knew that I only had to give her the records to copy.

'They were old wax 78s, and as I handed them to her, I told her to be extremely careful with them. They were unique and irreplaceable. She promised she would. We sat chatting for a short while. "Don't forget to take care of those records," I reminded her as she stood up. "I won't," she reassured me—and then we both realised that beneath her seat were the smashed remains of the precious records.'

For Petula, making *A Cabin in the Cotton* was one of the funniest experiences of that sad time: 'Edric Connor was an enormous man—coal black,' she recalls. 'He used to start off telling his Uncle Remus tales sitting in a chair. As he was narrating, he would slowly slide down until, eventually, he was lying flat on his back on the floor. This posed huge problems for the sound engineers who had to arrange for the mike to be lowered at an even pace the further down he slid. To keep the sound balance even, we had to follow him down. As it was a joky kind of programme it didn't matter too much if we giggled and we could ad-lib all over the place. It made wonderful radio.'

George Mitchell of 'Black and White Minstrel' fame remembers those days with affection, too. He was still an amateur at the time, working during the day as a chartered accountant in the Army Pay Corps and organising his choir work in the evenings. 'I remember giving her a lift home one evening. Leslie was going to collect her from my parents' home. I took her indoors and she saw my mother's harmonium. She was longing to play it but her feet wouldn't reach the pedals to puff the air so I sat her on my lap and punched the pedals for her while she played. The whole idea of having her around was to get a child's reaction to the stories.'

When Petula celebrated her fifteenth birthday, her time just didn't permit such a thing as a birthday party. Work came first. And in any case, even had such a treat been permitted, it is doubtful that she would have asked any friends of her own age to share the celebration. She simply didn't have any. But everyone in the BBC, including the canteen ladies, adored her and the supervisor in particular was keen to ensure that the day didn't pass without some kind of celebration.

Charles Chilton explains: 'When word got out, the canteen supervisor whispered to me that she had a surprise for Pet "off the ration". The whole *Cabin in the Cotton* team were invited. It turned out to be a rabbit pie. We all burst out laughing—and none of us could touch it. It would have been like eating Alan Keith and Benny Lee!'

She had reached her mid-teens. It was an age when teenagers around the world are beginning to find their feet and take an interest in the opposite sex. Physically, she was a woman. Yet, England still thought of her as 'Our Pet'—a delightful *little* girl.

CHAPTER SIX

HERE COME
THE HUGGETTS

At about this time, Petula met a man who was to have a huge influence on both her life and her career—pianist Joe Henderson.

They bumped into one another quite by chance at a time when he had just left the Army after completing his National Service and was an unknown song-plugger struggling to make a living with the firm of Peter Maurice Music Publishers, based in London's Denmark Street. He was twenty-seven—and new to the music business. She was fifteen and already a household name.

Leslie had gone with Pet to Peter Maurice's that fateful day looking for some new material for her Sunday afternoon TV spot. As was the custom, Joe listened carefully to her voice, chose a tune and played it over to her. It took him only about twenty minutes to fix the right arrangement for her, and both father and daughter were so impressed by the trouble he'd taken to get it right that Leslie asked him if he would be interested in accompanying Petula on the show. Until now she had always used a BBC pianist.

The BBC were very understanding about the introduction. She was a great favourite by virtue of her pleasing manner and sheer professionalism. If Leslie's insistence on discipline seemed harsh to those who saw it in action, it paid dividends in the polish of her performance and her impeccable behaviour. She always knew her scripts, her movements, how the cameras worked. Often when variety producers introduced newcomers to the screen, they would invite Petula onto their programmes. She could always be relied upon to pull people through 'first-night nerves'.

Television technology was still rather crude in the late forties. The cameramen were using the bulky, 1930s cameras which had been taken out of moth-balls at the reintroduction of the service. Focusing them was a highly skilled mixture of art and luck since the men behind the lenses saw upside-down the pictures they were beaming. The programmes were usually live and there could be no retakes when things went wrong.

Petula recalls one occasion—it was on one of her first shows with Joe—when things did get out of hand: 'The control-box ordered close-ups of me—and no one noticed that a bar used for rolling credits at the end of programmes had been accidentally left on the front of the camera. Every time the camera approached me to get the ordered close-up, I had to step backwards to avoid being hit by the bar.'

Since there was no way of informing anyone what the problem was, she spent the entire fifteen minutes of the programme doing what appeared to be a very odd jig around the studio every time the camera rolled towards her, much to the confusion of the controllers upstairs who were more accustomed to her totally conventional behaviour!

Joe was soon regarded as her regular personal accompanist. Right from the start, there was a musical sympathy between them which added a new dimension to her performance. It was a feeling which, she says, she has only ever found in one other partnership—with her American accompanist and great friend, Frank Owens.

Joe was the first person Petula had ever met of whom Leslie fully approved. She spent a great deal of time with him despite the difference in their ages, not only in the studios but rehearsing under Leslie's watchful eye at the house in

Salmon's Road. As the professional relationship matured, and Leslie began to trust him, so their private friendship grew.

It was to Joe that she confided her worries about her father's continual insistence on keeping her a child. He found himself in the role of amateur psychologist, advising her on how to handle the difficult situation. He was the first person in whom she'd been able to place her trust without fear of being reported to some gossip columnist.

In late 1949, she began work on another 'child' part in *Here Come the Huggetts*, the first in a series of three films being made by Rank under the Gainsborough Films banner, about the life of an 'ordinary' family. The Huggetts were based on the highly successful American *Hardy Family* series which starred names like Mickey Rooney and Judy Garland. It was produced and directed by Muriel, Sidney and Betty Box—a husband, wife and sister team. The idea had been engendered by the success of *Holiday Camp* in which Mr and Mrs Huggett (played by Jack Warner and Kathleen Harrison) were supposed to have had a grown-up family— but the appeal of the film was such that in the new series it was decided to give them a brood of unmarried and much younger offspring.

To give an even greater sense of 'reality', the Boxes decided that the film 'children' would be cast in their own Christian names. Hence Jane

Hylton became 'Jane', Susan Shaw 'Susan', Petula 'Pet', and Diana Doors who played a precocious cousin was still 'Diana'.

Probably the most revealing aspect of the series was that there was only a year's difference in age between Petula Clark and Diana Dors. Yet, while Diana was very much the blooming, bosomy pin-up, Petula had no difficulty at all in portraying a twelve-year-old.

Betty Box was struck not only by the physical irony of this, but by their mental disparity. 'Diana was all woman,' she says. 'She thought like a woman, acted like a woman and looked like a woman. After a hard day's shooting, we would go out for a meal together as a team; Tony Newley, who was Pet's age, came along too. But Petula was permitted no part in this off-stage ambience. When she finished work her father took her home.'

Tony Newley, although only a teenager himself, was aware of her personal misery at this treatment: 'I was a rough, tough tearaway from the East End of London,' he says. 'I had worked with her on *Vice-Versa* and I found her slightly forbidding; one of those little girls who is so bright that she's a daunting prospect for a young man with pimples.

'She always seemed so sad. She had a little director-type chair on the set with her name on it and she would sit on it with her back ramrod straight like a little sergeant-major. On one occasion, when we were on the set of the second "Huggett", *Vote for Huggett*, she confided in me.

'"I hate my father," she told me in an off-guard moment. At that time, I simply couldn't understand her. He'd always struck me as a very attractive and amusing man. But after that single conversation, we never discussed the subject.'

Another person who saw her unhappiness first-hand was one-time newspaper editor, all-time songwriter and best-selling author, Jack Fishman. He had met her some time before when he was News Editor of the *Sunday Empire News* and Petula was a child protégée. She called him 'Uncle Jack' on the 'Huggetts' filmset: her father always insisted that older colleagues were 'uncles' and 'aunties'.

'I had written a song called "Walking Backwards", in collaboration with my partner Peter Hart, which was to be Pet's first screen song in *Vote for Huggett* and it was my job to rehearse her,' he says. 'Peter and I took her into a rehearsal room and played it through to her. Just as she started to sing it, Leslie burst in. "You call that bloody singing," he screamed. "That's disgraceful. Absolute rubbish. I'll show you how people sing."

'With that,' Jack recalls, 'he flew out of the door slamming it behind him, announcing at the top of his voice how he was going to get some records of good singers and make her listen to them so that she would learn what singing was all about. She just stood there, dumbfounded and as white as a sheet, trembling.'

Jack was shaken, he says, because he felt it was all wrong. 'You couldn't blame her. He was treating her like dirt. Leslie thought he knew it all—but he knew nothing. He came back with a pile of American records and put them on. He made her listen to them while Peter and I sat in the background watching. When they were finished, he turned to her. "That's the way you've got to do it," he said. Pet was a natural mimic. She mimicked those records—and Leslie was satisfied!'

What Jack had discovered was that Leslie believed her gift for reproducing other people's work was the quickest way to stardom. Petula needed time in which to develop her own style. Leslie gave her no time at all. That incident made up both Jack and Peter's minds. They would never rehearse her in front of her father again.

Betty Box was well aware of the situation too, and it was left to her to find excuses to tear Leslie away from his daughter.

'It was a time-consuming operation,' Jack Fishman says. 'He was always interfering, always dominating. In the end, they banned him from the Gainsborough sets completely. Betty Box vowed that if he reappeared, she would never use Pet again.'

84

Since Betty both loved the girl and respected her work, this was quite some threat. 'Pet was a bloody good actress as well as a tremendous singer,' Jack says. 'She could have gone on to have a cracking career in films. But Leslie couldn't see any money in British films in those days. He saw it in singing. Pet was very frustrated. She never got the parts she really deserved—mostly because producers didn't want to have to contend with her father!'

The last picture in the series, *The Huggetts Abroad,* had an unusual history. Rank had sent a film crew to take some location shots in the desert without any particular film in which to put them. On seeing the rushes, the Boxes decided they could be turned to use in a 'Huggett'. 'It was at a time when a lot of people were emigrating to South Africa,' explains Betty Box. 'It was the "in" thing to do. We decided the Huggetts could emigrate.'

A desert had to be imported into the Islington film studios to match the location shots. Much to the cast's disgust, it came complete with sand-fleas which had the unpleasant habit of leaving their autographs, in the form of itchy pink spots, on everyone including Pet. And to get the full effect of tropical rainstorms, 10,000 gallons of water were blasted at the set—and the cast—by four enormous rain-making machines. In yet another attempt to enforce the 'little girl' image, the campaign leaflets which Rank sent around to local cinemas to help promote the films, included the story that the only person who was enthusiastic about the soaking was the Huggetts' youngest daughter, Petula. This was frankly laughable. Petula, at the time, was sixteen years old!

When the series ended, Rank gave a press-party to celebrate its success at London's Grosvenor House Hotel. Among the guests were Michael Wilding and Sir Alec Guinness, Dinah Sheridan and, of course, everybody who had featured in the films, including Petula. Rather pointedly, Leslie Clark did not receive an invitation.

Making 'The Huggetts' had, with the help of Betty Box, given Petula a little freedom from her father. She had enjoyed most of it except for, once again, having to have her breasts tightly bound to prevent them from showing her true age.

By now Petula was tugging with all her might at the kite-strings by which her father held her. She had so much that others of her age would have given anything for—fame, apparently a fortune from her films (although she was still only getting 2s. 6d. a week pocket-money), lovely clothes and a life among the stars. Even her cousin Shirley envied her this life, but Petula herself was yearning to enjoy just some of the pleasures other teenagers took for granted—such as freedom.

Among other things, she longed to have a boyfriend. But her first, innocent romance caught her when she was least expecting it. She found great comfort, when time allowed, in wandering alone amongst the tourists who flooded into the magnificent grounds of Hampton Court during the summer months. Ambling in the gardens of Henry VIII's old palace, she could dream, just as she used to do when she was a small girl picking raspberries in her own garden.

On one of her dream expeditions, she struck up a conversation with a Norwegian boy, Neils. She told him her name was 'Christina', her favourite pseudonym, and he thought she was just another English schoolgirl. After their first, brief encounter, they met whenever they could at Pet's favourite spot by Anne Boleyn's rose garden.

'We talked about anything and everything except show-business,' she says. 'He had absolutely no idea who I was, so I could just be myself. Of course, I fell in love. But, I didn't tell a soul. Not even Joe. My secret romance was just that. A secret that I could keep all to myself. My father would have been horrified to think that I'd been "picked up" by a fella in Hampton Court.'

Her secret life was very precious and very private. She is, by nature, a private person who guards certain sections of her life with a fierce jealousy and pride. Hardly surprising when one considers just how public and burdensome her lot must have seemed to her, even at a youthful sixteen.

And now, as she grew older and yearned for sophistication, another problem was rearing its head to add to her existing difficulties. For the first time in her life, the 'old trouper' was suffering from 'stage-nerves'. It was Joe Henderson who came to the rescue.

Years later, he told the story of how they were driving to an engagement together in his somewhat battered, ancient sports car when she began coughing and spluttering.

'Joe,' she cried in despair. 'My voice is going. I'd better stop and get a drink.' They stopped and Pet had her drink but a few miles further along, the coughing started again.

'I'll have to gargle,' she whimpered miserably. Again, they found a café, and she went into the ladies' room to gargle. Still she seemed no better, and the closer they came to their destination, the worse the problem seemed to become. Finally, just before their arrival, Joe the psychologist sprang into action.

'If it's that bad, I'd better stop and warn the management to find a replacement,' he said. 'You can't possibly top the bill in this state and if we don't give them at least a short warning, they'll be stuck.'

Pet got the message. She went on-stage, the

irritable throat forgotten—and gave her usual, perfect performance.

However, Joe wasn't always such a tower of strength, and travelling with him could at times have its drawbacks. Soon after the coughing incident, there was an occasion when they were booked at the last minute to fill a spot in Birmingham. In those pre-motorway days, it was a long and tedious journey. Pet, dressed in the frock she intended to wear for the performance, threw her make-up into a bag and off they went.

They had driven a mere twenty-five miles of the hundred-mile journey when it began to rain, lightly at first but then it turned into a deluge. To their dismay, they discovered that the windscreen wipers of the ancient sports car had gone on strike. Pet was given the job of working them from the inside of the car while Joe concentrated on his driving. Two and a half hours later, her oil-covered fingers raw, they arrived at their destination.

It was only then that Pet discovered that not only were her fingers covered in oil, but the dress in which she had to appear in front of an audience within half an hour was spattered with oil too. The management of the theatre went to work with tissues and cold water—but she was horribly embarrassed and extremely angry.

'Why didn't you check the mechanics of the thing before we started,' she demanded. After that, she refused to speak to Joe for two whole days!

★   ★   ★

Petula was undoubtedly Britain's most popular teenager. In between her other commitments, Rank were arranging personal appearances for her all over the country. In April 1948, she was invited to address some two hundred delegates of a British Youth Club Conference at a holiday camp at Gorleston-on-Sea, and, as usual, her role was to project the 'good girl' image so the subject of her speech was 'Let's make being a good neighbour an all-year round job'.

'Youth,' she declared in her prepared speech, 'must be ready to play its part in reshaping the future, to outlaw war and the hatred that leads to war . . .'

Afterwards, she entertained the youngsters, many of whom were the same age or just a little older than she was, and joined in the community singing and dancing.

'During a single "excuse-me" dance,' the Islington Studios' film bulletin reported, 'she changed partners no fewer than nineteen times.'

Since her father would never have allowed her to go to a local 'hop', there is no doubt that this was one personality stint she really enjoyed.

CHAPTER SEVEN

MUSIC, MUSIC, MUSIC

In early 1948, Britain faced a major fuel crisis, with the result that a national electricity emergency was called. Every possible avenue of conservation was explored. There were frequent power cuts—and the embryo TV service was temporarily suspended. Four of Petula's Sunday afternoon spots were cancelled—and for the first time in more than a year, she actually had Sunday afternoons to herself.

Even though she now had Gaby Rogers as her agent, Leslie continued to 'manage' her with single-minded determination. He was forever submitting ideas for programmes to TV producers, though few were acceptable. Once he wrote an entire script set in a kitchen. He suggested that Petula might be found working there and that he himself might appear as 'Mr Leslie Norman'. Obviously, despite having achieved a considerable measure of success for his daughter, he still had not recovered from his own, thwarted theatrical ambitions. The idea received a polite but firm 'no!'

Whilst Leslie was as busy as ever promoting Petula's career, another no-less ambitious stage-father—or step-father to be more precise—was still working on achieving full recognition for his little girl. Ted Andrews was as determined as ever to get young Julie on the air as fast as the law permitted.

He had been watching Petula's progress from the sidelines with jealous interest and now, the old, imagined feud of six years previously blew up again—but this time with such force that the blast rocked the entire British Broadcasting Corporation. The Andrews had never forgiven Cecil Madden for choosing to promote Petula's career in favour of Julie's. Nor had they forgotten how they had been axed to make time for her in the *It's All Yours* programme. And whereas that wartime programme had been heaven-sent for Petula, such opportunities no longer existed for Julie.

In March 1948, Julie Andrews had been appearing with Ted and Barbara at the London Hippodrome and Ted invited a BBC producer friend, Harry F. Pepper, to come and see her in action. Pepper was impressed—but the Andrews mistook his promise to try to help her for a vow to get her radio work immediately. They went to a great deal of trouble and expense having a script prepared so that their daughter would be ready when the moment came—and then, to their horror, they were informed that there was absolutely no chance of regular BBC work for Julie at that time.

They wrote a jealous and sarcastic letter to

Michael Standing, BBC's Variety Booking Manager, outlining their complaint. They said they couldn't understand why Petula Clark who, they claimed, was only slightly older than Julie's twelve years, should be offered entire series of her own both on radio and TV whilst Julie was simply not considered! They demanded to be told whether special exemptions existed to protect Petula, or whether there was some personal vendetta against them.

There followed a series of frustrated memos between various BBC departments to determine whether the Andrews had any justification for their fury. Despite the fact that she never seemed to be off the air, Petula, it was quickly discovered, had in fact given only eight broadcasts, in the years preceding her twelfth birthday.

Some four weeks after receipt of their letter and after searching investigations, Michael Standing replied: 'I do not believe that the treatment afforded by the BBC to Petula Clark is in fact very different from the way in which we have so far handled, and would like to continue to deal with, your daughter Julie. Petula Clark came to our notice when she was ten years old and was given in all six broadcasts over a period of twenty months until she became twelve. In the following year she received only two broadcasts and it is true to say that she did not make any regular appearances on the air until she was over fourteen.

'Julie, being only twelve at the moment, we are not prepared to feature in a series, and if you have got a wrong impression from Harry Pepper, then I can only apologise that we have inadvertently misled you. I hope, however, that she will continue to appear from time to time in our programmes and if, when she becomes a little more mature, she fulfils the wonderful promise that she now shows, I have no doubt that we shall be nearly on our knees, asking you to let her broadcast!'

In fact, the girls were absolutely no competition for each other. Their styles were totally different. Petula was the 'gutsy' pop-singer. Julie sang in purer, almost operatic, style. During the troop-concert era, they had often appeared together on the same stage. 'I used to watch her with the greatest admiration,' Petula says. 'I thought she had an exquisite voice.'

It must be said that neither Petula nor Julie had any part in the battle. Neither girl ever considered the other as a rival, even though their paths would cross many times in the years to come and, much to the chagrin of both, their careers would be frequently compared by the critics. When, in 1967, it was announced that MGM had signed Petula for *Goodbye Mr Chips*, Victor Davis wrote a news-feature in the *Sunday Express* headlined: 'It's Putting Her in the Julie

Andrews Class', in which he emphasised his point by saying: 'Metro-Goldwyn-Mayer are wooing her in a manner hitherto reserved for the Misses Julie Andrews and Audrey Hepburn.'

It was strange, too, how in later years their roles in the theatrical world seemed to reverse. As a child, Julie had few film roles—yet it was she who became the international film star first, in the very best Hollywood tradition. Petula, whose singing role as a child was more that of an impersonator than a vocalist of her own songs, and who proved her strong acting ability in no fewer than twenty-five films between 1944 and 1958, made her international name as a pop-star.

Although she sang 'Walking Backwards' in 'The Huggetts', Petula didn't cut her first, commercial disc until 1949 when she recorded 'Put Your Shoes On Lucy' for the Columbia label. It was never a hit to set the world alight but the sort of standard number which sells steadily through the years. Making it, Petula remembers, was an extraordinary experience:

'It was a very serious business. Everybody was very well-dressed for the occasion—dinner jackets and all that. The engineers wore white coats over their best suits and they didn't have any tapes in those days so the records went straight on to wax.'

Her first record producer was Norman Newell who has since produced many of the greatest names in the business, among them Johnny Mathis and Shirley Bassey. Her second record, made just a short time later for Decca, was 'The Shoemaker's Serenade'. And it was around this time that Joe Henderson introduced her to another man who was to have a great influence on both her career and her personal life—Alan Freeman.

Alan, too, had been a song-plugger, working for the Eddie Kaznar music publishing firm and, like so many of her friends, he had first seen her work long before he had encountered her professionally. 'I was attracted by her unusual name,' he says. 'Then she sang "It Had to be You", one of my favourites. That did it. At that time, I was a frustrated record producer in search of artistes and a song—and some money.'

In 1949, Alan inherited a small amount of money and decided to use it to fulfil his record-making dream. He had contacts in Australia who had asked him to make some English pop-records for them. He remembered the deep impression Petula had made on him and spoke to Leslie. It was just the sort of opportunity Leslie had been looking for and he agreed, not only to Petula singing for him but to invest some of his own money in the new company, Polygon Records.

Petula's first record for the new label, cut in late 1949 in a tiny hired studio, was 'Music,

Music, Music'. Her backing group, the newly formed 'Stargazers', included Dick James, Cliff Adams, Marie Benson with Jack Parnell on the drums and Ron Goodwin conducting. They were cutting their very first disc.

The song, vocalised by Teresa Brewer, went to the number one spot in both England and America. But in Australia, with the full force of the Rank Organisation behind her, it was Petula who had the hit—her very first! However, that wasn't enough to keep Polygon alive. To stay viable they had to prove themselves prolific. Pet followed 'Music, Music, Music' with 'Blossoms on the Bough' and 'Silver Dollar' in rapid succession. Apart from Auriel, there were then no other independent popular record companies in Britain; it was a 'dare' company—and it proved that it could be done.

Alan admits that even though she was only sixteen, he had at this time fallen head-over-heels in love with Petula: 'She was very young and obviously didn't know her own mind. I don't think she had any idea how I felt about her but I made up my mind to devote myself to her as number-one priority. She had such marvellous talent.

'I knew that by this time Joe was in love with her as much as he knew then. He was my best friend and I didn't want to hurt him. But I didn't have a chance of getting away from her.' Alan is a man who wears his heart on his sleeve.

Leslie recognised the symptoms and warned him to take care. He knew that for all the 'child-star' image he himself had created and would go on promoting, Petula was no longer physically a child, but at that difficult 'half-child, half-woman' in-between age.

'In Australia where her records were hugely popular she was accepted as a young woman,' Alan says. 'In Britain, she was still "Our Pet" and a little girl.'

'Be careful! You'll get hurt, Alan,' Leslie Clark warned him time and again. But Alan couldn't listen. He was hopelessly in love.

'I always knew that it was a love that would go unrequited,' he says. 'But I couldn't help it.'

*   *   *

In August 1948, the Clark family had moved to a slightly larger house in Riverside Drive, East Molsey. In early '49, the BBC decided to offer her a new TV series—'Pet's Parlour'. Originally, it was to have been called 'Pet's Corner' but Petula vehemently objected to the title, saying it sounded 'too much like the zoo'. The setting was supposedly the sitting-room in the Clark family's new home and much against her better judgment, Petula's sister, Barbara, then fourteen, was persuaded to take part to lend a 'family' atmosphere to the proceedings. She had never hankered after playing second fiddle to Petula's first violin but Leslie, in his characteristic manner of getting his own way when it came to his older daughter's career, coerced her into agreeing.

Joe, of course, was the accompanist and the two girls welcomed to their 'parlour' such guests as James Hayter and Harry Secombe. Invariably the songs she sang in that period were the youthful, innocent ballads which the public expected.

The time came, of course, when Petula, now seventeen, decided that she had to break the 'little-girl' mould. 'I sang a song called "When the World was Young". There was one line in it which went something like "Laying in the hay, games we used to play". The "shock, horror", mail I received was almost unbelievable. People wrote in saying "How dare I sing such words", and "Why wasn't I wearing little white socks any more?" The British public couldn't think of me as anything more than a ten-year-old. I resented it bitterly but my father assured me that nothing could be done about it.'

She made another film for Rank—*The Romantic Age*—in which she played the innocent schoolgirl daughter of the new master at a girl's exclusive finishing-school. The film was directed by Edmond Greville who had acquired the reputation in France of being a 'woman's director'. But seemingly, he failed to direct them with any degree of success in this unimpressive offering.

'The kindest thing to do about a film like *The Romantic Age* is to forget it,' wrote the *Daily Mail* critic. 'No, no, no, it won't do,' said the *Evening Standard*. 'I know critics are supposed to take a malicious delight in crabbing films but truly it breaks my heart to see so much misdirected energy.' The only decent remark in the entire lengthy piece were the words 'Petula Clark is good'.

She was Britain's most loved, and most envied, teenager. In those austere post-war days of utility clothing, she was an accepted fashion leader and often quoted as the country's best-dressed girl. Great play was made of the fact that the clothes she wore in films were often her own.

'Pet doesn't make the mistake of dressing "above" her age,' wrote *Picturegoer* in April 1950. 'She favours the simple styles—in fact the first thing that impresses you on looking through her wardrobe is the number of blouses, jumpers and skirts. One of her own skirts which she wears in *Dance Hall* (her latest film) is in accordian-pleated brown wool.'

Dance Hall, directed by Sir Michael Balcon, began shooting almost directly work on *The Romantic Age* ended. She was working with two old 'Huggett' friends—Diana Dors and Jane Hylton—and was permitted to grow up just a little, being cast this time not as a schoolgirl but as one of four friends who work side by side in a factory and relax at the local *palais-de-dance*. But once again poor Petula found herself in a 'goody-goody' role as Georgie, described by the Rank press release as 'young, happy and wholesome'. It was the same meat with different gravy, and how she was beginning to loathe the taste.

This time, not even Petula's appearance could lift the film from the doldrums in the opinion of the critics. If there was any praise, it went to Natasha Parry. '*Dance Hall* is about as embarrassing as a pair of broken braces at a wedding,' wrote the *Sunday Express*. Yet, even despite its lack of acclaim, Petula's popularity seemed harmed not at all.

Everyone, it seemed, now wanted her to associate her name with their particular club, society or cause. She received hundreds of letters each week inviting her to become president of this or chairman of that. One of the few she had the time or inclination to accept was the presidency of the newly formed Teenage Televiewers' Society. *Heiress*, the first magazine aimed at the teenage girl market and the forerunner of such papers as *Oh! Boy* and *My Guy* (in the more genteel style of the early fifties, of course), quoted her as saying: 'I *do* feel that the in-between-age has been left out in the cold.

'Were I not in the position of having seen TV from the inside, as well as from the ordinary viewer's angle, I should launch forth on ideas which I know would be quite impossible under existing conditions. Nevertheless, I *do* think that one half-hour per week could be set aside for teenage viewers.'

Daily Mail readers voted her 'Outstanding Woman TV Personality of the Year' in the annual contest—her first official, public accolade. It might have been imagined that she was one of the luckiest—and happiest—girls in the world. But this simply wasn't the case. Apart from the inner turmoil caused by her longing to be accepted for what she was, she had at this time other, more personal problems. It is to her credit—and superb acting ability—that few guessed the private stresses and strains beneath the happy-go-lucky exterior. But she had now entered one of the most deeply distressing periods of her young life.

Her mother Doris had never had a very strong constitution. She had suffered recurring flare-ups of the TB she had contracted whilst nursing and had been a semi-invalid for many years. Sadly, she lost her fight for life.

Leslie, no doubt feeling that both Petula and Barbara would be better kept in ignorance of how seriously ill their mother really was, arranged for the two girls to stay with Alan Freeman at his parents' home in South Kensington during the latter part of her illness. Petula had begun rehearsing for a new BBC series 'Study in A Flat' which was scheduled to go out once a week in the 'First House' slot, and the excuse he used for having them both billeted away from home was that it was so much easier for Pet to commute from Kensington to the Aeolian Hall in Bond Street from where the series was broadcast. The first programme went out on the night of Doris's death.

Bobby Jaye, now Head of Light Entertainment, Radio, was an engineer on the set that day and remembers: 'Leslie telephoned the control room at around lunch-time and told us it was all over. Petula was rehearsing on the studio floor at the time with Diana Decker, Gary Miller and the others. I told him I'd stop the show but he was quite insistent. "The show goes on; I'll tell her in my own way when the time is right." So the show went on.'

Others in the cast caught a hint of the tragedy and choked as they carried on, trying for all the world to appear as normal as possible.

The person who had to bear the brunt of keeping the secret was Alan Freeman. Leslie had rung him at 4.00 am to tell him that Doris had died two hours earlier. He made him swear not to tell the girls.

'He told me he wanted to tell them himself in his own way when I took them home,' Alan says. 'It was left to me to get Pet through the programme schedule that day. The girls knew of course that their mother was ill. At lunch-time,

Petula rang home as usual. She spoke to Leslie who told her that Doris had been taken into hospital but that things were otherwise much the same.'

The girls were both still in ignorance of the true situation when, after the live broadcast that night, Alan took them back to his parents' home. He was to take them home the following morning so that Leslie could break the news to them himself—and then collect them on Friday and keep them until after Saturday's funeral.

'Les told me he didn't want them at the funeral because he was frightened that the Welsh relations would make such a "do" of it and he didn't want them to think of it as a final break,' he explains. 'I took them home, just as he'd asked me to on the Thursday morning. I was so upset that I could hardly bear to listen to them chattering so gaily in the car—all the time knowing what was coming once we arrived.

'I knocked on the door and shook hands briefly with Leslie. He put his arms around his daughters and took them inside the house. I turned the car round in the cul-de-sac and drove round the corner where I burst into tears.' The enormous emotional burden he'd been carrying had just been too much, especially in view of his own feelings for Petula.

As arranged, Alan went back the following day to collect the girls. He had arranged with his sister that the four would spend the day picnicking on the Downs. He didn't know what else to do. He and Pet had a very close relationship, even if his feelings for her were not reciprocated in quite the same way. When he went to collect her that day, the greeting he received was one he will never forget. It was Petula herself who opened the door for him.

'How are you, darling?' Alan asked her.

'Oh! I'm all right. Why? Shouldn't I be?' was the only reply.

Petula knew, of course, that he'd kept the truth from her. A barrier had sprung up between them. Alan, naturally, was bitterly hurt and upset for her. He had known Doris well and counted himself her friend as well as her daughter's. He couldn't bear seeing Petula so pained. They picnicked as planned and then went on to Margate's 'Dreamland'. Neither Pet nor Barbara seemed able to show any emotion. Later he took them back to his parents' flat. Petula had to get through another week of rehearsals before the second broadcast. Leslie still had to sort out Doris's affairs. But her career had to go on!

Petula's grief was intensely private. To this day, she cannot discuss her mother's death. It must have hurt her more than words could ever describe that she, who had always been so close to her father, should have been excluded from sharing with him their joint loss; to have been barred from her own mother's funeral!

Later, Leslie took his daughters to the south of France for a brief holiday. For the first time in many years they were able to relax together, but even off duty Petula had to sing. One afternoon, the trio were sitting in a restaurant, drinking coffee, when a Frenchman sat down near them and began strumming a guitar. Petula began to hum along to herself, very quietly. Before she realised what was happening, a small crowd had gathered around her and, as she finished, they began to applaud.

A Frenchman leading a dog came across to the table. 'Mademoiselle,' he said. 'You have a very pretty voice. Eef you were French, we would make you a star.'

Little did that man know just how prophetic his words would prove.

CHAPTER EIGHT

CALLING ALL FORCES

When Petula had been launched into films back in 1944, Leslie had been keen to get as much expert advice as he could on how he could best help his daughter become a straight actress. He had written to numerous 'names' asking for their help—among them actress Googie Withers, now living in Australia.

She had written back with a single word. 'Don't.'

'That was always my advice to ambitious stage-parents,' she says. 'I believed, as I still do, that if children want to make a stage career, it should be their own doing and not that of their parents.'

Luckily, both for Leslie and the general public it was advice he had chosen to ignore—and in 1951, Petula found herself working alongside Googie in Rank's newest release, *White Corridors*, which also starred James Donald, Godfrey Tearle—Pet's old friend from *Medal for the General*, now in his sixtieth year as an actor, Megs Jenkins, Moira Lister, Jack Watling, Barry Jones, Bernard Lee and Basil Radford. Pat Jackson, considered at the time to be one of Britain's brightest directing hopes, took the direction of the film. It was, for once, a great success, widely acclaimed both in London and New York. It even received an 'honourable mention' at the Communist-sponsored international film festival at Karlsbad in Czechoslovakia, all the other awards being given to the Communist bloc countries—to Soviet, East German, Chinese and North Korean productions.

Petula's schedule for radio broadcasts—which now included one of the most important and best remembered programmes on which she had ever worked, *Calling All Forces* compèred by

Ted Ray—had to be carefully mapped to fit in with heavy filming schedules.

*   *   *

In this programme, which was sent overseas via the British Forces Network each week, Petula sang listeners' requests, bringing families together through music. She was backed by Geraldo's orchestra and the George Mitchell choir, which delighted her—but the programme seemed riddled with problems right from the start.

When it was first broadcast in December 1951, a tactless BBC announcer introduced the young woman who had been singing to troops through one medium or another since she was eight years old as 'The Forces' Sweetheart'. It was a title hard-earned and much treasured by Petula's old idol, Vera Lynn, and its apparent misuse caused a six-day war which involved not merely the BBC but the War Office, and thousands of British servicemen in all three forces who complained bitterly.

Once again, Petula found herself in the middle of a row in which she had played no part. She was, however, extremely contrite when she realised the furore which had been caused by the misuse of the affectionate nickname and wrote to Vera immediately, apologising for 'stealing' the title and assuring her that such a thing wouldn't happen again. But the press, as was to be expected, made great play on what they called 'the battle of the Sweethearts'. And Frank Cooper, the programme's co-producer, was entirely unrepentant.

Although the BBC themselves did not repeat the mistake, the newspapers continued to refer to Petula as 'the Forces' Sweetheart' for the next six months she spent on the programme—and passed it on to her successor, Carole Carr.

As on any request programme, it was necessary to 'balance' the songs used on *Calling All Forces*. It was all too easy to repeat the same favourites week after week. According to Leslie, there was a misunderstanding between Petula's new agent, E. W. Kent, and Michael Standing, Head of Variety, about pressures being brought to bear on her to sing certain kinds of songs on the programme—songs like 'The Mona Lisa' which, Leslie declared in a letter carefully preserved in the BBC archives, was 'quite out of her range'. It was finally agreed that, in order to achieve the correct balance of fast and slow, modern and nostalgic numbers, a request for 'Pet's own choice' could be slipped in if necessary to preserve this status quo.

Pet's sister Barbara, now fifteen, inevitably became drawn into the family 'business'. Each week, the BBC received sacks of request mail which they passed on to Leslie and Pet at home. Barbara was given the task of opening these letters and sorting through them before passing them on to her father and sister. Since Doris's death, the girls had become much closer and Barbara was anxious to do anything that would help her older sister.

Naturally, she had overheard the conversations between Leslie, Pet and Joe Henderson who was, as always, her accompanist on the programme and had rightly concluded that there were problems over the choice of material. This, she felt, was something she could sort out by herself.

In March 1951, during a particularly difficult week, she wrote five letters, topping and tailing them with genuine names and addresses but altering the requests to numbers which she knew Petula enjoyed singing. She changed her handwriting on each as best she could but when the letters were passed on for BBC approval, the similarity was noticed—and it almost cost Petula her unique, fifteen-minute, peak-time Sunday evening slot.

An angry Michael Standing contacted Leslie and demanded an explanation. Leslie, who quite genuinely knew nothing of his youngest daughter's well-intentioned antics, had none to offer. He was warned, in no uncertain terms, that should such a thing occur again, Petula would no longer be of use to the BBC.

The shock waves which reverberated around Broadcasting House echoed through to the house in Riverside Drive to which the Clarks had recently moved. It didn't take too much probing on Leslie's part to discover the culprit and he wrote a humble letter of apology to Standing. Neither he, Joe nor Pet herself, he explained, had had the least suspicion that the requests were anything but genuine.

In July 1952, it was announced that Petula had refused a further thirteen-week contract for the programme and that Carole Carr would succeed her. Her prime ambition had always been in the field of drama, anyway. The official reason given was that, with several films in the offing, Rank had first call on her services as 'their' contract artiste. She had even, it was rumoured, turned down an offer from Val Parnell to top the bill at the London Palladium. Of course, she announced, she would continue to accept BBC bookings but they would have to take second place to theatrical or film offers of straight parts.

During the *Calling All Forces* stint, Petula had had a slight altercation with a theatrical company over a role in *Gwith Loves Oswig* which Anthony Hawtrey was producing at the Embassy Theatre in Swiss Cottage—a London 'fringe' theatre. She had signed a contract, but then Leslie had announced that she would not be able to fulfil it because of ill-health. He produced a medical certificate which stated that she was suffering from 'nasal catarrh and needed a holiday'. Hawtrey was furious. His solicitors sent a doctor into the *Calling All Forces* studio to observe her—but the doctor declined to comment to the media and a lawsuit followed: the first in Pet's entire career. Actress Jane Barrett stepped into the breach—but Pet herself was as determined as ever to become an adult actress worthy of the kind of notices which her singing career had attracted.

Cecil Madden, who had played such a large part in bringing her to stardom within the BBC, was now frightened that he would lose her. In desperation, he wrote to Michael Barry, head of TV Drama, suggesting that she might be offered the part of 'the child' in *Daddy Long-Legs:* 'I think this casting would be a very popular move and help to put this very old play over. She is just at an age when she can look very young indeed.'

But this was exactly the sort of part Petula didn't want. The one-time child-star, now almost out of her teens, was becoming bitterly resentful about the efforts of all those around her, including her beloved father and Cecil Madden, to stunt her natural right to grow into womanhood. She still found herself dressing the way Leslie advised, accepting the roles her producers suggested, taking the film parts that promoted the pleasant, clean-living, perfect young girl image. It was an image she longed to dispel but so long as the public would only see her as 'Our Pet', it seemed she would never lose it.

In a desperate effort to fill out physically, she tried to stuff herself with the most fattening foods she could find. Doctors advised her to drink four pints of milk a day and to eat as many cream cakes and potatoes as she could manage. It was all to no avail. She worried about it so much that her weight hovered miserably around the six-stone mark.

In March 1952, her career suffered another, unexpected setback. Her Rank contract, which still had another year to run, stated plainly that she must not work for a month without a single day's rest. She was still, at this time, inviting guests to join her in *Pet's Parlour* on Sunday afternoons but now, it appeared, if she continued with her *Parlours*, she would be breaking the terms of that contract. Rank's insurance company were adamant. The show must be abandoned, temporarily at least. In fact, despite its popularity, and Leslie's frequent and vigorous attempt to revive it, it never had a regular showing again.

Leslie never gave up. He was still writing his scripts and submitting them to people like Ronnie Waldman—but by now they knew his mode of operation all too well. He was becoming something of a pest at the BBC. All this reflected in Petula's own attitude to work—and contributed to her increasingly difficult home life. While she wasn't as physically starved as she appeared, she was emotionally famished. Both Alan Freeman and Joe Henderson, her only two real friends, would have done anything to make her happy. But what she needed was something neither of them could provide: breathing-space and company of her own age. It was sheer luck that she found both these things for herself in the person of an American GI whom she met at her favourite Hampton Court and fell head-over-heels in love with. His name was Bill Foss.

'I would hate anyone to think that I was in the habit of picking up men at Hampton Court,' Petula says with a laugh. 'It was simply the only place I ever went to on my own. I was standing in my favourite spot, admiring Anne Boleyn's beautiful gardens one afternoon, when an American boy came up to me and started a conversation. He told me his name was Bill and that he was a GI and stationed at Bushey Park. He wasn't in the least stage-struck and at first he had absolutely no idea who I was. After a while, we began meeting regularly and, of course, we fell in love. For me, it was a very serious thing.'

Despite her heavy commitments in films, radio and TV, and Bill's duty rotas, the two began to see a great deal of each other—and this time there was no keeping the secret from Leslie. From the very first, he voiced strong objections to the friendship. America was a long way away. He could see no future for his daughter there. He could hardly have known that in the following decade, she would be more of a STAR in solid block capitals there than she could ever be in Britain despite the empire which he had built so painstakingly around her. He found every argument he could think of to dissuade her from continuing the relationship, but to no avail. For the first time in her life, Petula had decided to assert her own authority.

She turned to her two best friends, Alan and Joe, in desperation. Wouldn't they help her? They knew what she'd been going through! Couldn't they talk to her father and persuade him to give her the one thing she most wanted in the world. But there was little either of them could do. Alan was still in love with her himself although by this time he believed what Leslie had once told him—that she would never return his adoration.

Bill returned to his home in the Catskills in New York State in the autumn of 1951. They wrote to one another regularly—and in the end, Leslie, believing it was the only way he could get Bill out of her system, agreed to accompany Pet on a visit to the States so that she could see the hard reality for herself.

Cecil Madden got to hear of the proposed trip. He felt as sorry for her as he had always done and thought that if Leslie could be made to see that there were indeed possibilities of work for Petula in the USA he might relent and allow her to marry Bill.

She was due to arrive in New York on 28 December. The day before, Madden secretly cabled Commercial Broadcasts in New York City: 'Petula Clark outstanding nineteener television and radio singing star also top film personality here winner 1950 Daily Mail Television Award and altogether charming unspoilt personality arriving New York airwise tomorrow 10.00 GMT staying care William Foss Rock Hill New York before going Florida for rest would like to do guest television spot or so while there if conditions satisfactory stop Couldst notify networks or anyone you think fit + Cecil Madden.'

The Philadelphia newspapers got wind of the visit and announced that she would make her first American TV appearance on NBC singing 'The Golden Haired Boy from the Valleys'. But the show never materialised if, in fact, the offer to appear on it had even been made. Petula herself declares: 'I knew nothing about it and certainly didn't want to make a television appearance at that time. I had gone to see Bill and I wanted to be left alone to work things out for myself.'

Alan, too, was concerned about her. Polygon Records were not doing too well at this time, but if Pet was going to America, then Alan determined to go along too, just to keep an eye on her. Using his last cent, he booked himself a first-class ticket on a Monarch and arrived a few days later, ostensibly to talk to some American recording people. While Pet and Bill courted, Alan attempted to draw Leslie away from them and involve him in other things.

Bill's father owned a building company. During her brief stay, Bill showed her a magnificent house, set by a lake, which he said he was building for her. It would be their first home together. He took her out and bought her a small, diamond engagement ring which she hid in her bra. When the all-too-short visit was over, Pet and Leslie flew on to Florida for a four-week holiday and Petula led him to believe that it was all over between them. But only now, thirty years later, is Petula prepared to tell the real story.

'I was heartbroken when the time came to leave Bill,' she says. 'He'd bought me the ring and I considered myself engaged to him, whatever being engaged means. We went off for our Florida holiday, all the time my father reassuring me that I was too young to consider marriage and that I had done the right thing. Of course, he was right, although I didn't think so at the time. I had this inner feeling that if I left Bill, we would never marry. I wore his ring round my neck for a long time. I was terribly hurt and angry with my father for parting us, then. But there was absolutely no question of

117

me being allowed to stay in the States.'

Petula's instincts were right. It was many years before they met again, by which time they were both married to other people and Bill was living with his wife in the house he had built for her. She was living by another lake, too, many miles from her homeland.

For several months, the forbidden lovers continued to write, but little by little, just as Leslie had expected, the passions waned. 'Eventually,' says Petula, 'the whole thing died a natural death. But I think this had a lot to do with my growing affection for Joe. He was a great friend to me throughout it all.'

Joe was a gentle giant. He had loved Petula from the time she was a lonely child. He was married and by this time had a son, but he was happy to allow the equally lonely young woman to lean on him for support. Petula, depressed and desolate, was finding that the work which had once come so easily to her was becoming harder and harder, even despite Joe's encouragement:

'After Bill, my father had to realise that I was growing up. It was a fact of life he could no longer deny. The situation affected my work. Until this time, my father had chosen my clothes and my songs and advised which offers of work I should accept. I wanted to prove to myself as much as to anyone else, that I had the ability and aptitude to do some of this for

118

myself. My father told me he insisted on having things his way to prevent me from making mistakes—but I wanted to make mistakes for myself.'

Both Joe and Alan tried to persuade Leslie to understand how she felt. But he preferred to remain blind. He had brought Petula this far in her career and he wasn't being pushed aside after all his hard work simply because the years were flying away. The rows between father and daughter were becoming more frequent; the rift between them widening at every one. Petula was torn in two, knowing that she should express her gratitude but yearning to loosen the kite string and fly free for a while on her own.

When she returned to Britain in February, the press were quick to notice a 'new look' Pet. She had had her hair cut and styled in a more sophisticated fashion. The clothes she wore were stylish American models. Yet, however hard she tried, and whenever she returned to her homeland in future years, she couldn't shake off that childhood image. It stuck to her as closely as her own shadow and similarly appeared whenever the limelight struck her, no matter which way she stood.

The urge to act was stronger than ever. Yet the roles Rank offered were always those of a child or—at best—a sweet and innocent young woman. 'I'm simply not like that,' she protested, over and over again. 'No one knows the real ME.' But no one wanted to. They gave her the part of the pretty little mother of twins, opposite David Tomlinson, in *Made in Heaven* in 1952—but to Petula it represented yet another pliable, almost characterless part. That same year, they gave her the role of Nellie Cotterill in *The Card*. Another actress of that era may have rubbed her hands in glee at the chance to play with Alec Guinness, yet although the critics acclaimed it and her ability in it, she felt the part of the meek little dancing teacher's maid as nothing more than a gesture on Rank's part.

However, the story of the washerwoman's son who rises from a clerk in a rent-collector's office to become the youngest Mayor ever of the Five Towns—did permit Petula her first screen kiss. In the final scene Petula as Nellie is dragged somewhat dramatically from the ship which she is boarding with her mistress. As Machin (Alec Guinness) pushes her roughly into a conveniently parked hansom cab, she wrestles mildly with him.

'What is to become of me?' she pleads soulfully.

'I'm going to marry you, that's what,' he replies, pulling her masterfully towards him. In the best film traditions, their eyes meet. Hers are brimming with tears. For a haunting second, the look deepens. Then their lips draw closer and they kiss—a deep, passionate kiss spanning

120

a whole, tear-jerking thirty seconds.

It was a daring move on Rank's part. Pet's first real screen kiss was headline news in the movie magazines. The film company had acknowledged that she was no longer a little girl. Yet, still, she was dissatisfied. On 15 November 1952, her twentieth birthday, she told an *Evening Standard* reporter: 'Birthdays make me feel a little older. But the birthday present I'd really like most is a chance to play the gypsy heroine in a film of Jeffrey Farnol's novel *Peregrine's Progress.*' But, it seemed, there wasn't a producer who would take on the picture.

Even in the record industry—in which Alan Freeman and Leslie were both deeply involved—she couldn't cut herself free. When Polygon decided to make a record for Christmas 1952, 'Where Did My Snowman Go', with Steve Race at the piano and backing from a group of children from a Dr Barnado's home, it was an instant hit. So was 'Christopher Robin at Buckingham Palace' made just a few months later.

There had, of course, been other records; songs with grown-up words and a deeper meaning. Some were never released. Others made no impact at all and were best forgotten. Her only hits were coming with childish songs— and how she longed to leave them all behind forever.

CHAPTER NINE

WHITE CORRIDORS

Right from her babyhood, people seeing Petula in person for the first time had worried about her health, always without cause. The 'slim and wiry baby', as her Aunt Emma had described her, had grown into a petite, slender young woman. She had always looked frail—the sort of girl men instantly wanted to protect—yet apart from the usual childhood illnesses, she had never been ill in her life.

But in early 1953, when she finally had to admit, even to herself, that the romance with Bill Foss was really over, and at a time when she seemed to be fighting a never-ending, losing battle for independence with her father, all the nervous stresses and strains of the past eleven years seemed finally to be taking their toll. She didn't look well and there were constant rumours that she was losing weight, possibly even suffering from TB. Whether these originated from some twisted version of her late mother's illness, no one ever discovered. Naturally, she denied them strongly.

'I have not got TB. I am not losing weight. I have not had a nervous breakdown,' she told the ever-inquiring press. 'These rumours about me

122

are lies. I am in fact feeling better than at any time in my life and relaxing for the first time since I was a child.'

As though to prove her strength, she decided to take a stand with Rank and refused to co-star with Norman Wisdom in *Trouble in Store*, saying that she felt it was just another ineffectual role. The studio suspended her. Her contract still had one more year to run and they were quite within their rights. But so, she felt, was she.

Once more she decided that perhaps the answer to the more fleshy parts was to gain some real flesh herself and booked into Champneys, a huge country house in Tring, Hertfordshire, where most of the guests were paying twenty guineas a week to lose their excess flab. Petula was put on a diet guaranteed to make them drool; back to those hated four pints of milk a day, mounds of bread spread lavishly with butter, plenty of potatoes and cream and a strict programme of relaxation.

After two weeks, the treatment definitely seemed to be working. To her delight, she had gained six whole pounds and boasted a trim but curvacious 34" 21" 34" figure—'perfectly in proportion,' she told people proudly. Her radio career, too, was going from strength to strength. She was invited to appear on Henry Hall's popular *Guest Night*—but still they wouldn't allow her to sing the songs she most wanted to.

'I was a jazz influenced singer,' she says. 'I'd grown up with jazz and always wanted to sing that kind of music. I have always loved both Lena Horne and Peggy Lee and admired their styles. But if I broke the mould in which I'd been cast with even one single beat song, the anti-mail would flood into the BBC.'

In March, it became clear that despite her claims that she had never felt better, the wan complexion and general appearance of unwellness was due to more than exhaustion. She was rushed into hospital for an emergency appendectomy. 'I remember waking up thinking I must be dead because I was surrounded by nursing nuns,' she says. 'While I was in hospital, somebody gave me the book *Doctor in the House*. I fell around laughing as I read it, which was agony.'

It was, nevertheless, a pale little figure which emerged after two weeks in hospital to tell the world that she was 'fine' and would soon be back in full swing again. But somehow, she just couldn't seem to get back on her feet. She fulfilled her engagements in the same polished, professional way as she had always done but the sparkle was inexplicably missing.

In November, she was due to celebrate her twenty-first birthday—and twelve years in show business. Leslie, never one to miss an opportunity, wrote to his television producer friends informing them of this important fact and suggesting that since she was almost as much 'their' child as his, they might like to formulate some kind of public party to mark the occasion.

Cecil Madden, who loved her as dearly now as when he had first set eyes on her twelve years before, thought it was a marvellous idea. And he had another to add to it. He was now Head of Children's Television and as such had been deeply involved with such 1950s favourites as 'Mr Turnip', 'Andy-Pandy', 'Bill and Ben' the crackle-voiced flowerpot men and their close ally, 'Little Weed'. The Society of Puppeteers had voted him their president—and Madden asked Petula if she would be free, just before her birthday, to make a guest appearance at the Society. Of course, she accepted.

But, in the event, all the grand preparations were in vain and the publicity she received on her twenty-first birthday was not quite of the sort that any of her family or friends expected.

Leslie had remarried by this time. Both Petula and Barbara had known and admired their step-mother for a long time. Many years before, she had been Petula's governess on the Gainsborough film sets and, when their own mother had been too ill to follow their careers or do with them the many things a mother does, it had been Ann who had kindly stepped into the breach. Before her death, Doris had begged her to watch over her precious daughters and look

125

after them as her own and Ann had remained a close friend of the family throughout their troubles. From the time of her marriage to Leslie, both girls had looked on her as a mother.

Since her appendectomy, the pressures had eased a little. Perhaps it was his relationship with Ann that had softened Leslie's attitude to Pet's work although, of course, there was still room for improvement.

In October 1953, just before the birthday celebrations, Alan Freeman had arranged a recording session for her to cut a new title, 'Poppa Piccolino'. It was towards the end of that session that Petula complained of feeling ill. Then, to the horror of the entire studio, she collapsed in a heap on the floor. Alan picked her up carefully, lowered her gently into his car and drove her home. By the time she arrived, she insisted she felt better.

'She looked ghastly,' Alan says. 'Both Ann and I told Leslie he had better call a doctor, but Leslie had a quirk about doctors. He said he'd "see how it went".'

Petula went to bed, but in the middle of the night she awoke in excruciating pain. 'I knew I was dying. I just knew it,' she says. She hobbled into Leslie and Ann's room, doubled over in agony. Ann told her it was probably a 'woman's thing', gave her some hot gin and tucked her back into bed. But by 3.00 am, it was quite obvious, even to the stubborn Leslie, that

Petula was very ill indeed. Now he was in a blind panic as he rang for the doctor who came, still in his pyjamas.

It was a dank, foggy, mid-October night. The ambulance, its bells in full peal, picked its way cautiously through the deserted London streets to the South London Hospital for Women. She was put to bed. The agonising pain of just an hour before seemed to have disappeared.

'I slept through the rest of the night. I can remember waking in the morning and thinking that I must brush my teeth. I always had a thing about cleaning my teeth. I saw a wash-basin in the corner of the room. I can remember getting out of bed and going towards it. That was the last I knew.'

She had collapsed again. 'Nobody knew what the problem was but they decided to perform an emergency exploratory operation to find out,' she says. She has no memory of the anxious days that followed, but others close to her remember them all too vividly.

'Leslie rang me to tell me what was happening,' Alan Freeman says. '"Alan, I know you're not religious. Neither am I. But if you have a prayer inside you, say a little one for Petula now," he told me. That, coming from Les who didn't believe in very much at all shattered me. I broke down and cried and said that little prayer. Pet was within ninety minutes of death, they told us afterwards.'

The delicate operation was performed by a brilliant woman surgeon. She discovered that Pet had suffered from a strangulation of the intestine. It had possibly been caused, they said, because she had been kept in bed for a whole two weeks following her appendectomy. It was kindness which had almost killed her.

The surgeon had to remove a large amount of intestine in order to save her life. Speed had been an essential factor. For three days, she hung on to the world by a tenuous thread. For those seventy-two hours she was in intensive care, a nurse by her bedside day and night. Only her parents and Barbara were allowed to see her for brief moments. There were tubes everywhere, up her nose and down her throat.

'I remember,' she says, 'coming to and seeing the sun shining and the lovely blue sky outside the window. I can remember thinking how nice it all was and how I felt like just drifting back to sleep. Then an alarm went off in my mind. I knew if I went back to sleep, I would never awaken again. It was at that moment that I started to recover.'

Alan went to see her on the first day visitors were allowed: 'She lay there looking like some poor little thing from Belsen. Her arms were like matchsticks and she was still attached to all the tubes and things. It was awful.'

'A lot has been said about this illness,' Petula says, today. 'Rumour has it that they performed

128

a colostomy. It's absolutely untrue. There never was any question of it. I have a scar, of course, but there have never been any complications. I wear tight-fitting clothes and on the beach I wear a bikini if I must although I prefer to wear nothing at all if I can get away with it.

'I certainly wear no bags or other medical paraphernalia. Somehow or another, my name has appeared on a list of people who have undergone such operations and I still get a huge amount of mail from people who say to me: "We know you've had this done. What's your advice?" I have to tell them the truth. I haven't had it done and it's one rumour I'd like to dispel once and for all.'

Petula was in hospital for six weeks. Instead of enjoying the grand public celebrations which had been planned to celebrate her coming-of-age on 15 November 1953, she lay in hospital recovering with frequent visits from the ever-faithful Joe and Alan. As soon as she was well enough, the two men took her for a quiet, belated, celebration dinner at Ciro's, an exclusive London restaurant.

During Petula's illness, Leslie had had plenty of time to think. There is no doubt that for all his pushy, show-biz manner, he truly loved his daughter as much as she loved him. Coming so close to losing her had made him realise just how desperately he wanted her to be happy as well as famous. By the time she came home, he had formulated a whole new set of ideas which he hoped would please her.

'I plan to allow her to wear high heels to make her look taller when she comes out of hospital,' he told newspaper reporters. 'She will wear sophisticated clothes specially designed to accentuate the new, adult woman inside them. In her handbag will be her first cheque-book and there will be a sports car outside the front door which I've ordered for her as a special surprise.'

Petula had been taught to drive by a police driving instructor. She was an excellent driver and loved driving, finding great pleasure and freedom behind the wheel. A car of her own, Leslie knew, would be a great fillip to her morale. He had another plan up his sleeve, too, which he hoped would meet with her approval.

'I have been accused of exploiting her—claims I flatly deny', he said in self-defence, all too aware of the rumours which had been flying around about him. 'If I'd wanted to exploit her, I would have had her in Variety, earning three times as much as she does now rather than sticking to films, records and TV work as we have done. Petula's main ambition is to be a dramatic actress. I intend to help her achieve that.'

Leslie the father was making an extraordinary effort to be a father. But Leslie the manager hadn't given up the ghost. In an interview with

Donald Zec of the *Daily Mirror* on 22 October 1953—just a couple of days after her operation—he said: 'I am writing a film story specially for Petula. This encourages her to register every style from Gracie Fields to Sara Bernhardt. I am quite prepared to accept no fee for the script provided my daughter is given a starring role.'

Perhaps not surprisingly, the script was never heard of again. Donald Zec in the same feature summed up the situation: 'I hope she won't be too upset if this maturity campaign should fail to establish her womanhood. There is a shipload of plump, mature, ageing actresses who'd give an awful lot to be twenty-one, petite—and Petula.'

It was several months before Petula was fit enough to pick up her old pace again. As she grew stronger, she began trekking round the music publishers again. Eventually, she found the song which she thought was promising. She took it straight to Alan.

'Of course, I was extremely anxious to hear it,' Alan says. 'But when she played it to me for the first time, frankly I was amazed. "The Little Shoemaker" was a charming song—but it had a childlike quality which surprised me after all her talk about becoming a sophisticated woman and working with more mature material.'

Alan, nevertheless, routined it for her—Malcolm Lockier did the arrangements. Alan booked the orchestra for half a session. Money,

131

at Polygon, was as tight as ever and Pet had a reputation for having her work rehearsed and ready for immediate recording. Two hours should have given ample time to record two titles, 'The Little Shoemaker' and a 'B' side.

The orchestra arrived. Everyone was ready to go. And, for the first time he could remember, Petula was late. Alan stood anxiously glancing at his watch every few seconds and jigging from one foot to the other, growing angrier by the moment. She knew how precious time was. She knew how long the orchestra was booked for. She knew just how hard times were financially at Polygon. By the time she eventually arrived with Joe, Alan was in no mood for solicitous inquiries.

'Where the bloody hell have you been?' he bellowed.

Petula turned to Joe anxiously, unable to say a word.

'I was hoping to stop you yelling,' Joe told his friend. 'Les had a car smash and Pet nearly went through the window screen.'

Alan swallowed hard. Petula, already shaken by the smash, was livid.

'She has a flaming temper when she's roused,' he said. 'She wouldn't speak to me for the rest of the session. She made the recording with all that lovely charm coming over in her voice—and a thunder-black scowl on her face. It was all done in ten minutes and a single run-through. By the time they had finished, there were the usual hugs and kisses and all was forgiven.'

Despite the traumas in its making, 'The Little Shoemaker' was Pet's first entry in the British Top Ten. It hit number seven and stayed in the charts for nine weeks. She was back on top, again.

CHAPTER TEN

MAJORCA

With painful 1953 behind her—and 'The Little Shoemaker' riding high in the charts—it looked as though 1954 might prove to be the year of the breakthrough she'd been looking for so hard and for so long.

When, in February, it was announced that she had been cast in the role of the tragic waif, Tessa, in a stage revival of Edna Best's 1926 box-office hit *The Constant Nymph* at the 'Q' Theatre, Richmond, it seemed to endorse that prophetic feeling.

She had appeared at the 'Q' briefly once before in a nondescript comedy which had run for a mere week, but the chance she was now offered to portray this plum part opposite John Gregson seemed all she could have wished for.

In view of her own, recent dust with death,

the fragile Tessa was tailor-made for her to express all her own pent-up emotions, and it played to packed houses throughout its two-week run. But the critics' assessments of her performance on the live stage were mixed.

'Pet proved that she is something more than an appealing singer. Her Tessa was an excellent emotional study, pert and vivacious in health, tragically moving in sickness,' wrote John Balfour in the *Daily Sketch*. The *Daily Mail* reporter, however, was not as enthusiastic: 'Miss Clark's performance last night showed that for all her screen maturity, she still has far to go on the stage. It was a brisk performance in its jerky way and an appealing one but it seldom caught the real tragedy of a child lost in the woods of adult love.'

It was, perhaps, some compensation that the same critic was none too kind about Gregson's performance, either, saying that 'he ... underplayed the hapless idol in the manner of one who has made too many films in a row.'

It is probably just as well that the moment Petula herself best remembers from that run was one the critics missed. 'We had a bedroom scene towards the end of the play in which I had to have an attack and fall on to the bed and John Gregson falls with me,' she laughs. 'It was supposed to be a very dramatic moment. But on this particular night and with five minutes of the show left to run, we fell on to the bed and it collapsed underneath us. It was terribly hard to stop the scene from turning into a french farce. I had hysterics—although I didn't realise it until the moment was over. John Gregson, with his immense talent and *savoir faire* of the stage, managed to haul us both through with ad-libs. It seemed such a dreadful thing to happen, but I don't believe that the audience realised there was a problem at all.'

It would be another twenty-eight years before Petula appeared live on a London theatre stage again. And even though she had appeared so successfully in an adult role, the Rank Organisation, still smarting over her refusal to co-star in the Wisdom film, decided not to renew her contract.

She had spent seven years as a Rank contract star and in all that time, the only film with excellent reviews in which she had had a 'straight' and adult part was *White Corridors*. Another actress might have been hurt to be dropped thus after such a long time—but not Petula. To her, it came as something of a relief. A change of film company might also mean a change of image.

But if Rank were not yet convinced of her acting talent and potential, radio was. She was offered a starring part in a show which was to become a classic, *A Life of Bliss*. The show, in which she worked with Moira Lister, Percy Edwards and George Cole, satisfied her more than anything she had done for a very long time. As a 'Blisslet' she broadcast regularly for twenty-seven weeks from the BBC Playhouse at Charing Cross—a very long run for her indeed—and making the programme was an almost funnier experience than listening to it.

'There was always a problem with the *Life of Bliss* scripts,' she recalls. 'Sometimes, the audience would actually be filling the theatre and only six or seven pages of an eighteen-page script would be completed. The writer would be sitting in the basement sweating away at it while we began the show. We'd do the first twelve minutes to keep the audience happy and then the producer, Leslie Bridgmont, would announce that there had been a technical hitch. We'd all take it in turns to entertain the audience while we waited for the rest of the script to arrive. Sometimes, the half-hour programme could take five or six hours to record.'

It was almost a year now since Petula's illness. She had made a remarkable recovery—and an unremarkable film for the Republic Productions film company, *The Runaway Bus*, an improbable thriller in which she co-starred with Frankie Howerd, Kent Taylor, Margaret Rutherford and Renée Houston. It was her first film away from Rank—and she was no better off for it.

During her illness, Pet's two best friends, Joe

and Alan Freeman, had stood by her—and now, when Alan became ill, it was her turn to prove her friendship. Alan suffered a virulent attack of meningitis. For weeks he lay at home in a darkened room, unable to bear light of any kind. When the illness had struck, he had been in the middle of negotiating a deal with the record company Nixie to take it and Polygon under the newly formed Pye Records umbrella.

The doctors suggested that a holiday in the sun might aid his recovery and as he began to feel better, he accepted a friend's offer to lend him his villa at Camp Del Mar in Majorca; at that time a totally unspoiled Mediterranean island. But Alan could not travel alone—and when Pet heard he needed a companion, she volunteered herself.

'I was so weak that I couldn't even carry my own bag,' Alan says. 'It suited me down to the ground when Pet offered to come along. I was still very much in love with her, although she didn't give our relationship a second thought. By this time, too, she had realised that her feelings for Joe were too deep to be platonic any longer. No matter how much I loved her, I had no intention of coming between them.'

The holiday in Majorca with Alan, and a little later Joe, was one Pet herself will never forget: 'One day, after Joe arrived, the three of us had a particularly delightful Spanish concoction on the beach. We let our hair down and really went to town. That night, the three of us met in the corridors of the hotel in which we were staying by this time. All of us were gasping with thirst. The tap-water in the bedroom was undrinkable. Like thirsty dogs in a desert, we wandered round the deserted hotel looking for relief from the awful thirst, all of us in nightclothes. The kitchens were locked. There wasn't a drain of anything remotely drinkable to be had. Imagine! It was dawn before the first staff came on duty and offered us some fresh water which tasted like ambrosia.'

Within ten days of the threesome's arrival back in London, a strange coincidence occurred. Alan was offered a song called 'Majorca—Isle of Love', written by the French composer Phillipe Gaste. 'We've got to record this one,' he told Petula. It had already been a massive hit in France. It was the first song Alan cut under his new deal with Pye. In England, too, it was an instant hit.

When Gaste's wife, French singer Line Renaud, heard about Petula's huge success with the English version of her husband's song, she invited Pet to France to appear on her own TV show, *This is Your Life, Line Renaud*. Her first appearance on the French screen was sensational. She wore a strawberry pink ballgown—such gowns were later to become almost a hallmark for Petula Clark in France—and sang in English since she couldn't utter a single word in French. But it was very much a one-off thing. No one could then have foreseen the impact she would make when she returned to France four years later.

The success of 'Majorca' had another unexpected reaction on the British public. Much to the delight of the Spanish Tourist Office, it started a demand for holidays on the island. So excited were the tourist people by this development that they offered Petula, Joe and Alan a free holiday there the following year. It was an offer none of them were ever able to accept—due to pressure of work.

She made another film, released in November 1954, called *The Happiness of Three Women* and directed, to her immense joy, by Maurice Elvey, who had directed her very first film ten years before, *Medal for the General*, and who still sported his goatee beard with pride. This time, it was under the Adelphi Films banner and starred Donald Houston, Brenda De Ranzie and Gladys Hay in a romantic story centred around a wishing-well.

If Petula herself had been wishing for a huge film hit at last, then the well's powers were not as contrived as the plot would have had filmgoers believe. Even *The Times* critic raved about it: 'This is a film which, using any methods to hand determines to set the audience rolling in the aisles and reaching for their handkerchiefs at one and the same time.'

Yet, despite this success, Petula was becoming increasingly unhappy and self-doubting. The years of Leslie's drilling had left their mark. She was now twenty-four years old, yet at home and at work, he ruled the roost while she still did as she was told, when she was told and how she was told.

It is scarcely credible that, whilst she had been performing regularly for the BBC for fourteen years, she had never once during that time been offered a long-term contract. So far, all her contracts had been for single shows or series with constant renewals.

In early 1955, Leslie woke up to what he suddenly saw as a gross omission on the part of the Corporation and spoke to Cecil McGivern, BBC TV's Controller of Programmes and a close friend of Cecil Madden's, about it. McGivern sent an urgent memo on the subject to Ronnie Waldman, Head of TV Light Entertainment and by this time a close friend of Leslie's. 'Surely,' he wrote, 'it is madness not to try to put her under some sort of contract. If not, why not a series of films with an ISM pianist?'

'Agreed,' Waldman replied immediately. 'But how many shows a year are you willing to take?'

The subject of a contract for Petula was duly discussed with Waldman in April 1954 and it was agreed to offer her a yearly contract with options for the next two years and three months' notice on either side, starting from September.

They would expect her to make twelve appearances a year for a fixed fee of seven hundred guineas, with an extra fifty guineas for every show over and above the basic twelve. To this agreement, Petula and Leslie insisted on a rider. Of the twelve, two appearances must be 'straight' acting parts. There was, of course, an exclusivity clause, too, preventing her for working for the soon-to-be-launched commercial television companies.

But the contract was beset by problems right from the start. As her agent E. W. Kent—whom she affectionately called E. W.—was quick to point out, even before it was signed, the fee she was being offered was laughable when compared with the earnings of 'new' stars like Alma Cogan who would sign for no less than one thousand guineas a year, virtually for the same work.

Eventually, the BBC conceded and Petula's fee was matched to those received by Alma Cogan and Yana. She appeared in a series of *Starlight* shows but trouble began in earnest when, in November and true to their word, the BBC offered her her first dramatic part as a young girl, Joan Greenleaf in *Bird in the Hand*, a play to be broadcast on Christmas Day. She turned it down flatly, saying it was not an 'adult' part as she had expected:

'I won't do it. It will simply serve to re-establish me as a "sweet young thing." It is simply not the kind of part I'm looking for when my whole object is to grow up. You are treating me as a novice actress when in fact I have appeared in no fewer than twenty films from the time I was twelve years old.'

Television's Head of Drama, Michael Barry, was furious. 'Miss Clark has declined to play the part of Joan Greenleaf offered to her by us in *Bird in the Hand*. In my opinion, this was an attractive and suitable first part in drama that had the advantage of being the only girl's part in the play and was to be performed at a peak viewing period. The reasons passed to me for her refusal do not satisfy me as being professionally valid and I must therefore say that I consider this offer to constitute one of the two parts in drama which represent our contracted minimum commitment.'

The message was duly relayed, but Petula was not to be swayed. The part had been televised before, she protested. She didn't feel it was a particularly good one anyway, and although she had to admit that transmission on Christmas Day was sure to give high viewing figures, it was unlikely to be seen by the sort of people she was trying to impress nor would any sort of press be likely.

Michael Barry was equally as determined. 'It must be said,' he wrote, 'that it is a part which requires talent at the standard we aim for in this department and would not be offered to an actress who could not stand up to a carefully selected and first-rate company on a peak occasion.'

Petula did not take the part and her decision had repercussions throughout the life of the contract. As her failure to accept the role was regarded by the BBC as a breach of contract, one-twelfth of her fee was stopped. Michael Barry wrote her a letter in which he said that he hoped that in future they would be able to agree about the dramatic roles she was offered. But Petula was never again offered such a role, although, under the terms of the same contract, she had to be paid for the part she was never offered.

When the contract came up for renewal the following April, Michael Barry made it quite plain that he had no intention of taking up the option from the drama side. Ronnie Waldman wanted to renew her for Variety, but Petula refused to sign anything which would deny her the freedom to play serious dramatic roles on commercial television. Eventually, the BBC renewed their option but reduced her commitments to ten with a corresponding drop in fees, and exclusivity rights for straight plays only were waived. The immovable force had hit the irresistible object—and who could resist Pet?

Even with the new contract signed, she was unhappy. She was being offered small slots in which she considered were unimportant variety shows like *Starlight*. Both she and her father thought these a waste of both time and talent. In frustration, she wrote to Ronnie Waldman saying how she felt there was a lack of confidence in her ability and that she seemed to lack sex-appeal—or was it personality?—in their view. From that time, the shows she was offered were more to her liking but when the contract again came up for renewal a year later, the BBC declined to renew it further.

Petula was now entering one of the hardest phases of her life—and she knew it. The freshness had gone. She felt bitter and resentful at having put in so much for so long and now to be reaping so little in the way of recognition and reward.

CHAPTER ELEVEN

DEAR DADDY

There can be no doubt that Leslie honestly believed that he could please Petula by publicly announcing that she was now an adult: he'd given her high heels, a cheque-book, a car and a brand-new description as 'the girl with the figure of a miniature Jane Russell' to prove it! But even now, he was still writing to his old BBC chums with suggestions for the things he thought she ought to be doing. As late as May 1957, he wrote to producer Graeme Muir at Broadcasting House with the idea that she might read the part of Margery in the short playlet *The Captain* by A. J. C. Stevens, with narration by Brasby Williams. His private stack of rejection slips from the BBC might have papered *Pet's Parlour*.

For more than two years now, she had been desperately unhappy about the kind of bookings she was receiving from all sources. The devoted Cecil Madden insisted she must appear as one of only three paid artistes at the tea-party he was giving at the newly-opened Television Centre at Shepherds Bush, where he now held the impressive title of Assistant Director of TV programmes.

The idea of the party was to launch afternoon television and, at the same time, direct some attention away from the freshly-launched and hugely popular Independent Television Service. Madden was in charge—and to achieve his goal he invited some 2,500 of the best of British entertainment industry.

The entire operation, including the hiring of a dance floor to cover the breeze blocks at the bottom of the TV centre, engaging Edmundo Ross and another orchestra of his recommendation, Petula Clark and his other great protégées, the Beverley Sisters, and providing tea and cake for the masses was said to have cost less than thirty pounds—yet, as Cecil Madden admits with a laugh, 'even in those days, it was worth thousands in terms of publicity.' One thing was for sure. Names like Hermione Gingold, Bebe Daniels and Ben Lyon, Margaret Leighton, Terry Thomas, Sally Ann Howes, Robert Beatty, Richard Murdoch and Kenneth Horne didn't come just for the cup of tea and bun which was all the 'tea' they were given.

The event received an enormous press. One newspaper likened the hopeful smiles of the arriving guests to cheese. There was, they wrote, tortured cheese from Donald Gray; concentrated cheese from Diana Decker; brave, cigar-smoked cheese from Hermione Gingold; a cheeseless Bob Monkhouse and Lady Isobel Barnett; triple cream-cheese from the Beverley Sisters and 'model standard cheese from Petula Clark.' Little could the man who wrote those words have known that they were a perfect description of her mood of that moment.

The sparkle had gone. She was doing all the 'right' things: a three-week summer tour around the seaside resorts of the north-cast, a tour in the Isle of Wight and a week at the Odeon in Paignton, Devon. But this was not the kind of life she had expected after fifteen years as a top-ranking British entertainer. And whichever way she looked at it, her main problems all seemed to stem from her beloved, well-meaning but over-pushy father.

It was a problem both Alan Freeman and Joe Henderson had often discussed between themselves. 'In the end,' Alan says, 'early in 1957 we both decided that we would tell her, separately of course, that we felt that for the sake of her whole future she had to make a final break. We agreed to take her out for dinner on two consecutive nights and tell her that if she wanted to carry on working with us and if she wanted us to continue helping her then she would have to choose between us and her father.'

Petula listened to them both. She knew in her heart that they were merely expressing thoughts which she had tried to bury within herself for a very long time. Her sister, Barbara, had recently been rather ill, but Pet discussed it all with her and they agreed that it might be a good idea if the two made the break from home together.

'There was no final row as the papers have so often suggested,' Petula says. 'No one particular incident. It was a culmination of a number of things over a very long period of time. When we left home, the atmosphere wasn't exactly hostile but it was a little cold. My father was hurt that I'd finally done it. But let's face it—I was twenty-five. Not exactly young.

'We rented a small, unfurnished flat near Victoria. Money had never meant very much to me. I had always had a certain amount of pocket-money. I had my car and as many clothes as I wanted. When the subject had cropped up from time to time, my father had always told me that I had no need to worry. I was a very wealthy young lady. I had no reason to disbelieve him.

'We still lived in a semi-detached house and apart from the fact that my father now ran a Bentley—and why shouldn't he, after devoting himself to me for all those years?—there were no outward signs that he had spent lavishly. And I had been working for years, nonstop. It wasn't until I arrived at our new London flat that the shock came.

'I went to my accountant just to check on things,' she says. 'That's when I learned the truth. He studied the books which my father had kept with the aid of a local firm and then he said just four words.

'"My dear, you're broke."

'All I had left in the world was £500. I needed that money to buy carpets and furniture for the flat—and once it had gone, there'd be nothing left at all.'

The memory of that meeting pains her to this day. 'After all that work, all those years—I didn't even have enough to furnish my own first home,' she says sadly. 'I was completely bewildered. I asked my father what had happened to the money and he just shrugged his shoulders. He didn't know. It had just gone—

every penny.'

The night of her meeting with the accountant, a worried Barbara rang Alan and Joe. She told them what had happened and that Petula was distraught. Would they come over at once? They did. In the tiny apartment, they found Petula sitting on the threadbare carpets left by the previous owner, her eyes red-rimmed from crying. Barbara was desperately trying to comfort her.

'She sobbed her heart out,' Alan says. 'I kept telling her that she still had her talent and that nobody would take that away from her. But she couldn't be comforted. Not then.'

It was the lowest ebb of her entire career. She was not a rock 'n' roll singer and this was the era of rock 'n' roll. With the possible exceptions of Belinda Lee and Connie Francis, women singers were out of vogue. This was the heyday of Bill Hayley, Elvis Presley, Billy Fury, Adam Faith and Tommy Steele. But, if she was down, it wasn't in her character to allow anyone to think she was out:

'I remember going on a train to a horrible place to do a cabaret-type show. Everyone in the club was drunk and it was awful. Joe had his own career just beginning at this time so I had an accompanist who was not very good. I couldn't afford a good one. But after the show, they paid me in cash—£75. I came back and bought a fridge with the money. That was when

I started realising what money was. I could go and sing. Make some money. Then I could buy something with it. For the first time, it all made sense. That's what it's for, I thought. That's how it's done.'

And Petula remembers, smilingly, just how close she and her sister became through their trouble. 'Barbara was now thc one who was keeping an eye on everything for me. I had to get a petty-cash book. Everything had to be organised and every penny counted. Little by little I began to get back on my feet.'

Her new accountant advised Petula to form a company. Petula Clark Limited was duly registered, with Petula S. Clark and Barbara A. Clark and the accountant, T. E. Southey Banks, listed as its directors. They rented an office in Monmouth Street, above a dirty-book shop. Joe took the room next-door and furnished it with a piano and Barbara became Pet's secretary.

For the first time in her career she was making mistakes, but they were her own mistakes. And she was proud of them. Until now, she hadn't realised the complete hold Leslie had had over her life.

But if she lost a manager, she still had Joe. She and Joe had been very much a 'couple' for several years. Their friends believed that they were simply waiting for the right moment to announce their engagement. Not only did they work closely together but by this time he was renting an apartment above Petula's Victoria flat and they were rarely apart.

'He was a quiet, very gentle man,' Petula says softly. 'I had loved him from the first day we met when I was still a child. And, he was the most marvellous accompanist. Not such a marvellous soloist but there's a great art to being a good accompanist.

'At first, it was our joint love for music and the almost telepathic communication between us on stage which drew Joe and me together. We became so close that in the end it was invitable that we would fall in love. But Joe was married and he had a son. Later, he divorced his wife. Our love for one another was of a very special kind. There was nothing sordid about it. It was wonderful.'

It was at about this time that journalist-turned-songwriter Jack Fishman, now a very involved member of the 'Pet Set', wrote the highly emotive words to one of Joe's musical compositions. It was, he insists, never intended as a song for Petula, but when Jack and Joe were working on it in the next-door office she, of course, heard it.

'I remember that she came into the room, humming it,' Jack recalls. 'She told us that she'd love to do it. We, of course, agreed. Petula was always very hard to resist. The title of the song was "Dear Daddy".

'She made the most sensational record—the

best, I believe, of her life. As she sang it in the studio the day we cut the disc, she tore our guts out. But as soon as the session was over, Petula refused to plug it or ever sing it again. What she had subconsciously put into it was the love-hate she had for her own father. The lyrics were terribly relevant to Leslie and herself. It was only when she recognised in those potent words her own, rather sad, situation that she realised she just couldn't work it. So, it died.'

Petula's relationship with her father remained, for a while, rather tense. He found it hard to forgive her for leaving him—but, to his credit, he had decided that the time had come to build a new life for himself. He bought a post office-cum-general-store at Lodsworth, a small village in Sussex and a world away from broadcasting, television and recording studios, theatres, film sets and the show-biz people who had filled his life and his thoughts for nearly twenty years. Instead, he sold corned-beef and stamps to the fascinated locals who never tired of hearing the stories he had to tell and revelled in seeing Petula's pink sports car with its distinctive PET 1 number plate parked outside the unpretentious shop.

He began to declare himself totally uninterested in the show-business world— claiming, one could say somewhat justifiably, that it was a false world which held out meaningless promises to those who courted its favour and who were quickly forgotten once their usefulness had disappeared. He was proud that he had given to it a sweet little girl called Petula, proud that he had turned her into a glittering star. But that was all behind him. Now he was going to forget it—and make his own life the best that he could.

CHAPTER TWELVE

WHY DON'T THEY UNDERSTAND

Petula's love for Joe extended into every aspect of both their lives. She knew that one of his dearest wishes was to be known not only as her accompanist or as a composer and publisher but as a star in his own right—and she was determined whenever possible to help him.

'I'll never forget,' Alan Freeman recalls, 'how on one occasion Petula rang me and asked me if I would give Joe a recording audition. Of course, both Joe and I saw it as a huge joke. In the end, we agreed to do it just to please her. She came with him to the IBC studios in Portland Place and she addressed me very properly as "Mr Freeman" and insisted I call her "Miss Clark". Both Joe and I were falling about laughing but she was in deadly earnest.

She has a superb sense of humour but just this once, she couldn't see the joke. She was furious with us for not taking it all seriously.'

'This is a professional meeting,' she told the two men as they gagged around with tears of laughter running down their cheeks. 'Why don't you behave yourselves properly. Forget you know one another. Pretend you're strangers and get on with it. How can you expect to get a proper chance, Joe, with all this giggling going on?'

Alan, of course, knew Joe and his work too well to need an audition. They made two LPs together: 'Sing Along with Joe' and 'Sing it Again with Joe'. Both discs needed backing singers so Alan and Petula mucked-in in the background, anonymously of course.

'It was cheaper than employing a proper backing group,' laughs Alan.

It was now becoming apparent to those around them that, for all the closeness of their relationship and for all her encouragement, the careers of Petula and Joe were taking very separate roads. And, for the first time, this difference was coming between them.

Joe was still accompanying her occasionally, but now he was taking on as much commissioned work as he could get in order to finance his dream—the Joe Henderson Music Publishing Company. He even had an employee; an office boy called Ian Ralfini who aimed for a career in song-plugging but was content to fetch and carry and make tea for Pet and Joe while he learned the business and waited for it all to happen.

Joe had by this time built up a catalogue of his own and was delighted when he was invited to write the score for *Privates on Parade*, a film in which Anthony Newley had the starring-role as a phoney rock 'n' roll star. As Tony, a very old friend of Petula's from the *Vice-Versa/* 'Huggetts' days, had never sung rock or been pushed as a singer, it was left to Joe to teach him how to do it.

Like Pet herself, Tony was a natural mimic. Joe rehearsed him in the Monmouth Street office next-door to Pet's and she popped in from time to time to see how they were getting on. The result was the renewal of an old friendship as well as a highly successful film which was to embark Tony on a real career as a rock 'n' roll singer. Decca Records were so impressed by the way he aped the part of a rock star that they put him under contract to become one.

But rumours of a split between Joe and Petula were now running rife. She was appearing in a variety show at the Palace Theatre in Cambridge Circus when a photographer approached Joe on one occasion when he went to meet her after a performance.

'Can I have a picture of the two of you together,' the photographer asked cunningly.

Joe was as wise as the photographer. 'Of course,' he answered, obligingly putting his arm around her as they both smiled broadly.

'Would you mind looking a little more serious,' he asked politely.

'Yes!' Joe replied. 'We would mind. You want us to look serious so you can take a heartbreak picture. That's just what you're not getting.'

The couple said goodnight and parted, Joe leaving via the stage-door. But there, the same photographer was lurking in the shadows.

'Could I have another picture of you,' said the photographer, pouncing from the gloom. Joe was now furious. The photographer wanted to catch a dejected Joe, but Joe was far from dejected.

'Of course,' he answered, obligingly, turning down his collar and beaming as merrily as though he'd just won the football pools. But, beneath the surface, both he and Petula were beginning to feel the strain.

Joe could foresee that if he went ahead and married Petula, it wouldn't be long before all that would be left of the old Joe Henderson would be 'Mr Petula Clark'. Or that all that remained of the old Petula Clark would be 'Mrs Joe Henderson'. He had known Petula long enough and well enough to realise that it was the wrong thing for both of them. They had been together for a very long time and he knew the time had come for them to make a decision.

Joe and Jack Fishman had a very successful song-writing partnership going between them by now. They usually worked together in the evenings, after Jack had finished his shift as News Editor of the *Sunday Empire News,* and when Joe was unlikely to be disturbed by telephone interruptions. It was on one such evening that Joe turned to Jack for advice.

They had, as usual, bought themselves some sandwiches from the 'Dairy' across the road and settled down to work on a teenage song, but although they sat at it for hours, they were both stuck. At around 1.00 am, according to Jack Fishman, both feeling tired and frustrated, they decided to have a break and make themselves some coffee to go with the sandwiches. It was then that Joe opened his heart to his friend.

'Maybe I'm not in the mood for a song,' he said. 'I've got too much on my mind. It's Pet. We've come to a crossroads. I've got to make up my mind. She wants to get married and so do I but I feel that if we marry, I'll always be Mr Pet Clark. I don't want to be Mr Pet Clark. I want to be Mr Joe Henderson.'

'What are you going to do?' asked Jack kindly.

'I don't know,' Joe replied miserably. 'I'm still struggling with it. But I'm determined to make up my mind by the end of this week.'

As they talked, Jack suddenly had an idea for

157

the song they'd been struggling with. Together they set to to work it out. Totally absorbed and with tiredness and misery forgotten, the two tinkled out the music and chanted lyrics until 4.00 am. Outside, the streets of London were eerie and deserted. When it was finished, they sat back, delighted by the song born of Joe's deep misery and Jack's attempts to help him. They had written 'Why Don't They Understand'.

As they were about to leave the smoke-filled little office and descend the three rickety flights of stairs to the real world, Joe suddenly turned to Jack. 'You know what. I don't think I can do it. I'll tell her today. It's all over. I've got to stay Joe Henderson.'

'If you let the news slip, you'll be swamped by reporters,' Jack told him. 'You both hate that. Talk it over with Pet and if you decide that you've got to stay two people apart, then let me know. If you want the news broken, I'll break it for you. I'll do it in a way which softens it. It will be broken your way.'

Jack knew that both Pet and Joe trusted him. It was a trust he wouldn't betray.

That morning, within hours of completing the song, Petula and Joe sat in her little flat and he told her how he felt. They talked a long while and agreed that, after sharing so much together, they would always remain friends. But the romance was over. That same afternoon, they rang Jack and agreed to meet in Joe's office. Jack worked out how he proposed to approach the story and wrote the copy there and then for their joint approval. It ran in the *Sunday Empire News* that week as a page lead. Once the story broke, every other newspaper in Fleet Street was hot on its heels. To every inquiry they repeated the story they had devised with Jack Fishman.

For both of them, this was a turning-point. And the song Joe had written the night he made up his mind was to have important implications for his future.

Both Jack and Joe thought that 'Why Don't They Understand' was hit material. They toured it round the usual sources but without success. Eventually, they took it to Alan Freeman. He, Petula and Barbara all thought it was great so Alan signed up a Shakespearian actor, John Fraser, who was looking for a musical break, to sing it for Pye. Nothing happened.

Nobody thought it was a suitable song for Petula so it was sent to America. Lou Levy, who had managed the Andrews' Sisters, tried it. Still nothing. In the end, they decided to ask David Platz, who had promoted Tony Newley in the States, to see if he could get a recording that would sell. To their horror, he did. When the record came back with the then unknown American singer George Hamilton IV vocalising it in a twangy, Western voice, they thought it was a complete dead duck.

Joe was the most disappointed. For him, who had co-written it the night he had decided to make the final break from Petula, the song had a very special meaning. But then came the big surprise.

Hamilton's record reached number two in the US charts. It sold more than a million copies. Jack and Joe were jointly awarded the British Musical Industries Award for one of the best songs of the year. Cliff Richard recorded it in England; so did Bobby Vinton. And, some time later, so did Petula Clark. Their traumatic love-life had given Joe his first big international hit. A turning-point, for sure.

Petula was also making something of an international success in a much smaller way. She had been doing a fair amount of work touring in shows in Holland, Belgium and the Scandinavian countries. Barbara, her sister, spoke fluent French, but Petula herself spoke no other than her native language. As these were mainly English-comprehending countries, she could work them quite successfully in English, and Copenhagen was a particular favourite.

'I felt a certain musical freedom over there,' she explains. 'They are a modern kind of people who appreciate the sort of modern music I love to sing. I could go there and they liked whatever I did whereas in England, I was still, even at this time, having to live down the old child-star image. You still meet people for whom the forties were the best years of their lives. And I was part of their memories. If they acknowledged that I was a woman, then it meant acknowledging that for themselves, the fun years were over and they were growing old!'

Somewhat coincidentally as it later turned out, a new Petula Clark film was released in 1957. She co-starred with Phyllis Kirk, Dan O'Herlihy and Wilfred Hyde White in *That Woman Opposite*, the setting for which was a little French town called La Bandelette.

The coincidence lay in France. In late '57, she made two records, 'With All My Heart' and 'Alone'. Both were stupendous hits, putting her back in the charts again for the first time in a very long while.

'When I made "With All My Heart" I felt that I was finally beginning to shake free of that awful childhood thing,' she says. 'I had almost made up my mind to leave show-business and go and do something really worthwhile with my life like joining Dr Schweitzer.' It was one idea she never had time to put into practice. 'With All My Heart' was a catchy song—and the French caught it. A French singer, Dalida, who had been copying Petula's English songs in French for some time, sang it in her own language, translated to 'Prend Mon Coeur' with lyrics by the French poet Pierre Delanoe who was, at that

161

time, also joint station manager of Europe Number One, Europe's newest and most important radio station.

Pye, who had released the English version, had a tie-up with Vogue Records in Paris, owned by the legendary Leon Cabat. Cabat decided that it would be a good idea to import Petula and invite her to sing her own song on 'Musicarama' which was broadcast from the Olympia Music Hall in Paris.

'At the time, Europe Number One had just got off the ground and had already found its place as the most important radio station on the Continent,' Petula explains. 'They had never had anything like it in Europe before. The station played a lot of American music and it was all happening. When Vogue and Europe Number One first invited me I wasn't interested. They told me that Dalida was copying me so I said: "Good luck to the girl if that's what she wants, she's welcome to it."'

'At that time, I didn't like Paris. I thought it was a dirty, smelly place. I didn't speak a word of French and if I had to perform abroad, it was about the last place on earth I would have chosen. I resisted for as long as I could, but then Leon Cabat persuaded me by saying that it was silly for Dalida to be cashing in on my hit—and anyway, if I came to France I could do a lot of shopping.'

Eventually, she conceded. For two weeks

prior to her arrival, Vogue plugged 'With All My Heart' for all it was worth in its original, English version. But, when Petula arrived, she felt anything but a starlet about to set the heavens ablaze with her glorious voice.

'It was winter and I had a terrible cold,' she remembers. 'I was shooting a film at that time and my hair had been dyed bright red. My nose was scarlet and I had a green complexion. Just to finish the effect, the dress I had taken with me was a pink, flouncy affair with lots of sequins. Lampshade dresses were the latest rage in England. By the time I arrived, my cold was so bad that I couldn't sing a note. I thought to myself that the whole exercise seemed rather pointless—just a nasty nightmare.'

Alan, who was travelling with Petula and Barbara, took Petula to a doctor. She couldn't understand a single word he said.

'He was a very strange man,' she said. 'His consulting room was full of antiques and I felt as though I was meeting Napoleon himself. He gave me a prescription for suppositories. Uh! Uh! I thought to myself. Now we're in France.'

'You don't speak,' the doctor told her.

'But tonight I must sing,' she replied.

'Yes, tonight you sing. But for now'—a finger went to the thin, French lips—'not a word.'

Petula, Barbara and Alan were booked into the Hotel de Paris on Rue Hausmann, almost next-door to the theatre. All afternoon, as ordered, she kept silent, a scrappy piece of paper and a pencil her only means of communication with Alan and her sister. When the time came for the performance, Petula dressed in her hotel bedroom. Then Alan wrapped her in a green blanket from the bed and carried her carefully out and through the stage-door.

In her dressing-room, she found several good-luck messages, but among them was one telegram which shocked her. It bore the single word *Meurtre* and the signature, 'Charles Aznavour.'

'Barbara,' she asked her sister anxiously. 'Does this mean what I think it does?'

'Murder,' exclaimed an equally stunned Barbara. 'Yes, it does.'

'What a weird thing for a man like Aznavour to do to a foreigner,' she exclaimed. At that time, nobody had told her that in France, to wish a performer *'bonne chance'* in a dressing-room was tantamount to mentioning Macbeth behind the scenes in an English theatre where he is always referred to as 'that man'.

Petula had carefully practised saying *'bonsoir'* to her audience, but by the time she finally appeared on the stage that night, she didn't dare try.

'I didn't know until I opened my mouth whether anything would come out or not,' she says. 'I sang four songs in English—and because of the cold, not particularly well. To my amazement, I pulled the place down. I don't know to this day whether it was because they liked the way I sang or because I was the weirdest thing they had ever seen!'

At the end of the performance, in mid-ovation, Petula threw her arms round the neck of the conductor for that auspicious night, Raymonde Legrand, father of the great Michel. The audience responded to this spontaneous gesture with thunderous applause, rising to their feet in a unified mass and cheering the funny little English Miss until their throats were as sore as hers was. But, always the perfectionist, she was all too conscious that the performance she had given was far from her best. Neither nerves nor her cold had been very much help.

However, next morning the French press were loud and generous with their reviews. They called the girl who'd taken the great Paris Olympia and 'Musicarama' by storm the 'bon-bon anglaise' because of her frothy pink frock, so very different from the kind of slinky, sexy clothes worn by their own top performers.

That same afternoon, she had an appointment at the offices of Vogue Records to discuss a possible tour to promote 'With All My Heart'. Still feeling extremely unwell, she protested meekly that all she really wanted to do was go home to England and curl up in her own familiar bed with a hot-water bottle. It was to no avail. The appointment, Alan assured her, must be kept.

When she arrived at Vogue, intent on refusing whatever offers might be made she had reckoned without the persuasive powers of the short, stocky figure of Leon Cabat, who delights in loudly checked American-style jackets and has a habit of lifting the lenses of his silver-framed spectacles to take a closer look at one.

Today, he sits in a rather grander, oak-panelled, antiques-filled office at Epinay-Villetaneuse with a harmonium in the corner and an instant ice-machine hidden behind an elegant false bookshelf, laughing as he remembers that first meeting in a tiny, smoke-filled room which was, in 1957, his central Paris headquarters.

As she entered the room, a tiny figure with dyed red hair, in a jumper and skirt, he jumped up to meet her and shower her with kisses of effusive congratulation before seating her in a rickety chair. The airless room full of the stench of Gauloise cigarettes did nothing to soothe her sore throat and streaming eyes.

'I think the time has come for the French to have an English-style singer,' M. Cabat told her.

'I'm not interested,' Petula replied. 'I can't speak a word of French. I don't like France. I don't particularly want the hassle of it all. I want to go back to England; to my own flat and my little car. I've got hits in England. My career is good there now. I don't want to leave it, not even for another day.'

As she spoke, the single light-bulb above their heads popped, plunging them into total darkness. Cabat screamed something in French, and a tall figure loomed in the doorway and clambered on to the desk to reach the high French ceiling. When the light was restored, Petula found herself staring up at the most beautiful man she had ever seen.

'Aren't you going to introduce us,' the man asked Cabat from his perch.

'Mademoiselle Clark—this is Monsieur Claude Wolff,' Cabat obliged.

She had no way of knowing it then, but that broken electric light-bulb had just re-energised her life.

CHAPTER THIRTEEN

WITH ALL MY HEART

Petula claims she fell in love with Claude the moment she first set eyes on him.

'For me it was instant, but not so for him.'

But the clever Cabat caught the expression on her face as he introduced them.

'If you come to Paris, Mademoiselle, Claude

167

Wolff who is our promotions manager will be looking after you. He's the best promotions man in the country.'

'He will?' she gasped. In the two minutes since the bulb had blown, her fluey cold, her general weariness and her dislike of everything and everyone French had flown with the speed of light.

Claude had been born in Paris of Jewish parents in 1931. His father was an architect, his mother a housewife, and he had one sister, nine years his senior. Until 1939, he had lived the life of a normal, middle-class Parisian child but when war broke out things changed dramatically.

At the outbreak of hostilities, he was on holiday with his parents in Bordeaux. As news came through of the occupation of Paris and the deportation of Jews to unknown 'work camps', his father decided to remain away from the capital. The family did not return to their home until 1942. Then, just as Petula was making her début at the Criterion, the Wolff family were walking round the streets of the French capital with the telling yellow star pinned prominently to their clothing. As she entertained the troops in Britain, he was banned from visiting theatres, cinemas or music-halls. He couldn't even go to a normal school.

'Coming back to Paris was a gamble my father decided we had to take. We knew, in 1942, that

168

Jews were being deported to camps but we did not believe they would be killed. We thought the camps were to work, manufacturing war-armoury for the Germans. We didn't know of the gas-chambers, then,' he says.

'We had one bad fright in 1944. Two huge Gestapo came to the flat and said they had information that we had guns. As Jews, suspected of having guns, they should have just taken us away without searching or questioning. We were lucky. They searched the flat but when they didn't find any guns they went away. Being alive is a lucky accident.'

Claude had been clever at school, before the Germans forbade him an education as a birthright. He had wanted to study law, but the Nazis banned Jews from entering the professions so his father apprenticed him in the design business and he attended classes. Claude desperately missed the freedom to enjoy the theatres, cinemas and concerts he loved so much. 'Sometimes, my friends and I would hug our books close to our chests to hide our yellow stars and sneak into the cinemas,' he says. 'We couldn't do it very often. It was too dangerous.'

In 1944, Paris was liberated by the allies. The Jews now had a chance to try to rebuild their lives. For Claude, it came too late to try to fulfil his dreams of a career as an attorney-at-law. He didn't feel he could ever catch up on his missed education.

As soon as he could once more attend theatres as often as his pocket would allow, he discovered a new love—jazz. Some afternoons he would play truant from his courses to listen to jazz musicians in St Germain-des-Prés. Among the players at that time was a young singer, Sacha Distel. The owner of one of the clubs was Andre Reweliotty. And, when Claude and his friends needed a stage for their own little orchestra, Reweliotty allowed them to practise in his club during quiet afternoons.

The reputation of the little band soon spread. Friends at the local high school asked if they could play at a school party and almost before he knew it, Claude had become their manager. They began giving regular concerts and instead of trying to get into Reweliotty's place for free and being grateful for the chance, they now found themselves invited to play there with Claude negotiating the fee. He was learning fast—and when the great jazz musician Sidney Bechet arrived in Paris and needed management, Reweliotty recommended Claude for the job. Together Bechet and Claude toured the Continent and came to England, where Bechet joined Chris Barber for a tour of Birmingham, Manchester, Cardiff and Edinburgh.

Bechet was recording at this time for Vogue and Leon Cabat. He introduced Claude to Cabat, who took an instant liking to the tall young man with dark curly hair and sparkling brown eyes. But when they asked him what he could do, he had to be honest and say that he knew nothing about the business at all!

Cabat put him in the stock department to begin with but just two weeks before he was due to take up his new position, he broke a leg. Nevertheless, he turned up for work on that first day, his leg in plaster from ankle to knee, and humped himself around getting to know the catalogue. Gradually he worked his way up from general dogsbody to the company's chief public relations man.

'I was a good public relations man,' he says. It is not a boast; merely a statement of fact borne out by everyone who knows him. And it was this young man with his startling good looks, fresh to the business of record-making which had been so much a part of Petula's life for so many years already, who changed a light-bulb in that stuffy little office—and was to change Petula's entire way of life.

She fell in love with the dark, handsome Frenchman, but he was frankly not as enthusiastic about her—at that first meeting at least: 'I thought she was quite an attractive girl, but I also thought she had a very odd way of dressing herself. She had this terrible red hair and when I had seen her the night before at the Olympia she was wearing a dress which was shaped like two pink lampshades and I thought she must be a very strange lady. I thought it terrible taste to wear her hair like that. I didn't know it had been dyed for a film. I thought she had done it to seek attention.'

The mode of the French stars was reflected in their simple, almost casual attire. Piaf usually sported plain black dresses; the men tended to wear open-necked shirts. To them, Petula in her frilly, garish, English clothes was an enigma.

That evening, Claude, Petula and Barbara were invited to dine at the Cabats' home. Since Petula could speak no French and Claude's English was confined to what Petula describes as 'American musician's gutter slang' picked up from Bechet, any conversation between them was necessarily conducted through Barbara. It was not an easy relationship—and as Petula quickly discovered, falling instantly in love can prove to be only the beginning of a dangerous obstacle race. The first hurdle she had to overcome was Claude's current girlfriend, an elegant, slinky model called Françoise.

Next to this tall French clothes-peg, the petite Petula felt ordinary and insignificant. Yet she was sure that this time, her love for Claude was the real thing.

After her first trip to Paris, she returned to London for a brief three weeks to record the French version of 'With All My Heart'—'Prend Mon Coeur'—with Alan Freeman, for the French market. Her French was so bad that he had to write the words out for her phonetically.

She was invited on to Radio Television Français' equivalent to 'Top of the Pops', an enormous boost for a foreigner since French audiences are notoriously conservative in their acceptance of stars.

Radio was more of a problem. Although Pierre Delanoe, the station manager of Europe Number One, was a close friend of Claude's and had, in fact, initiated her first visit to Paris, his co-manager Lucien Morisse was at this time in love with Dalida, the girl who had copied Pet's English hits. Delanoe found himself in the centre of a battle about her use. On the strength of her television success, he eventually won through.

'I told Morisse that the interests of the station had to come first,' he says. 'I told him that the most important radio station in Europe would look very stupid if they didn't promote Petula when she was so much in demand by everybody else.'

Claude, the PR man, was revelling in the success she was having—and determined to expand the scope of her French stardom. When he heard that TV producer Marcel Cravenne was planning to screen *L'Anglais tel qu'on le Parle* by George Bernard Shaw, he told Cravenne that he knew just the person to take the part of the English girl who comes to Paris and falls in at the deep end. Cravenne thought it was a brilliant idea.

Claude rang Petula who was back in England and told her the news, expecting her to be delighted. 'It will only need two weeks rehearsals,' he told her.

'I can't do it. No way,' Petula replied. 'I just don't have the time.'

'If you like it, Cravenne will cut down the rehearsal time. He's very keen to have you.' Petula wavered. Claude put the phone down and rang Cravenne back.

'I told him she'd love to do it. He said he'd send her the script so I called her back and said it was in the post and that he wouldn't take no for an answer.'

With Barbara's help, she learned the script quite quickly.

'The first couple of rehearsals were quite risky,' Claude admits. 'I thought one or other of them would let the cat out of the bag but everything went OK. The play was a great success.'

Her career in Britain, so recently in the doldrums, was now picking up nicely again. She signed with the BBC for a twenty-six week radio series with Joe Henderson—the man she had almost married. It was to be her last, long-term radio series in Britain and the last time she ever worked with Joe. Called *Pet and Mr Piano*, it gave Joe the break he'd been chasing for so long.

Leslie Clark, who had now almost totally

faded from her professional life was, none-the-less, not too pleased about his daughter's success in France. 'I'm a bit of a confirmed John Bull,' he told anyone who asked why he didn't seem over the moon at his daughter's Continental breakthrough. If the truth were known, he was highly suspicious of the whole thing and not a little afraid of where it might lead.

'My dad had an inborn dislike of the French and everything to do with them,' Petula says. 'When they served him rare meat flavoured with garlic, he thought it was "off". He thought French cheese was "soapy". In fact, everything across the Channel was to be distrusted because it wasn't British.'

But perhaps he was shrewder than even his daughter realised. He hadn't been her father and her manager for so many years without being able to creep into the deepest recesses of her mind when she wasn't looking. Her enthusiastic return to France had encouraged him to believe that there must be more to it than a single night's success.

She was yearning to love and be loved. The break from Joe had left her feeling lonely and vulnerable, even though they were still friends. It became obvious to those who knew her best when, in January 1958, she went 'home' to Wales for her cousin Shirley's wedding to David Vaughan.

Shirley remembered that she was all on her own and insisted there should be no fuss. She wanted to be part of the family—not a star. When reporters tried to collar her outside the church, she told them firmly: 'This is my cousin's wedding. It's her day and nothing to do with me so please leave me alone.'

When the ceremony and reception were over, it was Petula who went upstairs with her cousin to help her change into her 'going-away' outfit. As Shirley made-up her face in the bathroom, Pet perched on the edge of the bath and chatted to her.

'You are lucky, Shirley,' she said suddenly, with just a tinge of envy in her voice.

'I knew that of course I was lucky. I had just got married to the man I loved and I was very happy. But I couldn't understand why Petula should say that to me. I couldn't understand it with all that she herself had.'

'I want to get married and have a family, too,' Pet told her quietly.

For Shirley, it was the first time she'd had a glimpse of Pet's 'other' life.

It seemed that she was looking inside herself and was not too happy with what she saw there. She was reputedly earning a vast salary of around £20,000 a year—not bad for a girl who, eighteen months previously, had thought of giving up show-business forever. But she was searching for something which no amount of work or money could provide. In June that year, she took the unusual step for a woman of that age of studying and becoming confirmed by the Bishop of Croydon, the Right Rev John Hughes, at the Church of St. John the Baptist in West Wickham, Kent. Perhaps, she felt, religion could bring her an inner peace.

There was no question now of her needing persuasion to cross the Channel. She toured France with Claude, playing in large towns and tiny villages, and Claude promoted both her image and her records. It seemed that whatever she touched was flecked with gold. And then came her second big chance when she was booked to appear as top of the bill among some of France's greatest, native stars at the Alhambra Theatre in Paris, including Claude's old friend Sacha Distel, the rubber-faced comedian Henri Salvador, and Charles Aznavour, with musical direction by Michel Legrand.

Today, the great French variety theatre has been replaced by a concrete multi-storey car-park. If its foundations could speak to its present residents, one of the funniest tales they might hear would be of the events leading up to Petula's début in the grand old music-hall.

'They had arranged for a new song, written especially for me with music by Joe Henderson and lyrics by Steelman and Vian called "Java pour Petula",' she says. 'The lyrics were in idiomatic Paris-argot, the slang of the back streets. For the first time in my entire career, I found I simply couldn't learn them.'

She couldn't understand a single word of the complicated-sounding verses and had to believe as she was told that it was all about an English girl who arrives in Paris for the first time and is taught the facts of life by a taxi-driver.

'I looked at the lyrics and they didn't even look like French to me. I tried rehearsing it with Barbara who spoke very good French, but— *comme il faut*. I had learnt all my other songs for that show with no problem at all, but this one wouldn't go into my head and it was desperately important that I get it right.'

As the opening night drew closer, Petula, normally so calm and well-rehearsed, began to panic. The more panicky she became, the less chance she had of learning it by any conventional means. For this woman who had possessed a remarkable gift of memorising both music and lyrics instantly from childhood, it was a most uncomfortable feeling:

'I've always had extremely good ears—so sensitive that they often frighten me because they hear things they shouldn't. I can hear a single wrong note in an orchestra, particularly in bass, as my bass players will tell you,' she says. 'They're all warned before they start working with me that I'm a bass freak. One wrong note can stop me in the middle of a song—but an exceptionally good one can really get me going.'

But on this single occasion, with strange words in a foreign tongue that bore no resemblance to anything she'd ever sung before, her gift failed her. Then she was told of a man who might be able to help; hypnotist Roberto Risselli.

'Berto was Italian and the first time I went to see him I thought he was very strange,' she said with a smile. 'He was wearing one of those striped jerseys, rather like a bumblebee, and that made me giggle.'

Her first visit to Berto lasted about twenty minutes. He sat and talked to her very quietly but as far as she could see, nothing happened. The first twenty minutes or so of her second visit was spent in much the same way—and then, unexpectedly, Berto told her: 'Now.'

'Now, what?' asked Pet, bemused.

'Now you're under.'

'I had expected something extraordinary to happen but as far as I could see, nothing had,' she says.

'I'll leave the room,' Berto told her. 'When I've gone take out your lyrics and read them. I will come back in half an hour and when I do you will know them.'

'That,' says Petula, 'is exactly what happened. By the time he came back I knew the lyrics, and I've never forgotten them. There are many songs which I've performed in the past and can't recall at all now, but that one has always stuck. If at any time I've felt I might be losing it, all I've had to do is recall Berto and sitting in that room and back it comes.'

Berto told her that he was sure he might be able to help her in other ways, but she declined the offer, firmly. 'I found it an amazing but somewhat scary experience,' she says. 'I never used him again.'

Now she was all set for the Alhambra show; to sing to a French audience in their own language for the first time, live. Once again, she chose a pink frothy frock for the occasion, much to Claude's amazement, and the amusement of her co-stars, including Sacha Distel.

'In that pink frock, the audience thought she was cute and when she sang with such a strong English accent they found it very, very funny,' he says.

Charles Aznavour, too, remembers that début with pride—and a sense of fun. 'She was all pink and young and sweet and curly—something French audiences knew nothing of,' he says. 'And she had a wonderful voice. When she had conquered Paris, she conquered the whole of France. The French are one of the hardest audiences to impress in the entire world but Petula did the impossible and pleased them instantly.'

On that opening night, 14 November 1958, she began with her first French hit, 'Prend Mon

Coeur'. 'Java pour Petula' she saved for her finale.

'She sang it instead of singing one of her own repertoire translated into French,' says Aznavour. 'The audience thought this was an unusual and amusing thing to do. As she finished, they showed their full appreciation. They stood and clapped and stamped their feet and cheered until she gave them an encore—and then they cheered for more. Echoes of the "bravos" rang round the theatre. They loved her funny clothes. They adored her English accent. They respected the time she'd taken to learn to sing them a song of her own in their tongue.'

In France, almost overnight, she'd become a star. They wanted her, not as an import, but as a star of their own. They even Frenchified her name, calling her Petu La Clark. And, La Clark was all woman. Her new audiences knew nothing of the enchanting little girl the British wouldn't let grow up. They saw and accepted her as the attractive, sexy woman she then was with a sweet and amazingly powerful voice. To them, her attraction lay in her maturity and professionalism, not in a memory.

Her excitement at her coup was heightened by the fact that for the first time in years, her public and private lives seemed to be running along parallel lines. She had fallen in love with Claude Wolff when first they met. But it had taken over a year, commuting cross-channel to work with him promoting her discs, to persuade him that he loved her.

Yet, when he did finally propose, she couldn't feel the happiness she'd hoped for. Both wanted a family. But due to her illness seven years before, she didn't know whether she would ever be able to bear a child.

'At the time of my hasty emergency operation, the surgeon had told me she couldn't be sure that I could have a baby,' she says. 'They had had to operate very quickly to save my life. They didn't know whether it had affected my ability to have a child and there was no test they could give me that would prove whether I could or not. It was a case of "wait and see".

'There had always been this thing in my mind about possibly not being able to have children. I felt it would be unfair to tie Claude to me for life under those circumstances, knowing how much it meant to him to have a family,' she says. 'So for a while, we lived together. I promised him I would marry him the moment I became pregnant—and that's how it was.'

Now, with commitments on both sides of the Channel and the added draw of Claude in France, they set up a base in Claude's bachelor pad in Paris. By this time, he had earned the reputation of being the most dynamic PR man in the French record business and as Petula says, 'We couldn't live in the middle of the

Channel.'

With her heart so much in France and the delights of her new French career stretching before her, she was spending less and less time in England and, as a result, her career there was suffering. Even the BBC seemed to have lost interest. She was doing occasional TVs but as her British agent, E. W. Kent, was the first to point out, she was not being rewarded in keeping with her status. Alma Cogan, Joan Reagan and Jill Day were being paid £105 for *Starlight* spots, yet Petula was being offered half that sum for the same show. It was grudgingly agreed to offer her seventy-five guineas for each programme when she agreed to appear on a series of six *Juke Box Jury* programmes.

Christmas 1959 was her first with Claude. She had been booked that year to appear in her first ever live pantomime at Southampton and it seemed to provide the ideal opportunity for Pet to introduce the tall Frenchman to her family for the first time. That trip to England proved quite an ordeal—not least because it almost led to Claude finding himself enlisted in the British Army.

'Oompty Doompty', as Claude called it, was booked for a two-week run.

'It was great fun to do,' Petula says. 'Tommy Cooper played the King and Derek Roy was among the cast. I'm a champion giggler on stage and I have a terrible sense of humour. Once

Tommy Cooper discovered this, well, that was it. I hardly ever got a word out. Edmund Hockeridge was the Prince and we had two duets in the show, but I never managed to sing them as a duet. I used to laugh all the way through them.

'Anyway, Claude arrived in London and I gave him directions to Southampton. By the time he arrived, it was dark and there was quite a fog. The stage-door entrance was down a little back alley. When he saw a light at the end, he thought that must be it and went inside.

'He'd actually walked into a British Army recruiting office,' Petula laughs. 'They saw this strapping young man with a suitcase and it was a case of "Come in, my boy, and welcome". There was a brief moment of panic on both sides before they realised they'd nearly signed up a Frenchman who spoke hardly any English at all. Claude scurried out rather rapidly.'

Leslie, a committed anglophile, was not happy about the idea of his daughter sharing her life with a Frenchman. In his opinion, even an American would have been an improvement. At least they spoke the same language.

'I realised Claude would be good for her and I soon learned to respect his excellent business sense,' Leslie said at the time. There was only one thing about his prospective son-in-law that Leslie would never learn to accept—his mode of embrace. He never relished the dubious pleasure of being kissed on both cheeks by another man.

Before he could become an accepted member of the family, however, there was just one more torture Claude had to endure—a British Christmas dinner.

'Christmas dinner in England and the equivalent meal in France are two rather different things,' Petula explains. 'The French meal might start with oysters, followed by a little chicken or turkey and ending with champagne and a fluffy chocolate cake. When Claude sat down for his first Christmas dinner with the family, he faced crackers, funny hats, stuffed turkey, Christmas pudding and plenty of beer. He had never seen anything quite like it.' He struggled manfully through the meal knowing he was under scrutiny from the entire Clark clan—until they reached the traditional flaming pudding. He picked at it, obviously disliking the taste.

'Do I have to eat this?' he asked, surveying the stodgy dark mess on his plate.

'Yes, you've got to eat it,' she replied.

He took some cream and tried again. 'I have to?' he asked mournfully, mixing in some custard, followed by brandy butter and sugar.

'You have to,' she insisted as he spooned in another mouthful gingerly. But it simply wouldn't go down.

'By this time, it looked like a plate of sick,'

Petula laughs.

Her entire family were now staring at the foreigner who didn't like Christmas pudding in fascination. But by the end of the meal they were all laughing with him and he was forgiven after doing something 'funny' with the jelly.

★　　★　　★

As the New Year dawned, Petula was, for almost the first time in her life, completely content. She had finally met a man she knew she could settle down with; a man who would protect her as her father had done, but without dominating her. A man who would promote her career without needing to compete with it. She had always been at her best with a strong man behind her. Both Alan Freeman and Joe Henderson had loved her—but neither of them had had the strength that she needed in a partner. From that fateful morning when she and Claude had first met under the famous light-bulb, things had changed. Now, as she swayed into the swinging sixties, she was introduced to another man whose effect on her career was to be almost as dramatic as Claude's. He was at that time a young, regular Coldstream guardsman—and his name was Tony Hatch.

CHAPTER FOURTEEN

MY FRIEND THE SEA

When Petula first met Tony Hatch, she was twenty-seven years old and had notched up a grand total of twenty years in show-business, already. Her career had begun in earnest the year he was born. He was very much a newcomer to the record industry although he had already had two remarkable successes— 'Messing About on the River' and 'Look for a Star', the theme song he'd written for a film called *Circus of Horrors*.

He had spent eighteen months working for Top Rank Records before signing up with the Army for three years, and had never really stopped his involvement with the business as he was in barracks in London and could do as he pleased once his duties were finished for the day. It was all quite legal and within Queen's Regulations.

When Top Rank folded, Alan Freeman, who was still Petula's recording manager and confidant, invited the promising young composer to join Pye. He had to tell him—and Pye's joint Managing Director Louis Benjamin—that he wouldn't be able to work for them full-time as he was on call to the army between 9.00 am and 1.00 pm each day but that he could give them most afternoons and evenings—and even all night if necessary. And there always remained the possibility that he would be shipped off to Germany or America at short notice. To his surprise, they accepted this arrangement and offered him a position as a Junior Recording Manager. All meetings involving him would be scheduled for the afternoons to fit in with his army duties.

Petula was on his roster of artistes at Pye. He could not, of course, produce her records. His job was to find artistes of his own and to assist Alan and help with the general record production of the company. She was somewhat sceptical of the 'new boy'.

'I don't think I'm going to like your Mr Hatch,' she told Alan after their first meeting. She couldn't have misjudged any relationship more in her life. Later, the musical chemistry between them produced sheer magic which would conquer the world. But at that time, the one thing Tony himself is the first to admit that he lacked, was tact.

Lonnie Donnegan had once stormed out of a session with Tony, after Tony thoughtlessly asked him to play his guitar like Duane Eddy.

'You should just have told him to pitch a bit lower,' Alan told the young man afterwards. 'Stars of Donnegan's status don't like to be compared with anyone else.' And when Joan

Reagan played him a song she was to sing with Edmund Hockeridge at the London Palladium, he told her he thought it was 'lovely, but for a much younger woman'.

For a while, Tony worked with Alan on Petula's sessions using arrangements by Peter Knight or Bill Shepherd—and Petula herself had little time to give much thought to young Mr Hatch away from the studios. She was totally involved with Claude and her new Continental career.

Under his clever management, her career in France was in full swing. In the summer of 1960, she went on her first full tour of the French provinces with Sacha Distel—and, of course, Claude. But as Claude points out, she was shocked at the conditions under which she was expected to perform, even allowing that she had worked in many repertory theatres in England and trodden the boards everywhere, from little shacks in Puddlington to the great Albert Hall itself. But the French summer circuit is a world of its own.

'In some places, you literally have to clear up the blood on the floor before you can work there,' Claude explains. 'On one occasion we had three different shows to do seventy miles apart. The first two were in France and the third across the border in Belgium. When Petula woke that morning, she had a terrible cold and a very bad sore throat. She saw a doctor who told her she shouldn't sing—but when we arrived at our first stop in Mauborg, the manager said: "Please! She has to perform just four or five songs." So she did. Knowing these places, I insisted always on being paid before the show and afterwards, when the management were not very happy, I told them it was their own fault because they had insisted that she perform in the first place.

'The second show was in a small village some distance away. It was now obvious that Petula wouldn't be able to sing for the rest of the day. I rang the Casino at Spa in Belgium and the manager, a friend of mine, understood so that was OK but then I had to get in touch with the other Frenchman.

'The booking was in a little village—part of the celebrations for the Canesse de Vin Rouge. I looked up the phone numbers but the only telephones in the village were those at the town hall, the police station, the post office and the pub.'

He rang the pub and asked to speak to the show manager. 'He's on his farm,' the publican told him.

'It's urgent,' Claude explained. 'About tonight's show.'

'Give me your number,' the man said kindly. 'I'll go and fetch him and ask him to ring you back.'

The manager called him back and Claude

explained the position and offered him a doctor's certificate. 'She will be better in four days. We'll come then,' he said.

'Impossible!' exclaimed the manager/farmer. 'My place is fully booked for tonight. Anyway, in four days' time it will not be possible. The place will be full of hay.' The theatre, that night, would have been a converted barn.

Her first stop on this tour had been at Cherbourg. She used to take her own pianist, an Englishman called Ralph Tomoborg with her because, at this time, she couldn't afford a four-piece band. Ralph would usually rehearse three or four locals supplied by the management to accompany her.

'I don't think either Pet or I will ever forget that first stop', says Claude. 'We rehearsed the three locals and at the end of the rehearsal, Ralph said to them: "See you tonight."

'"Yes," said the first one, "but it won't be me. It will be my brother. He is fishing today but he plays much better guitar than me."

'"It won't be me either," said the second. "My brother is the bass player. He is a plumber and he is working all day so he sent me to the rehearsal instead."'

Of the three players with whom she'd spent all afternoon rehearsing, only one was to be with her on the stage that evening.

And when they arrived at Belle Plage, a spa renowned for its medicinal air for chest patients, particularly those suffering from TB—there was yet another problem. The stage appeared to be a very long way from the audience.

'I would like the audience to be closer,' Petula told Claude and the management. 'I don't like to feel they are so far away from me.'

'Don't worry,' the proprietor reassured her. 'They will be closer to you.' The situation wasn't improved when it was discovered that the microphone was not in working order. 'I'll bring another one with me for this evening,' he promised.

That evening, Petula arrived and peeped through the curtains to see whether her instructions about moving the audience forward had been carried out. To her surprise, the front of the auditorium was packed with folding beds, filled by patients from the sanatorium. Then the manager appeared with the new 'mike'. A megaphone. 'It was so huge,' Claude laughs, 'that you couldn't see her face behind it.'

The eventful tour ended with a visit to Salon de Provence—and for once, a magical, open-air setting sent straight from the set of a Hollywood musical.

'Our stage was the beautiful Roman arena,' Sacha Distel remembers. 'I was a big star and Petula was well on the way up. She had the *veudette Americaine* spot, closing the first half of the show, and then the whole fifty minutes of the second half was supposed to be mine.'

But things didn't work out quite as planned. 'She stayed on for over an hour,' Sacha laughs. 'It was getting chilly and I was looking at my watch and sending little hate signals.'

After Petula had been on-stage for an hour and twenty minutes without a break—and with no end to the marathon in sight—Sacha began to get really mad. Each time she took a bow and came into the wings, the crowd demanded '*encore*' and Claude would give her a shove back on-stage again.

'When she finally came off, I said to her: "That's what you want. OK. Be happy!"' he says. At the time, the great Distel was annoyed—but not offended. His friendship with both Claude and Petula was too deep for that. He actually saw the whole thing as a huge joke, and he found it rather amusing in retrospect that Claude should be thrusting forward the English girl to overbalance his old friend on a one-night stand.

But the French tour route was not always fun and games. When she played San Raphael, the manager ran a forged ticket racket and tried to con them out of their promised fee. The result was a fisticuffs fight between Claude and the manager.

Claude had not built his reputation on promises. While he was in no way the Svengali figure her father had been and never tried to tell her how to dress or conduct herself—but merely kept at his job as her manager, a job he was proving to excel at—he had promoted Petula not only in France but across the entire European continent.

Since meeting Claude, she had toured in Germany, Italy and Belgium as well as in the French provinces. She had sung in three languages, despite her lack of linguistic skills, using the phonetical method of learning lyrics she had first employed for her French songs. This was something greatly appreciated by the Continental audiences who had no idea at all that she couldn't understand a word of her songs.

E. W. Kent now felt that it was time the BBC was aware of the enormous impact she was having abroad. In a letter he wrote to producer Eric Maschwitz in August 1960, he told him how her diary was now filled with the best French, Belgium, Italian and German stage and cabaret bookings. How she had been acclaimed all over the Continent through Eurovision shows which had sadly not been networked to the BBC. And how he felt that, having become an international show-business personality, she might still be of some use to the British entertainment industry.

Petula herself was no longer very interested in what happened to her British career—a new development which somewhat irritated old friends like Jack Fishman. Jack had written a song called 'Thank You' to music composed by a German priest.

'It had a double meaning—it could either be a religious-type song or a love-song,' he explains. 'Pet did the song on one of her now rare trips to England and it made a bloody good record. But in those years when there were no commercial radio stations, you had to have an artist to plug a record. Claude and Pet both said they were far too busy with Pet's Continental career to come to England to plug that record. Without the personal plugging we knew it might just as well be thrown away.'

'Thank You' never did become a chart-topper. But it did better than anyone, even Jack Fishman, could have believed: 'It became one of the most performed of all Clark records and is, to this day, never off the air. It was played on the "God" spot on TV, before the early morning sermon on radio, and somehow it even got into the official hymn books. Children all over the country still sing it in morning assembly. The song Pet Clark didn't have time to plug continues to promote her all over the world.'

Despite the initial disappointment over the non-promotion of 'Thank You', Alan Freeman wasn't giving up. In late 1960, he received a call from Don Agnes at Cyril Simons' music publishing company, Leeds Music. Don told Alan he had a new song and he believed it would be a smash-hit for Pet.

Alan listened to a few bars of 'Sailor' down the phone, caught Don's enthusiasm and rang Petula in Paris.

'As it happens, I have a free day tomorrow. I'll pop over,' she said, making it sound as though she was popping across the road to buy some toffees. She came with Claude, but when they heard the song for the first time, they were frankly unenthusiastic.

'It's quite a nice song,' she said. 'But I don't think it's hit material.'

Alan, supported by Tony Hatch, persuaded her to do it. For the 'B' side, they recorded another title, 'My Heart', which was a sentimental ballad with plenty of violins. As soon as they heard the playbacks, both Claude and Petula told Alan that they felt the sides ought to be reversed.

Alan was now faced with a dilemma. On the strength of her huge Continental success, he had arranged for her to promote 'Sailor' at a show she was booked in at the London Palladium. Since he had great faith in her judgment, however, he now had to decide whether to stick with his original decision or change his promotion plans. Despite her feelings, he made up his mind to stick with it.

Within days of its release on the British market, 'Sailor' navigated to number two in the British charts—and held its own there for five weeks. The news reached the ears of Petula's old mentor, Cecil Madden, and he dropped her a line congratulating her on her success. She was delighted that he still followed her progress.

★　　　★　　　★

She had her new hit—and she also had a very special secret. In May 1961, Petula discovered that her dearest private wish had been granted. She was pregnant. Now she would marry Claude.

8 June 1961 was a bumper day for brides. In York Minster, the Duke of Kent was marrying Katharine Worsley. In London, Shirley Bassey wed film director Kenneth Hume. And, at Bourg-la-Reine in Paris, Petula took her vows before the local mayor, M. Etienne Thaullin, in a simple, private ceremony at the town hall. The mayor was so excited by his clients that he forgot to hand over the twin gold rings and the couple had to put them on after the ceremony.

'Because of the baby, we didn't want a big fuss with people counting on their fingers,' Claude says. Even Leslie didn't come to Paris for the nuptials.

Petula wore a short dress of fine, white chiffon with a ruffle around the neck and a pintucked bodice with a little veiled Juliet cap on her head—and afterwards, with Claude's father, sister and their closest friends, Sacha Distel,

Pierre Delanoe, Leon and Dorothy Cabat and Paul Claude, the General Secretary of Vogue, they retreated to the Moulin Deux restaurant in the south of Paris for a celebration, gourmet meal.

Sixteen days later, on 24 June, it was the turn of British friends and relatives to share the wedding party. Petula particularly wanted her marriage blessed in church so a simple ceremony was arranged at the parish church at Lodsworth where Leslie and Ann now lived. Pet arrived there with Claude—'After all, we're already married'—and, as Claude remembers all too clearly, the celebration meal at a small, local pub was not quite the gourmet outing of the splendid Moulin Deux.

'It was a terrible meal,' he says, 'lamb cooked without garlic or herbs and wobbly jelly which I hate.'

It was far removed from the grand-scale, Hollywood-type wedding that Leslie must have dreamed of for his star daughter. But he could no longer argue with a daughter who had inherited his own strong will, and this was what she wanted.

The short honeymoon which followed in London was a disaster. The day after the Lodsworth ceremony, Claude started to feel ill.

'We called the doctor and he said I had a fever of 40°C and it must be a virus,' he says. 'He gave me penicillin. I told him penicillin had no effect on me at all but he insisted. He came back four days later and said, "You're right. Penicillin doesn't work on you"; and then he gave me another drug which had me on my feet twenty-four hours later. But our honeymoon was over by then. Poor Petula had spent all of it in a hotel bedroom, nursing me. Some honeymoon!'

CHAPTER FIFTEEN

TWO RIVERS

With 'Sailor', or 'Marin' as it was titled in France, her luck in England had changed, almost against her will. She had a French husband, a French home, and the French public had adopted her in a way formerly reserved only for home-grown personalities.

'I was actually beginning to feel French,' she says. 'As when you live almost anywhere in the world, you begin to pick up the characteristics of that country without noticing what is happening. I had shed my flouncy English clothes and had begun to dress the simpler, more sophisticated French way. I loved France and I was starting to speak the language and enjoy the food; imbibing, in fact, the whole atmosphere of the place. I didn't feel able to cope with a British career as well, especially with a child on the way.'

Perhaps to bring her two backgrounds closer together, she wrote the music for a new song. Pierre Delanoe caught its mood and composed a lyric which spoke of two rivers, the Seine and the Thames, and their importance in her life. He called it 'La Seine et La Tamise'. Jack Fishman wrote the English version and named it 'Two Rivers'.

Alan Freeman, meanwhile, had bought the rights to another song which originated on the Continent, 'Romeo'. This time, both of them agreed there was great potential. She recorded it first in English but when Leon Cabat at Vogue heard it, he demanded a French version. 'I want it to recreate the sound of the English version exactly,' he insisted.

'We had the French lyrics but recreating a sound when you've already got it absolutely right is one of the hardest things in the world to do,' Alan Freeman explains.

Yet, it was done. And the French adored it as much as the English. But now came a problem. Petula was needed to plug it—and she was seven months pregnant. The French are generally rather prudish and public pregnancies are frowned on. The idea of presenting a heavily pregnant Pet was rather more than the French TV producers were prepared to cope with. However, much to Petula's amusement they discovered quite an original solution.

'They built a sort of cylinder around me to hide the bump—I really was enormous—and while I sang they flashed pictures on to the cylinder,' she laughs. In fact, all that could be seen of her on screen was her pixie-like face and her feet! It worked. 'Romeo' was a runaway success and sold more than a million EPs in France alone.

Two weeks before the baby was due, Alan received yet another song and he felt sure it would complete the trio for 1961: 'My Friend the Sea'. As usual, his instincts were right. Petula and Claude had moved back to England to await the baby's birth. She would have her child at the South London Hospital for Women in accordance with the medical advice she'd been given so many years before. But the lady-in-waiting could not sit idle. Three weeks before her 'due' date, she was a guest on BBC's *Juke Box Jury* and as if that wasn't enough, she agreed to fill in time by recording Alan's new record.

The session itself was hilarious. Petula was now so hugely pregnant that using a normal stand microphone was out of the question. She simply couldn't get close enough to it for accurate sound reproduction. The engineers lowered a boom down to her amid merry mirth from everyone on the studio floor. Then, unusually for the girl who always got it right first time, she sang a wrong note midway through the recording. Everything stopped. Petula stood in the centre quite unabashed.

'Excuse me. It wasn't my fault. It was the baby,' she said seriously. And then carried on as though nothing untoward had happened while Alan, Tony Hatch and the rest of the recording gang doubled up laughing.

By the time that Barbara Michelle Wolff—Barra as she was soon nicknamed—entered the world on 11 December 1961, obviously determined to prove to the world that she had inherited her mother's stupendous lung power, 'My Friend the Sea' was topping the British hit parade. The congratulations she received as she lay in hospital recovering from the birth were twofold: she had a much longed for daughter and her third hit of the year. Among all the messages of love she received was a very special one from Cecil Madden.

'Dear Petula, Well done! And all my love. I must see the baby soon,' he wrote.

'I was so excited when I heard the news,' Madden says. 'It was almost like becoming a grandfather myself.'

To everyone's relief, not least Claude's, little Barra's birth had, in itself, been perfectly normal. But Petula had had a long, hard labour and had taken a great deal of gas:

'When they said "take a deep breath" they had forgotten I was a singer. I guess I took too much. Under the influence of the drugs I had this terrible experience of a voice booming at me that there was no such thing as love and that this was all a big joke! A nasty trick! I wasn't really loved. I wasn't really a mother. Then I woke up but the awful feeling stayed with me.

'People sent me the most beautiful flowers in hospital but I couldn't look at them. They seemed to be like monsters coming at me. If somebody smiled at me, it would seem like the most distasteful, obscene thing. It was like a bad trip. Even when we got home, I couldn't go out at first. Eventually, it faded although it came back very mildly about six months later,' she says.

Claude was astute enough to recognise and accept his wife's post-natal emotions and to try to alleviate them the best way he could. The little family planned to stay at their London flat in Great Peter Street for the first six weeks after Barra's birth, before returning to the apartment they had bought at Montparnasse in Paris. Claude's bachelor pad where they had spent two such happy years was no longer big enough for the three of them.

Moving back to Paris with a new baby was, as one might expect, somewhat traumatic. Everything had to be shipped in advance—including the baby's cradle.

'Barra had to sleep in an apple box for a couple of nights but she seemed to sleep there very well indeed,' Petula laughs. She was extremely anxious to get back to work.

'I got myself pretty well organised with a woman to come in and cook and another to take care of Barra but I soon realised that it was very difficult to have both a baby and a career. I was not happy,' she says. 'My mind was always with her. I felt very close to her. The tie between mother and baby is very strong and I was being pulled in two directions.

'Nobody had warned me about the mystique of having a child. I thought I could just have a baby and that would be it. For me, it was not like that at all. I could sense her needs, even when I wasn't with her. I always knew when she wasn't well. When I went back to work, there was no conscious sort of guilt, but with a first baby, particularly, you don't know quite how to cope with your emotions.'

Petula Clark, the one-time child star, was now very much a wife and mother in her own right. She came to London regularly to make her French records. She liked to have Alan Freeman's reassurance and, after an incident in France when he found great difficulty working with French engineers and technicians, Alan had flatly refused to record there.

The music world was now entering what quaintly became known as the 'yeah yeah' period. The Beatles were exploding British talent into the world charts and Petula had a moderate success with one French recording called the 'Ya Ya Twist' which was released in both countries simultaneously. But, for the most part, she stuck to her Continental career and was almost forgotten by the fickle British public.

On the Continent, the musical style was ripe for her. Charles Aznavour believes that she was probably the only singer of that period in France who could sing 'ya ya' without a false, Franco-American twang. Always a jazz-orientated vocalist, this was the music she most enjoyed and for which, physically and vocally, she was best prepared. In 1961, the French set their official seal of approval on her when they voted her top female French vocalist of the year.

Along with Françoise Hardy, Sacha Distel and Charles Aznavour, she toured the French circuit of night-clubs and worked Les Comedies de Festivities which occur for two days at a time all over France during the summer months. She had not earned the title without working for it—but it was an added mark of acclaim that it had been awarded to a British-born girl.

In the early autumn of 1962, when baby Barra was just six months old, Petula found she was pregnant again. After all those years of waiting and wondering, she would have two children just fifteen months apart.

Of course, they had to move again—this time to a magnificent apartment overlooking the Bois du Boulogne—and by the time little Catherine

Nathalie was born on 23 May, she was to discover that it had another bonus.

'We bought the flat in winter when the trees were bare,' she explains. 'When spring came, the cherry trees outside the windows were a mass of gorgeous pink blossoms. They were so bright that they reflected right through the flat giving it a wonderful, pink glow in every room.'

Katy was born at the Hertford Hospital in Paris and, with the all too recent traumas surrounding Barra's birth, this time she declined any drugs.

'It was a marvellous experience,' she says. 'A wonderful, easy birth.'

Just two days before her second daughter's appearance, a new Petula Clark title 'Chariot' was released in France by Vogue. It sprang instantly to number one in the charts there. In England, with the slightly less enthralling title of 'Casanova', it reached only thirty-nine—but it seemed to be almost an omen. Babies, it seemed, brought her special luck.

With two small babies and a husband to consider, she might have been forgiven for taking leave of absence from show-business for a while—but slowing down, even for her children, was simply not in Petula's character after the gruelling years of Leslie's training. She was a particularly consistent artiste, a quality greatly appreciated by her French audiences, and her popularity was no longer due to the gimmick value of her English accent. They loved her for herself, for her gentle personality, strong, versatile voice and bubbly British charm.

Petula was now thirty years old and had had six big Continental hits. Three of them, 'Je chante doucement', 'Les Colimaçons' and 'La Seine et La Tamise' had been musical compositions of her own with lyrics by Pierre Delanoe. It was clear that her talents reached far beyond those of the mimic-singer actress. She was performing all over the Continent, giving concerts in Belgium, Italy and Germany.

Apart from the odd TV, she had done very little in Britain over the past two years—but now the British were beginning to take notice of the girl they'd born and bred and almost forgotten.

On 2 February 1964, Petula was the amazed subject of Eamonn Andrews' famous star-shocker, *This Is Your Life*. Once again, it was her surrogate media 'father', Cecil Madden, who was the power behind it all.

She had come to London to take part in a BBC variety show with Russ Conway and Stéphane Grappelli, produced by Yvonne Littlewood. Yvonne had lured her into a rehearsal room at Shepherd's Bush where, to her utter amazement, the man with his famous 'red book' sprang on her and reunited her with a host of old friends ranging from Kathleen

Harrison and Jack Warner from the 'Huggett' days to Tony Newley, Jack Fishman, Joe Henderson, Peter Ustinov and Diana Dors. Claude was there of course, and there were three stupendous surprises in store. First she found herself crying in the arms of USAAF Sergeant Ernie Tassin who had organised the Christmas Day delivery in 1944. Then, as the programme drew to its finale, the curtains opened to reveal Pet's sister Barbara with Barra, then two-and-a-half, and Katy, just nine months old. What Petula didn't know was that they almost hadn't made it at all.

As the trio had set out for Boulogne that morning, a thick fog had descended, blanketing both sides of the Channel and the water in-between. Barbara, terrified of an accident and all too well aware that she was responsible for her sister's most precious possessions, had declined to travel further. And Cecil Madden, who had of course made all the arrangements with Claude's full approval, couldn't argue with her.

'Not only was I worried sick about the responsibility of flying the children over in those conditions,' he says. 'I was scared of Petula's reaction. When they arrived at the very last possible moment after we had already gone on the air, I was delighted. When I saw her face as they appeared from behind those curtains, I knew it had been worth while.'

A glaring omission that day seemed to be Leslie Clark. He flatly refused an invitation to appear on the programme saying: 'I don't want to be there. Our lives have drifted apart. My life is completely divorced from Pet's show-biz world and I want to keep it that way. We're not enemies. But I've seen very little of my daughter since she married and I can't help feeling a little bitter at what has happened. If I'd invested money in a business, I would have something to show for it. But building a person ... there's nothing.'

At first, Leslie had refused to co-operate with the *This Is Your Life* researchers in any way. In the end, Alan Freeman was designated as intermediary and went down to the Lodsworth store to persuade Leslie to tell him some of the essential, but missing, details only he could supply.

In fact, although Petula continued to keep an eye on her father through her sister, Barbara, to ensure that he wanted nothing, it was almost another two years before the rift was totally healed and she began to see him properly again.

CHAPTER SIXTEEN

DOWNTOWN

Just eight months after moving to the magnificent Bois du Boulogne apartment, Petula and Claude realised that they would have to move again. The luxurious flat wasn't big enough for them now they were four—and despite its glorious outlook, there was no garden for the children to romp in. Claude and Petula, who had both been robbed of romping-time during their own childhoods, for vastly different reasons, were determined that their own youngsters would have all the time and space they needed.

They bought a ten-bedroomed mansion at Ciel St Cloud, reputedly costing £40,000. Both of them adored antiques so it was furnished slowly and carefully with the best they could find on their travels. Yet, even in this new home, Petula seemed unable to put down firm roots. She was still recording for the English and French markets in Pye's London studios, under Alan Freeman's watchful eye. Alan had now moved up to executive producer of the Company and his shoes as senior producer had been filled by Tony Hatch although Pet still preferred to have Alan around while she worked, whenever possible.

They had graduated to a new routine whereby Claude would look at the diary and as soon as a few spare days came into view he would ring Tony in London and ask him to arrange a recording session. Tony would then fly over to Paris, taking with him some of his own compositions as well as demo discs, and Petula would choose those she liked. Tony would routine them with her, sitting at her grand piano in the elegant, yet still home-like sitting room of the new house and a week or so later, she would follow him back to London for the session.

At first, it seemed there was no electricity in the Clark/Hatch partnership. He wrote three English titles for her—'Valentino' inspired by 'Romeo', 'Baby It's Me' and a third so obscure that Tony himself can't remember the name. None of them even hovered above the ground.

In the summer of '64, she completed a grand Continental tour embracing France, as usual, followed by Belgium and Germany, ending in Italy. She had been hailed as Britain's biggest export since brown ale—but on the final lap, at Lecce, a tiny resort on the Adriatic coast, she encountered a situation which displeased her. She was in full song when some of the more exuberant among the audience began to dance. At first, she ignored them but as the pace hotted up and more joined in she began to get angry. She had not come all the way to Lecce as the front-girl for the band. In the end, she marched off the stage in disgust. When, a few days later, she arrived to perform in Milan, Italian impresario Claude Scaffidi refused to pay her for what he considered a less than perfect performance. She was later ordered to pay £737 damages for not completing the act, but the balance was redressed when she was awarded £840 against Scaffidi's non payment. These were the usual kind of hiccoughs one encounters when dealing with often temperamental show-biz management around the world, and didn't bother her too much at the time.

'Walter', a song released in Germany, had done extremely well there. Her French version of 'Hello Dolly' with lyrics by Delanoe was a big hit. It didn't matter whether or not she had hits in Britain any more.

In October, she had to come to London to fulfil acceptance of a long-standing invitation. Cecil Madden, now an MBE, was retiring at the age of sixty-two after serving the BBC in almost every capacity in a career spanning over thirty years. The man who had pioneered both television and radio and had worked with the greatest artists in the world, including the Von Trapps, Walt Disney, Bing Crosby and Bob Hope—the man who had launched afternoon television and children's programmes—was finally retiring. The Variety Club of Great Britain were honouring him with a luncheon of tribute at the Savoy Hotel and Petula Clark was top of the list of guests which he was asked to submit.

The list of guests that day read almost like a roll-call of the famous. Wynford Vaughan-Thomas, Anona Wynn, Frank Lawton and Victor Silvester, Harry Secombe, Valerie Hobson, Billy Cotton and Geraldo, Bessie Love, Lady Kathleen Grade and, of course, Madden's own, pet protégées, the Beverley Sisters and Petula Clark.

The late Peter Haig was MC for the occasion and Edmundo Ross supported the toast to the Guest of Honour.

A few days before their arrival for the party, Claude had rung Tony with his usual, 'We'll be in London for a few days and how about a session' message. 'While we're there, we might as well record something for the English market,' he said.

'After the last three English "misses", he made it perfectly plain to me that unless we had a success in the British charts, she wouldn't try again,' Tony says. Tony was all too well aware that he meant it. And both Alan Freeman and Louis Benjamin were very anxious that he should come back from Paris with a 'Pet loves it' response.

'As I hadn't been having any success with my own compositions, I decided not to push myself this time,' Tony says. 'I booked the usual studio and orchestra and instead of taking something of my own, I took what I thought were three hot American hits. Claude, as usual, met me at the airport and dropped me off at the Ciel St Cloud house before going off on a mission of his own. He was very good about leaving us to work alone and then only coming back when the session was over.'

But as soon as Tony arrived, he smelt panic in the air. Although it wasn't her birthday, Barra, then aged three, was having a children's party that afternoon.

'We'll have to be quick, Tony,' Pet said. 'The children are arriving about three o'clock.'

They sat at the piano while he set the French songs she wanted him to orchestrate in the right key.

'Petula is a black-note player and had written them in either "G" flat or "D" flat. "G" flat is an especially horrible key for me to play in,' he says.

The French songs rehearsed, Tony played her the discs he'd bought. 'As I played, I watched her face for reaction as I always do,' he says. 'It was quite clear that she was desperately disappointed.'

She decided that the time had come to give him a quick lunch and went into the kitchen to put the kettle on. He sat by the piano, thinking hard. Although he knew his job with Pye was safe, he also knew that the shape of his entire career from here on depended on the result of this trip and Petula's reaction to the songs he'd taken her.

'While I'd been in the States, I'd been greatly inspired by the atmosphere in New York and the life there,' he says. 'I had picked up the word "Downtown" and when I got back to England I remember sitting in a studio after a session doodling at the piano. All I had was a few basic bars of the melody with the Americanism "Downtown" sprinkled through it.'

At the time he had formulated it, he had thought it would be a perfect song for Ben E. King and the Drifters if only he could fix a lyric to it. They had already had great success with 'Under the Boardwalk' and 'On Broadway'.

'"Downtown" was just a song in my head,' he says. 'About the last person I thought was right to record it was Petula Clark. It seemed to me an entirely "Black music" song and my aim had been to finish it and either send it or better still take it to America and hope that one of the Black singers or groups would do it.'

But now he was desperate.

'Have you got anything else?' Petula called from the kitchen.

'Only one song. It's got a title but it doesn't have a lyric,' Tony replied.

He played it to her, la-la-ing it until he got to the key-word 'Downtown'. She returned instantly, without the promised tea.

'That's the one I want to record,' she said. 'It's great.' Tony was in no position to argue. Claude's promise that she would forget the English market was still ringing loudly in his ears.

They had to stop the rehearsal then as the children began to arrive. 'Uncle' Tony played the piano 'rum-de-dum-de-diddle-de-dum' for them to pass the parcel and dance around for musical chairs. He did not, he says firmly, give those little ones a sneak preview of Petula's new song. At six o'clock, when the children had gone, Claude took him to the airport and he sat, chainsmoking, as he waited for the flight home, worrying about the forthcoming session.

Back in London, he wrote the first verse and the chorus and sent them over to her. She loved it.

'Don't worry, Tony,' she said, sensing his anxiety. 'It's going to live up to expectations.' But having had the idea for a very different kind of singer in the first place, he was unconvinced. And even when Petula arrived at Pye to cut the disc some three weeks later, the lyric still was not finished. Tony explains:

'The session was fixed for 7.00 pm. I arrived at the studio a quarter of an hour early and made straight for the men's loos where I locked myself in to work on it. It was the only place where I could be out of the way and on my own.

'Pet hadn't even seen the second verse when she arrived. It hadn't been written. And cutting a disc in those days was very different to the way it is done today. We worked on just three or four track machines then. There were no multi-track instruments with the same scope to take away instruments or voices as you go along. Petula would sing—the orchestra would go on two tracks, the vocal backing group on the third and Pet on the fourth.

'Getting a good take at that time was rather like having an orgasm. Everyone had to reach the peak at the same time. You needed the best performance from the orchestra, the right tempo, the best from your balance engineer, and the best vocal performance from the singer. It could have been done in bits, to some extent, even then, but Pet herself preferred to sing with the orchestra and it was the peak, that orgasm, that I had to attain.'

The disc cut, Tony found Claude and asked him what he thought of it. 'Eets vary good,' he said.

But although Tony, too, thought it sounded 'pretty good', he was still not convinced that the right person was singing the right song.

'Pet's experience had been honed over so many years of experience and she's a damned good singer,' he says. 'She has a remarkable feeling for white "soul". But when we played the take, she still sounded very "English".'

217

What Tony didn't realise was that it was that very English accent, which he felt marred his song, which gave it its unique appeal to the American market. It was the same gimmick which, in quite a different way, had set the French market on fire. Instead of projecting a slurred eastern or mid-atlantic drawl as Tony had intended it should, the colloquial Americanese interpreted by the pure English Petula had a magic all of its own. It was an attraction Petula herself had recognised as she was brewing Tony's tea before the children's party.

After the recording, Petula and Claude went home to Paris and their babies. Tony was left to present the song at the weekly meeting attended by all the Pye executives. Alan Freeman, with his super-talent for spotting hit material, loved it at once. The rest of the team, although less enthusiastic, thought it quite pleasant. It was released on to the British market on 12 November 1964.

'I still didn't believe what was going to happen to it, although it was rising rapidly in the charts to hit second place to the unconquerable Beatles who were at number one with "I Feel Fine". It stayed in the British charts for twelve weeks,' Tony says proudly.

At the time of 'Downtown's' release, Joe Smith of Warner Brothers was on a trip to England and Tony decided to play him his newest record in Louis Benjamin's office.

'He snapped it up immediately for the States,' Tony says. 'It was released in America just before Christmas and there it even toppled the Beatles. It was a hit of hits.'

She had, in fact, captured the entire world. 'Downtown' was translated into Spanish, French, Italian and German for her. It peaked to number one in Japan. Perhaps the only place in the world where it didn't reach the number one spot was, rather surprisingly, in her adopted France.

'"Downtown" was a word the French simply didn't understand,' Tony explains. 'The song was a hit wherever Americanese was acceptable. But neither the lyrics nor the music had any special appeal to the French.'

The one person totally unprepared for all the fuss and flush of such a success was Petula herself: 'I wasn't ready for it. As far as I was concerned, I had my career wrapped up. I was a big star on the Continent and that was enough work for me. But the Beatles had opened all doors for British artistes in the States and when Joe Smith picked up "Downtown" and decided to release it in America in its original form instead of getting an American artist to cover it, it was an instant hit without me having to go there to plug it.'

When 'Downtown' hit the number one spot in New York, Petula was fulfilling a long-standing engagement in Canada. Her French hit songs like 'Chariot', 'Romeo' and 'Marin' had already earned her a special place in the hearts of the French-speaking Canadians. Her one-woman show in Quebec and Montreal was packing them in.

In Montreal, she was reunited for the first time in years—and to her enormous delight—with the soulmate of her childhood days, her cousin Clive Rose.

Clive had emigrated to Canada some years earlier and was working as a remedial teacher in Montreal. When he heard that his beloved cousin was appearing at the Valleyfield Theatre he applied for tickets for her concert and was dismayed to find it was sold out. The news of her success with 'Downtown' had swept across the entire North American continent. But, whatever happened, he was determined not to be deprived of seeing her perform, even if it meant resorting to the old techniques of entering a theatre undetected—the tricks he and Petula herself had shared back in the old days in Pontlottyn when they had to climb through the toilet windows to get into the local 'flea-pit'.

He climbed up a fire-escape and in through a half-open window to find himself standing in the wings, watching the waif-like figure in her shimmering dress pouring her powerful voice out over an enthralled audience.

'Afterwards we decided to have a meal

together to talk about the old times,' Clive says. 'We stopped off at the Chateaubriand Restaurant on the outskirts of Montreal but they wouldn't serve us because, by the time we arrived, it was well past midnight. We ended up at Rudyfoos—a Chinese restaurant where we sat dipping meat into a kind of fondue and talking and talking. Suddenly, we both realised that it was 7.00 am. I didn't even have time to go home to have a shave so I had to shave right there in the restaurant and go straight to school to take lessons.'

After the Canadian tour, Petula returned to Paris and her tiny daughters. As always, she had missed them enormously. She had a long-standing engagement to fulfil the Saturday after her return at a benefit for a Paris school, but then came the ultimate accolade—an invitation from the legendary Ed Sullivan to appear on his live TV chat show in New York. Undoubtedly, it was the most important network show on American television at that time. Sullivan always had the best and always at precisely the right time. The Beatles had been on the show. The Stones had too. Now, he wanted Petula Clark.

'He rang me himself and said, "You're coming over, right".' It was a command, not a request. No star who wanted to stay big refused Ed Sullivan. 'Ed asked me to be in New York on Thursday for rehearsals before the Sunday night performance. Short of cancelling out on the school engagement, there was just no way I could do it. I told him I'd be there on the Sunday afternoon and Sullivan, who respected my professional attitude, agreed.'

On the Saturday afternoon, she did the Paris show as planned. She and Claude had arranged to catch the first plane to New York on the Sunday morning. Allowing for the six-hour time difference in her favour, it should have given her ample time. But, to their joint horror, the plane was cancelled. The next one wouldn't arrive in New York until late on Sunday afternoon and when it landed the route from the airport to town was jammed with Sunday afternoon sightseers and trippers. She arrived, utterly exhausted and only just in time for the dress rehearsal.

'Nobody told me that Sullivan always overbooked his shows and that he only chose the acts he would finally use after seeing the reaction of a live audience at the dress-rehearsal,' Petula giggles. 'I had never seen or heard the orchestra and I had never met Sullivan personally. As I arrived in the studio, my music was already playing so I merely had time to jump on-stage and straight into the song.'

But, as she did so, she realised that the tempo was wrong. 'I did the unforgivable and stopped the show. It was something which, I gather, had never happened before. I told them about the wrong tempo and they got it right. Ignorance is bliss. From then on, I couldn't lose. "Downtown" had become like their national anthem and I pulled the place down. At that moment, I had made it. I was there.'

'Downtown' stayed in the American hit parade for an incredible fifteen weeks. It was played by paraders along Fifth Avenue; in every home and store in the country the English Petula's voice belted out the pure American lyric. It earned her her first 'Grammy' award with sales topping the three-million mark.

Tony Hatch had not accompanied Pet and Claude to the States to share the adulation. 'I was too busy working on other songs for my fourteen other artistes,' he says. Claude, always the astute businessman, knew Tony ought to be there.

'He rang me and told me I had to go over to meet the trade press and be part of the celebrations,' Tony says. 'They got permission from Louis Benjamin for me to fly over for just three days. It was one long round of parties. But then I had to come back to get on with the work in hand. I just didn't have time for anything else. To me, "Downtown" was an accident—a wonderful, beautiful accident.'

CHAPTER SEVENTEEN

I KNOW A PLACE

Tony Hatch had produced Joan Reagan's records until she had left the Pye label in 1963. Then he was left without a female singer of his 'own' and in that year before 'Downtown's' grand success, he had signed a girl of whom he had high hopes, Jackie Trent.

'I didn't feel that Petula was really my artiste. I always felt she still belonged to Alan Freeman,' he says. By 1964, Alan had, of course, given him *carte blanche* to write, produce and orchestrate for Petula. But she still liked to have Alan around when she was recording. He represented security to her—although it often left Tony feeling ill at ease.

Tony had first heard Jackie Trent perform in a London club and her voice had interested him. Her manager, Eve Taylor, brought her to Pye for an audition and he put her under contract. At first, success seemed to elude her until Tony, who wrote the theme for the soap-opera *Crossroads*, was commissioned to write another theme song for a Granada TV series called *It's Dark Outside*. The song was to be part of the plot and Granada had asked Tony to find a female vocalist, who had not had a hit, to perform it.

He asked Jackie if she would do it at Pye's annual Christmas party, held at the Lotus House, one of London's most famous Chinese restaurants. Although she was due to leave for a South African tour within the week, she accepted happily. Two days later they were cutting the disc of 'Where Are you Now' with music by Tony Hatch and lyrics by Jackie Trent. It was released in May 1965 and swept straight to number one in the British charts.

It seemed that this was Tony's lucky year. Whatever he touched turned to gold—first 'Downtown', then 'Where Are You Now'. He knocked himself off the top of the charts with another newcomer, Sandie Shaw, singing 'There's Always Something There to Remind Me' and his own group, The Searchers, had a big success with 'Goodbye My Love'. He was almost living in the studio.

Not surprisingly, his work was having an unwelcome side-effect on his home life. He had married his wife, Jean, when he was just twenty. She was a qualified teacher and ran her own dancing school. By the time he was twenty-five, he had two children and a home he rarely visited—and no marriage. He was working almost twenty-four hours a day in the studio and Jean saw very little of him.

Petula and Claude were quite unaware of Tony's private troubles, but they knew that he worked hard and badly needed a holiday. They had bought a holiday home at Valiteneuse on the Côte d'Azur and generously offered to lend it to Tony and Jean for a couple of weeks. They jumped at the chance of time alone together— but its effect was not long-lasting. They separated in early October.

Petula, who knew and liked Jean, was upset when Tony told her they were parting. Although he had not, he insists, become emotionally involved with Jackie until just before his marriage broke up, she had for some time been helping him with his lyrics, including those he was submitting to Petula. In the circumstances, he felt it would be undiplomatic to mention his new partnership to her—and Jackie agreed.

In January 1965, the Hatch/Trent partnership came up with a new title for Petula, 'I Know a Place'. It was, as Tony explains, the natural successor to 'Downtown': 'I had learned a special trick from "Downtown" and that was to appeal as far as possible to the American market'.

The new song was released in February and earned Petula her second 'Grammy' in six months. It hit number two in the States and number seventeen in Britain. Tony's instincts had been right.

Petula was now a recognised American star. Offers of work were coming at her from every angle. The path ahead was split into two distinct forks—the rock 'n' roll concert scene or the ballad-type cabaret route.

'Claude and my agents advised me to follow the cabaret route,' she says. 'They decided that was the kind of work where I would be listened to. At rock concerts, they just hear the hits—and that's it!'

She was in desperate need, now, of an American musical director who understood the pace of the States and could blend with her in the same way as Joe Henderson had once done in England. Claus Oberman, a mutual friend of both Claude and Sammy Davis Jnr., put Claude in touch with Frank Owens, a Black musician of outstanding promise.

'We met in a little studio on Sixth Avenue in New York and went over her music. She didn't have any with her at the time but it just happened that I knew most of her hits like "Downtown" and "I Know A Place". I can remember that Claude didn't speak English too well at the time—and I was so anxious to get the job that I practised my French on him,' Frank laughs. 'It was a big thrill when they hired me to play with her at the Coppa Cabana in November.'

Petula herself had been thrilled when the invitation to perform at the Coppa—New York's most glittering nightspot—had been confirmed. This time, they decided to take the children along, too. Barra was four years old, Katy three, and she found total relaxation from the pressures around her when she had them with her. The afternoon before the big opening night, she took them skating at the Rockefeller Centre outdoor rink before tucking them into bed and making the début of a lifetime.

It hadn't been quite as glamorous as she'd expected though, when she arrived for rehearsals at the club which regularly featured such stars as Sammy Davis Jnr. and Frank Sinatra.

'I had never been in a club like that in daytime. The Coppa Cabana was the hot spot of New York and both Claude and I were shattered when we saw it as it really was by the light of a single, naked bulb. Denuded of its pink shaded lights and elegant patrons, it looked filthy dirty. There were cobwebs everywhere. The fabulous Coppa Cabana showgirls came to rehearsals with holes in their tights and stood around chewing gum. It was dreadful.'

As though the reality of the dream-world in daylight was not bad enough, there was another shock to come. The Coppa's manager, Jules Podell, told Petula that before she could work she had to pay a visit to the police headquarters, ironically enough in 'downtown' New York, to have her fingerprints taken.

'You had to go there with a photograph,' Claude explains. 'They give you an identity card and you have to put your fingerprints on it with another set going into the police records. In those days, the rules about working in New York night-clubs were very strict.'

Podell had earned himself a reputation for meanness, but it was a side of his character which was never revealed to either Petula or Claude.

'I couldn't understand a word of his English and he couldn't understand a word of my French,' Claude says. 'So he communicated with me through champagne. He used to send cases of it round to the dressing-room. We had never seen anything like it before. We drank a lot together and it was quite obvious that he thought that this was the way to please a Frenchman.'

That New York booking was one which Petula herself can only describe as 'an amazing experience... One of the first things you realise, and I felt it even more later in Las Vegas, is the amazing energy level of American show-biz people. It is something we don't have in Europe. It tingles.'

The smart New Yorkers worshipped Petula as much as she was stimulated by them. Not a single night went by at the Coppa when she didn't have a standing ovation and such a deluge of flowers on-stage that they almost drowned her from view. She was no longer Britain's 'Our Pet' or France's 'Petulante Petula'. She was an international star of magnitudal proportions, fêted and followed wherever she went.

The musical chemistry between Petula and Tony Hatch had formulated to precisely the right balance to produce the hits, with— unknown to Petula—a gentle prod from Jackie Trent in the background. Both Petula and Tony stress emphatically that there was never any emotional entanglement between them, as has at times been hinted. They were fond of each other, naturally, but it was a fondness born of mutual respect for the other's talent.

'Everyone assumed that because I was always rushing off to Paris or New York whenever Pet called, there must be a great thing going between us. But every time I arrived to see her, it was always Claude who met me at the airport and Claude who returned me there. The three of us got on extremely well together. Claude knew where she was every moment of the day and night and I always made it my business to stick to business. It gave us both a good feeling and I know that Claude trusted me completely.'

Jackie was now regularly helping Tony write the lyrics for Pet's songs. The first had been 'I Know a Place'—but still Tony dared not tell her where the magical inspiration was coming from.

'Jackie had a gift for it,' he says. 'It's easy when you write a tune because you've got lots of bits and pieces here and there which repeat. When you have a verse which then has to be repeated musically but with a whole new set of words, it's not so simple. I used to get tied up in knots.'

He decided that the time had come to make a clean breast of his relationship with Jackie to Petula and Claude. They had decided to take up a 'trial residence' together. Tony was unsure about marrying again after his disastrous marriage to Jean.

'Claude's reaction was predictable,' he says. 'He told me he knew something would happen the moment I had success. Petula's was much the same. She had liked Jean—and Jean who was not in the business posed no threat to her.'

But even having told them that he was now living with Jackie, he still omitted to mention that Jackie was writing most of the lyrics.

While Petula had been in New York, she had asked Tony for a new song. He had written one called 'Life and Soul of the Party' and had been taking it to her when, on the plane, he got into conversation with a fellow passenger. The man had asked Tony his business and Tony had told him what he did and that he was taking a new song over to Petula.

'What's it called?' the man asked.

'"Life and Soul of the Party",' Tony told him happily.

'I know the meaning of "life" and I know the meaning of "soul",' the man replied, puzzled. 'But what is a "life and soul of the party"?'

'I knew then,' Tony says, 'that it was the wrong title for America. I had to do some quick changes. Luckily, the plane was half empty so I moved to a seat on my own and started working on it frantically. Midway across the Atlantic, I had the music for "My Love" but no lyrics. On arrival in New York, I pleaded jet-lag as an excuse for not producing the song immediately and checked into my hotel suite quickly to call Jackie in London. I hummed her the tune I'd written down the phone and she hummed it in turn into a tape-recorder.

'In the morning, she rang me back with a completed lyric which I duly presented to Petula. She was delighted with it and used it right away.'

'My Love', written in such a panic transatlantically, flipped straight to number one in the American charts. Claude and Petula had finished the New York engagement and had gone to Megève in the Swiss Alps for a Christmas holiday. After that, they were due for an engagement at the Olympia in Paris and a booking at the London Palladium. Claude knew that for these engagements Petula would, as usual, need some new material. He rang Tony and invited him to join them in Megève.

'We must work on some new English and French songs,' he said. 'Come and spend three days with us and then Pet would love you to come on to Paris to see her performance. I'll

232

pick up your fares.'

'I'd like to bring Jackie with me,' Tony said.

'Fine,' said Claude, 'we'll be happy to have her. I'll book you into a hotel.'

Jackie and Tony arrived at Megève at about 10.00 pm and they were both tired and hungry. Claude and Petula, they discovered, had already eaten and gone on to an *après ski* disco bar in town. Tony and Jackie decided to join them there immediately.

'Jackie and I walked into the crowded bar together and although we were sure that Pet had seen us, she made no acknowledgement,' Tony says. 'I knew that the reason had to be Jackie and that I had made a terrible mistake bringing her along. Still, I felt that my personal life had to carry on. I felt that I had to have the freedom to do as I pleased without censorship from anyone—even Pet.'

Finally, a frustrated Tony approached Claude. 'Hello,' he said. '"My Love's" at number one in the States. Aren't you going to invite us to sit down and share some champagne to celebrate?'

'Of course,' replied an embarrassed Claude. He ordered them drinks and the two sat nursing them miserably, feeling very much on the outside of an 'in' clique.

The next three days, Tony describes as 'sheer hell'. No matter how hard she tried, Jackie simply couldn't break the ice-barrier that seemed to have developed—a barrier which Petula can erect instantly when she's unhappy with her company. It was a mode of self-protection and defence she had developed during the traumatic, self-doubting years of her late teens and early twenties when her father's dominance had sapped her confidence—and when all her efforts to 'go it alone' had proved so fruitless.

'The second evening we all four sat down for a meal together and I told Petula of an idea I'd had for a medley for the Palladium show,' Tony says. 'Jackie was terribly enthusiastic and said—"Oh! Pet. It's a wonderful idea. Tony's talked to me about it and you could do so much with it." Instead of replying, Pet stood up, her face very white, and stormed away from the table. Within hours, she had made it very plain to me that she wouldn't have anyone else involved in the planning of her songs, the recording sessions, lyrics, orchestrations, ideas or anything else. It was me—and me alone—or not me at all.'

Says Tony: 'All Jackie had done was to try to get Pet to like her. She wanted to tell her that she wasn't a threat—that she was genuinely wearing two hats. As long as Pet and I were making hit songs, she would be with me writing the lyrics, not pinching them. But Pet didn't believe that was the case.

'The next afternoon, Pet was having a siesta

and Jackie knocked tremulously on her door. She's a northern girl—very open and down to earth and very determined not to sweep the dust under the carpet. She begged Petula to let her explain how it was between her and me. But Pet, basically a sensitive person, had no wish to discuss the matter any further. "It takes me a long time to get to like people," she told the distressed Jackie. "At the moment, we have a problem."'

The following day, the four flew from Geneva to Paris for the Olympia booking. Tony was disappointed to find that while Claude had booked first-class tickets for himself and his wife, he and Jackie were travelling in the economy class cabin.

It took several months before Petula was willing to accept Jackie Trent as a friend and even then, theirs was never a close relationship.

'I found Jackie Trent rather vulgar and uninteresting,' Claude says. 'I felt that a person like that couldn't write good songs. Pet had nothing in common with Jackie. I was afraid that if she was going to write all the lyrics, they weren't going to be terribly good!'

Tony, however, believed that it was possible for the two to build a relationship—and he felt he had got it going.

Whatever the personal feelings between the two couples, Petula was voted Top European TV personality of the year in Austria after

'Downtown'. The Italians claimed her as their Juke Box Queen and the American Greater Reno Chamber of Commerce gave her their award for 'her contribution to sheer joy'. In the swiftly growing avalanche of accolades, Tony was not forgotten. He received several BMI Special Citation Certificates, each representing a million broadcasts of 'Downtown', a gold disc and recognition from the Association of Song Writers, Composers and Publishers.

In March 1966, she toured the Continent, ending with a booking in Ankara, Turkey. Just as she arrived, it was announced that the Turkish President, Gursel, was seriously ill, having suffered partial paralysis as the result of a stroke. He had undergone urgent treatment at the Walter Reed Army Hospital in Washington—but when he suffered two further strokes and it became clear that no treatment would cure him, he was flown home.

The day following his return, Petula opened to a packed house and the promise of a sell-out for the rest of the week-long engagement. But the morning after her first night, the club's manager paid them a visit at their hotel.

'There's no show tonight,' he told the surprised Wolffs.

'What do you mean?' Claude asked. 'Petula had a fantastic reception last night.'

'Our President is desperately ill. He's had a heart attack to add to his other troubles and everything is closed. There are no restaurants, no night-clubs, nothing is open. We have to close, too. Don't worry. You will be paid. It's an act of God.'

'I'm not asking you to pay us,' Claude protested. 'I'm just asking what is going to happen.'

'If he dies in two days, then we will have two days official mourning and then you can go on,' he told them.

'You mean,' protested Claude, 'that we have to sit for four days doing nothing. I mean the man no harm, but I hope he dies tonight.'

They sat it out for two more days, both intensely frustrated.

'We can't stay here any longer,' Claude finally told the management. 'We have other engagements and this could go on forever.'

On the afternoon of 13 March, a declaration signed by thirty-seven doctors was read to the Turkish National Assembly informing them that President Gursel would be unable to resume his Presidential duties due to ill-health. The new President was elected and sworn in; the restaurants and nightclubs reopened immediately and Petula Clark was back in business. As President Gursel lingered for another six months before finally passing away on 16 September, it was, as Claude says, just as well that they hadn't been held to their contract until his death!

In April, '66, Petula returned to Canada and Montreal where they cheered her French repertoire once more and allowed her the privilege of singing 'Downtown' in English. The next stop was the Capital Theatre in Ottawa—but after her tumultuous reception in Montreal, her reception in this other Canadian city took her by surprise. As in Montreal she sang in French, thinking she was pleasing them. To her sheer horror, a thousand people stalked out of the theatre in disgust. Those who remained took up a solemn chant—'Sing in English, sing in English.'

'Nobody told me that English is spoken in nine out of ten of the Canadian provinces,' she said. But, always the professional, she was quick to retrieve the situation. She switched languages and wisecracked her way through the remainder of the programme, delighting those who remained.

From Canada, she went on to the mecca of American show-biz—the Coconut Grove night-club attached to the Ambassador Hotel, Los Angeles (where Bobby Kennedy was to meet his untimely end just two years later). This time, Barra and Katy came too. And, as Claude explains, travelling with small children is not always easy.

'We booked into the Beverley Wiltshire Hotel. Katy, who was then about four years old, was going through a phase of refusing her meals.

Whatever she was offered, she would say "I'm not hungry" and turn it away. I could see that this was worrying Petula, so one night I decided I had to be firm with her.

'When she said she wasn't hungry, I made her go to her room and told her to stay there. She screamed and screamed. It was so loud that I thought it would disturb the whole hotel. I had just acquired a new toy at the time—a cassette tape-recorder. I don't know what made me do it but I turned it on and recorded all the screaming. Eventually, she wore herself out and went to sleep.

'The next day she woke up and ate breakfast. Fine! Lunch! Fine! But at dinner-time she started again, with "Daddy, I'm not hungry".

'"OK," I said. "Then we do the same as last night." Before she could answer me, I turned on the recorder. When she heard her own screams she started to cry. "Stop it, Daddy. Stop it. I won't do it again." With that, she ate her dinner and she never repeated the performance.'

Petula had persuaded Frank Owens, with whom she found she shared a similar musical rapport to the wonderful togetherness she'd had with Joe Henderson, to accompany her for her big chance in Los Angeles. Her opening night there is one she will never forget. When a new star comes to Hollywood for the first time, the established planets descend in a meteoric mass to give them that welcome which only

Hollywood knows how. And it was this stupendous greeting which they bestowed upon Petula.

In the audience that night were Barbra Streisand and Frank Sinatra, Sammy Davis Jnr, and Lucille Ball, Fred Astaire and Jack Warner from Warner Brothers' films. The compère was a very old friend, Anthony Newley.

As the theatre filled, Petula peeped through the curtains—rather like a child taking part in her first school play.

'What are all those stars doing out there?' she asked Claude nervously.

'They've come to see *you*,' he replied gently.

'I can't go out there. I just can't,' she whispered.

'You can, and you will,' he told her firmly. 'You're going to wow them in just the same way as you did in Paris and London and New York.'

Anthony Newley came on-stage and introduced his old friend as 'Petula Clark—the girl from London, England'. The lights lowered. The orchestra, under Frank Owens' careful direction struck up the opening notes of 'Downtown'—and off she went.

'It should have been a strange sensation working with her again after all those years but it wasn't,' Newley says. 'There was a rightness about it as though it was preordained. I still held Pet in the same high regard that I did when we worked together as children. And they loved her. How they loved her.'

Petula herself, used as she was to the appreciation of her audiences, was overwhelmed by it all.

'They stood to greet me almost before I had a chance to open my mouth,' she says. 'It was as though they were saying—"Go on. Be great. We know you can do it. We know you're the best. If you weren't you wouldn't be here".

'Everywhere else in the world, the audience's attitude is: "We've heard you're good. Now prove it." But when you open live in Hollywood, the proving time is over. You've shown them already. Just by being there on the stage, I was a real star in a way I had never been before in England or on the Continent.' And she was.

Tony Newley claims that as he stood there watching her, his mind ran backwards more than twenty years to another opening night. 'Petula was wearing a white dress and ankle socks and we stood on the steps of the Odeon in Leicester Square having press pictures taken before the opening of *Vice-Versa*. I'd slipped her a piece of crumpled cake that I had in my pocket to keep her going. Now, I had to realise that this glamorous woman singing to the world's greatest entertainers was the same as that shy, aloof little girl I'd worshipped from afar.'

With the echo of her sensational performance still ringing in his ears, Newley found himself chatting to Jack Warner after the show.

'She's got everything Julie Andrews has got—plus,' he told Warner. Warner nodded in agreement. The following morning, Warner's musical director, Quincy Jones, telephoned her.

'We're doing a remake of *Finian's Rainbow!* You wanna screen test for me?' he asked her.

Only a few weeks before, she had turned down a screen offer to appear with Elvis Presley, not because she didn't want to work with the world's greatest rock 'n' roll star but 'because I can't see myself dancing around on a beach with bikini girls and guitars. I'm thirty-three now,' she'd said. 'Although in the States they seem to think I'm a teenage pop-star, I'm definitely not.'

She had also refused a 'Peggy Lee'-type part in *Valley of the Dolls*, although she was one of Peggy's greatest fans, because she couldn't see herself in 'that kind of sexy-and-black-sequinned role.'

However, the role she was now being offered, that of Sharon, the Irish colleen daughter of the immigrant Finian, was just the kind of part she'd been hoping for. But first, she went on a tour of the West Coast with Claude, and Frank Owens as guide.

'All she knew of America at that time was the big cities like New York and Los Angeles,' Owens says. 'She didn't know about the little Western towns. So we played in Montana and in Oregon to give her an idea of how the country is.

America is so diverse in terrain. We did one-nighters in all the little one-horse towns across the West. It was a tremendously exciting tour.'

With her American adventure over, she returned to Italy and Paris for brief engagements before coming home to Britain. The British, not to be outdone, wanted to give the new super-star a chance to show her that they adored her, too.

CHAPTER EIGHTEEN

THIS IS MY SONG

Summer 1966. Petula's popularity was at an all-time peak in America. Yet, despite having spent the most part of the past seven years working first in France and on the Continent and latterly in the United States, she was still as basically British as ever, loving nothing more than a British breakfast of bacon and eggs, the British sense of humour and, of course, British applause. It was this that now drew her home.

With her engagement diary on the Continent so full, it was a long time since she had appeared in a top notch on BBC TV. Over the past few years, she had made guest appearances on panel games like *Juke Box Jury* and there had been the surprise of *This Is Your Life* but now she was invited to star as hostess in her own TV spectacular series, *This Is Petula Clark*—six programmes with an international flavour produced by the great Yvonne Littlewood who, in the years ahead, was to become not only her favourite producer but one of the few close, personal friends Petula ever had.

Petula and Yvonne first met back in the *Pet's Parlour* days of the late forties and early fifties when Yvonne was secretary to the show's producer, Michael Mills. They had become friendly during rehearsals when Yvonne had discovered Petula's pickled onion passion and had sneaked pots of her favourite relish in to her from the café across the road. They had met again in 1964 when Yvonne produced *The Best of Both Worlds* and Pet had sung 'Funny Valentine' with Robert Farnham and 'Boom— Why Does My Heart Go Boom' by Charles Trenet.

In this new series, Petula introduced to Britain many of the stars she had worked with on the Continent—people like Rafael, Claude François and Les Surfs from France, Germany's Conny Frobuss and Fred Bongusto and his troupe from Italy, as well as Danish jazz violinist Svend Amussn—all under the musical direction of Harry Rabinowitz.

A private market research report carried out for the BBC at the time showed that the public were thrilled to have her back.

'She is an artiste of immense charm, great sincerity and exceptional talent. A further series would be most welcome,' the report concluded.

But even while it was in the making, she was appearing live at one of London's most glittering and exclusive night-spots—the Savoy Hotel—with her new, all-star image and her new repertoire. It was a booking which obviously delighted her.

'One nice thing is that people here know all about me and when I walk on-stage, nobody is going to be disappointed to see a woman in her thirties,' she said gleefully. 'In America, where my records sell in millions to the teenage market, they think I'm a teenager myself.'

Among the new songs she sang to the celebrated Savoy audience was one which Tony Hatch felt was particularly significant in the sometimes stormy relationship between Petula and Jackie Trent, who had now become his wife.

'Jackie wrote the words of "I Couldn't Live Without Your Love" as a private tribute to me,' he says. 'She was in cabaret in Birmingham at the time and I wrote the music one day for no particular reason. She loved it and asked me to put it on a cassette for her. Journeying up to Birmingham for her cabaret booking, she played the music to herself in the car and wrote the lyrics as personal poetry; a way of expressing the relationship we shared from her point of view.'

Certainly, the words of that song were distinctly pertinent to Jackie and Tony:

'You're the only one that I rely on
A shoulder there for me to cry on
And the hours that I spend without you
All I ever do is think about you,
No one knows that you're so understanding
Even though I'm so demanding,
I couldn't live without your love,
Now I know you're really mine
Gotta have you all the time.'

'After waiting for my own divorce and with all the personal problems we'd had, the words were aimed just at me,' he says. 'But then Claude rang in his usual panic and asked if we had a new song which Pet could use for her comeback to Britain. That was the only one we had. I had to be persuasive but, in the end, Jackie graciously conceded it to Pet. She knew that Pet was running with the hits so she was prepared to wear her lyricist's hat so that Pet could continue to have success with a joint composition of ours. It was instances like that that made it so hard for me to understand Petula's reluctance to be Jackie's friend.'

It was the song which Petula featured both in her international TV series and at the Savoy where the Wolff family were now based. Despite all that was happening to her, she

246

needed to spend time with her children and they needed her. Each night, before appearing on-stage, she would disappear to her suite to bathe Barra and Katy and to romp with them and read them a story before tucking them into bed for the night.

'Whilst I'm with the children, I don't want to know about work at all,' she said. 'I just want to be their mother. But as soon as I start working again, everything else is forgotten. When I'm performing, I'm certainly not a "Mum" and I don't want the audience to think of me as one.'

There was no way they could. Paris had adopted her, Hollywood had fêted her, and now London merely wanted the chance to show its appreciation too.

'Sharp at midnight, Petula Clark returned to sing in London on the most gilded rung of the cabaret ladder, the Savoy Hotel,' wrote Gerrard Garrett in the *Evening Standard*. 'Slim, fair and elfin-faced, or so she appeared in a red and purple spotlight, she looked a bit like a Cinderella who'd forgotten the way home.

'Miss Clark wooed them with a Beatle number and a burst of "My Fair Lady". It's easy to see why she's become Britain's Continental Queen of Song.'

It was adulation as great as she had received from anywhere in the world—all the more precious because it came from home. She'd lost that awful 'little girl' image, at last. And in the audience that night, full of praise and excitement, was her father, Leslie. He was now watching her career from the sidelines, but what he saw pleased him beyond description.

From the time when she had first discovered that the fortune she'd earned as a teenage star had disappeared, the relationship between them had been somewhat cold. Since her return to England, however, she had been to see Leslie and Ann who had now moved to Bognor Regis. Leslie had found it hard to make a go of the post-office at Lodsworth and now had a job with the Sussex School Meals Service as a stock-man. He had put the showbiz life behind him long ago.

Petula, who now reputedly earned around £250,000 a year, could no longer bear a grudge. She had sung in some twenty countries around the world. She had a luxurious ten-bedroomed mansion at Ciel St Cloud in Paris and a magnificent holiday home on the Côte d'Azur where the children could stay in familiar surroundings while she did her regular summer tours of the French provinces. She holidayed with the Distels at Megève in the French Alps where she and Claude were considering building another holiday home. It was estimated that her records had achieved world-wide sales in the eighteen months since she'd been launched on her new American career.

However, at the beginning of 1967, just as she

was all set to start work on *Finian's Rainbow*, a new problem faced her.

Early the previous year, when Petula had been in London for a *Show of the Week* with Sacha Distel, Cyril Simons of the Leeds Musical Publishing Company had spoken to Claude about a film-score which Charlie Chaplin was writing for what sadly proved to be his very last film, *The Countess from Hong Kong*. Simons had suggested to Louise Benjamin that he would like Petula to record the theme song. 'This Is My Song'.

Claude had agreed that it sounded a good idea—but nothing happened. In late October, when Petula was appearing at Caesar's Palace in Las Vegas, Claude suddenly remembered it. He rang Simons.

'What happened to the Chaplin song?' he asked him.

'Frankly, Claude, we've done a demonstration and it's lousy,' Simons told him. 'I wouldn't insult Pet by asking her to do it. We've been touting it around and the only person who makes any sense of it at all is Harry Secombe. I don't think it's really the sort of song Petula wants to sing.'

Claude was intrigued. He was a great Chaplin fan and knew Chaplin's seemingly unbounded talents.

'Why don't you send it to me anyway, just for fun,' he said. 'I can only make a judgement on it when I've heard it.' The demonstration disc arrived and after listening, Claude had to agree he was right. It was late in the afternoon, however, when he suddenly heard the tune being whistled by the family's Australian nanny. Petula heard it too.

'What's that?' she inquired.

'Chaplin's new song. It's a lousy tape and the words are dreadfully old-fashioned but there's a melody in it I like and it's obviously catching,' he told her.

He played her the disc and she had to agree that she didn't think much of the lyrics. But Claude was getting quite a 'feel' for it.

'Maybe it isn't very good for the English-speaking market but I bet the French will love it,' he said and rang Pierre Delanoe in Paris. Pierre started work on the French lyrics while Claude sorted out an arranger, recorded the music properly and sent Delanoe the tapes.

The Americans had been clamouring to see what Petula would release to follow 'Downtown', 'I Know a Place' and 'I Couldn't Live Without Your Love'. 'This Is My Song', Claude knew, was no new 'Downtown' rock song but a much more middle-of-the-road ballad. He rang Jack Fishman in London and explained about the old-fashioned words. 'We can't use sentences like: "I care not what the world may say." Petula thinks they've come out of the ark. But be subtle. Chaplin would hate to think anyone else had altered a word.'

Fishman did what he thought was a brilliant job, changing Chaplin's words as little as possible while modernising the song. Delanoe in France had worked equally cleverly, keeping as close as he could to the original version within the bounds of language. When both were completed, Chaplin suddenly asked to hear the English version with the music. Jack Warner played it to him, convinced that the old man wouldn't notice the difference. But Chaplin was not so easily fooled.

'If a single word of the English version is changed, then you don't get the song,' he bellowed. 'I wrote it and it will be sung as I wrote, word for word. No song—no film.'

Warner had no option but to agree and relayed the message to an anxious Claude who had always been doubtful about the English-language potential of the whole thing anyway. Petula had just completed her highly successful Vegas booking and had returned to New York for a second run at the Coppa Cabana. Louis Benjamin from Pye joined her there.

Petula was having serious second thoughts about the whole thing. Despite the problems between herself and Jackie, she had had a remarkable run of luck with Tony Hatch. If she were now to sing a song written by somebody else, even the talented legend Chaplin, would Tony take offence? Louis Benjamin remembers:

'I had booked into the Pierre Hotel where Claude and Pet were staying and I went along to see Petula at the Coppa. As usual, she. was superb. Everyone was there that night; The Kinks, Nat King Cole and Alan Klein. Afterwards, we had a party in my suite and King Cole gave us a private performance. But I could see that Petula was worrying about something. She told me it was the Chaplin song.

'I spent the next forty-eight hours with Claude and Pet, agonising and arguing about it. Despite the differences between Jackie and Petula, Pet was worried about breaking what she felt was an unwritten contract between them. The arguments raged between the Ziegfeld Theatre, the. Stage Deli on Sixth Avenue and my suite at the Pierre where we used to sit up half the night, nibbling salt-beef sandwiches. We never left one another's sides. In the end, she agreed to record the song.'

What she had agreed to do was to record 'This Is My Song' in French and German, leaving English aside for the time being. The Wolffs were due to fulfil an engagement in Reno, Nevada, and it became a matter of some urgency to find a top-flight arranger at short notice. Jack Warner obligingly agreed to supply Ernie Freeman. But Claude had a shock when he went to meet Ernie from the airport the morning after they themselves had arrived from New York.

'He was being escorted through the airport

lounge in a highly inebriated state,' Claude laughs. 'In all the hurry, Warner forgot to tell me that Ernie hated flying and was likely to console himself with large tots of the hard stuff on the journey.'

On a Saturday morning in late January, they were all in a recording studio in Reno. It took just three hours to record 'This Is My Song' in French and German.

'We didn't intend to make an English version but as we were there with everything set up, we decided to do an English version at the very last minute,' Claude explains.

Almost immediately following the session, Petula was booked to do *Orswood Palace*, a networked TV show.

'The producer asked if she had any new material and as "This Is My Song" was the only one we played it through to him,' Claude says.

'It's not meant for the British market,' Petula protested.

'Do it on the show, anyway,' the producer said. 'We'll see what the audience's reaction is. If they don't like it, we'll just cut it out.'

To both Claude and Petula's amazement, the studio audience responded with a passion which could only be compared with the sensational reaction she'd first had to 'Downtown'. As Louis Benjamin says: 'For Pet, it was yet another change of pace; something entirely different. They loved not just the music and lyrics which bore Chaplin's name—but Petula's versatility.'

'This Is My Song', or *'C'est Ma Chanson'* as the French called it, with music and lyrics by Charlie Chaplin in the English version and words for the French version written by Pierre Delanoe, was at number one in the charts within days of its release; not only in Great Britain and the United States; not only in France, Italy, Germany and Spain, but in the Scandinavian countries, in Dubai and Japan. If 'Downtown' had been a monster, then 'This Is My Song' was a dinosaur. The only other British stars to have demonstrated the same, universe-conquering magic were the Beatles!

The English never could, and never would, comprehend the adulation which surrounded Petula in the United States. Her talent was acknowledged there from the humblest home to the most extravagant. When she returned to Paris in the spring of '67, she carried with her an invitation from President Lyndon B. Johnson to sing for him at a private benefit in Washington alongside other stars like Victor Borge—for her that was a compliment which said it all.

Chaplin himself was thrilled by the furore of its success and began work on another song for her immediately. But, it was not to be. Claude explains:

'We went to see Chaplin in Geneva just before he died and he played me a tape of another song he'd written. It was a kind of can-can.'

'It's for Petula,' Chaplin told Claude, 'but you can't have it yet. It isn't finished. As soon as I've completed it, I'll send it to you.'

He was then a frail old man in his eighties, confined to a wheelchair—the bowler-hatted, trouble-prone, moustachioed imp the world adored, reduced by the cruel tricks of old age to a white-haired shell who could hardly see and who was losing his hearing. When he died, the song intended for Petula was lost.

'Nobody knows what happened to it—not even Chaplin's wife, Oona,' Claude says. 'After his death, I spoke to her about it and she searched for it but it had gone.'

'This Is My Song' hit the charts in February. In March that year Petula was back in London again, working with Yvonne Littlewood and Harry Rabinowitz in cabaret at the Talk of the Town. The show they were producing, again for the BBC, was in the old, spectacular traditions—and Frank Owens came over specially to accompany her. Petula was supposed to make her grand entrance on a stage lift which would rise from the basement bearing her to the cabaret floor. Says Yvonne Littlewood:

'Petula went down to position herself there with just one sound engineer—but as the lift began its ascent, it stuck. It took thirty-five minutes to repair it—and all that time, Petula was trapped, unable to get up or down and with no communication with anyone except that single engineer. When the panic was over, the lift moved up on to the stage and Petula, as though nothing had happened, gave a one-woman show which defies description for its sheer excellence.

'There was one song in the programme that night called "My Name is Petula" in which she laughed at herself and all the various ways in which her name had ever been pronounced all around the world—PetUlah; Petoonia; Petu La. At the end, she sang "I Know a Place" and brought the house down.'

Wherever she went, Petula usually found herself with an invitation to return as quickly as possible—and, usually, she was delighted to be able to return. But there was one exception. Soon after her appearance at the Savoy, the management contacted Claude and asked him if they could book her two years in advance. Claude was delighted.

'Of course,' he said, thinking ahead to the summer of '68. He laughs as he recalls their reaction.

'Oh, no! Not in the summer!' said an anxious management. 'Petula Clark is a winter artist.'

'What do you mean—a "winter" artist?' asked a puzzled Claude. 'What difference does it make?'

'Well,' explained a tactful manager, 'When

she sang here last time it was very hot. We had to open all the windows but with a big orchestra and her powerful voice, the neighbours complained it was too noisy. As we can't guarantee the weather in England, it is better that she performs here in the winter when the windows stay closed.'

It was left to Claude to explain, equally tactfully, that he couldn't commit her to 'winter only' bookings, not even for the doyenne of London hotels.

'So far,' he says with a smile, 'we haven't ever managed to make it back there.'

CHAPTER NINETEEN

FINIAN'S RAINBOW

As 'This Is My Song' gathered the gold discs— and the Grammys—Petula and her family moved to Los Angeles for the start of work on *Finian's Rainbow* with Fred Astaire and Tommy Steele. This was her twenty-sixth commitment to celluloid—but the first time she'd worked on a major musical since *London Town* over twenty years before.

'Jack Warner hadn't especially wanted to make *Finian's Rainbow* because he'd had such a terrible time with *Camelot*,' Petula explains.

'But he'd bought an option on the contract and time was running out. He had to decide whether to make it or lose it. Luckily for me, he took the gamble. I never enjoyed working on any film as much before or since.'

The film was a remake of the original, first released just a year after *London Town*, and was based on the book and lyrics by the original writers H. Y. Harburg and Fred Saidy but with an updated storyline. It was directed by the brilliant, but then relatively unknown, Francis Ford Coppola.

Working on *Rainbow* meant three months of rehearsals and one of Petula's initial worries was that she had to dance a duet with twinkle-toed Astaire. As had been noted by Gladys Day, the dancing teacher engaged by Cecil Madden some twenty-three years earlier to assess her potential, dancing had never been Petula's forte. And she herself could only agree.

'I am a real fairy elephant,' she says. 'Astaire heard about my worries and lent me his own choreographer, Hermes Pan. We worked together on the routine for a solid three weeks. At the end of it I was so nervous that when Astaire took my hand to begin the dance, I was trembling at the knees.'

Feeling her anxiety, Astaire whirled her round and suddenly, she felt as though she was the world's most marvellous dancer: 'It all came together in a way it never had before. Working with Astaire was the experience of a lifetime!'

If Petula had been anxious about dancing with Astaire, Astaire let it be known that he had been equally anxious about singing with Petula. When they had completed the first shot of their duet together, Astaire leapt into the air with glee.

'I did it. I did it,' he screamed. 'I sang with Petula Clark.'

'The great Astaire—the man who is a legend in his own lifetime seemed genuinely pleased that he'd sung with me. It was a very strange feeling,' Petula says.

Coppola, Petula soon discovered, is a perfectionist. One of his private quirks is that before he will commit his work to the can, he likes to see a live run-through from start to finish, but without the whirling cameras.

'We played it out on the studio back-lot,' Petula remembers. 'I had to wear a wig with masses of long black hair in the film—and for the run-through—but we had no scenery, no props and no music apart from a couple of drums. There was an audience of about sixty, mainly the film crews and their families.

'Astaire and I became real buddies. We would go around together, laughing and talking the whole time. He was terribly anxious to know about the pop-scene.'

Their admiration was mutual. 'Working with Petula was a delightful experience,' Astaire

259

commented years later. He was not always so enthusiastic about his leading ladies!

'It had been crossing our minds to move to the United States permanently,' Petula says. 'If I had really wanted to cash in on my status there, I could have done so. Personally, I wasn't crazy about Los Angeles. What made it marvellous at that time was that I was working with such marvellous people. But when you're not working—and Claude wasn't really working once I was on the film—it's easy to get bored. There was nothing for him to do except to join the tennis/swimming pool set and it all became rather tedious. In the end, we decided to defer the decision and come home to Europe.'

Claude was European through and through. He loved concerts, particularly jazz concerts, as did Petula. He enjoyed live theatre and gourmet restaurants. Los Angeles is not renowned as the cultural capital of the world and these particular luxuries were rather thin on the ground, once the initial rounds had been outworn. There was also the question of the girls' education. Petula felt that her family's happiness had to come before the great American opportunity which now lay there waiting for her to claim.

'I've seen many unhappy marriages. Claude and I weren't too young when we met and we'd both been around. Our marriage works because we want it to work—but we both have to make sacrifices,' she said.

When *Finian's Rainbow* was released in London in October 1968, it received mixed reviews ranging from the over-poweringly enthusiastic to the blatantly disappointed. 'A really brilliant film musical which can stand comparison with the best the great days of MGM have to offer,' wrote John Russell Taylor in *The Times*. '... Petula Clark sings and acts appealingly, outside her usual range, as Finian's daughter.' In the *Daily Express*, however, Ian Christie was less impressed: '... the film is so whimsical, so illogical and sentimental that it defies any attempt at rational explanation. It does have some good tunes embedded in it, mind you, and Petula and her sweetheart (Don Francks) are a lovely couple and they sing pleasantly.'

This latter, in Petula's opinion, was an unfair assessment. 'It's often described as a classic now,' she defends boldly. 'It was really an almost impossible subject, particularly at that time because the whole black problem had been handled in a more adult way in the States and the social side of the down-trodden Irish was a bit passé. It was an odd story to put on film, where it seemed even odder, but I think it was a wonderful movie.'

★   ★   ★

While Petula was wrapped up in *Rainbow*, Tony

Hatch back in London was concerned with his future in her recording career. As a team, they had had thirteen smash-hits in America, the latest, 'Colour My World' and 'Who Am I' having been released in late 1966.

'I couldn't really blame Petula for doing "This Is My Song",' says Tony. 'She wasn't under any personal contract to me and despite my own chagrin at her success with it, I knew she was right to have done it. What had really upset me was that I felt that I should have been asked to produce it and I wasn't asked. That had to mean I was slipping.'

By now relations had improved between Petula and Jackie. Jackie had purposely kept a low profile on her own singing career although she never stopped working. They had reached a stage where Petula would record a song in French, using the French music and lyrics and then, of her own volition, she would ask Jackie if she would write the lyrics for the English version. Now, after the crowning glory of 'This Is My Song', Tony made a private vow that he and Jackie would break back in with her again.

'Claude had always been very fair to me. In the spring of 1967, he rang me and asked me for a new song for instant recording. He said that Petula wanted something a little more clever and sophisticated,' Tony explains. 'He said she felt that "This Is My Song" was so simple that it was virtually a pop-song and that it was time for a change.'

Tony, as usual, left everything to the last minute. 'I was working with Jackie in a double-act at the Golden Garter Club in Manchester. It was a freezing cold, wet Manchester Monday. There was no heating in the club and the double doors were wide open, blowing a gale through the place. They were cleaning so the vacuum cleaners were making the darndest noise and I had sent Jackie away because I could never doodle around and form a basic melody with anyone else around. I had to be on my own. And, to cap it all, I was working on a borrowed piano which was out of tune—hoping that by some miracle I would be able to produce a song to take to Petula Clark in Paris the following morning.'

When Jackie returned to the club some two hours later, all Tony had managed was: '... half a melody here and a little bit of a tune there. I had a perfectly crude working title "Don't Shit in the Custard"—just something to sing at the right moment in the melody I'd got.'

Tony told his wife he felt frantic. 'I had two different tunes—one in "G" major which was a lilting sort of folksong, and the other in "E" flat—a kind of Beach Boys' riff.'

'Why won't they work together?' Jackie asked. 'You've always been able to bridge things like that. Make the Beach Boys' bit the chorus, the other bit the verse, and think of something smart to put in the middle.'

Tony played some Tchaikovsky on the piano—just the chords.

'That's it,' said Jackie.

Tony wrote a new melody for that part. The following morning, he caught the only flight to Paris from Manchester—and he had a song. The lyrics, he says, were based on a private row he and Jackie had had a few weeks before:

'I'd packed my bags and gone downstairs when suddenly I realized that I'd forgotten my razor. I went upstairs again and when Jackie answered the door with a cold "What do you want?" and I explained, she said, "Come in, you silly sod," and we made it up with kisses and cuddles.'

But the incident had set him thinking. 'I imagined all the down-and-outs who had no homes and sought refuge in the comparative warmth and comfort of the London Underground,' he says. 'I called it "Don't Sleep in the Subway" rather than the Tube—Americanese again—because we felt it would work better in the States that way.'

He was right, of course. 'Don't Sleep in the Subway' rocketed to number two in the States and although never the hit that 'Downtown' and 'This Is My Song' were—reaching a mere number seventeen in the British charts—it became a 'standard' selling millions but at a steady pace.

In late 1967, Petula's old friend, Yvonne Littlewood, suddenly found herself with an unusual free patch and ten days' leave due. On the spur of the moment, she decided to pay her first visit to Los Angeles to see Petula and meet up with some other American friends.

'When I told my boss that I was taking a holiday and flying to LA the following morning, he was horrified,' she smiles. 'He said that a trip like that should be carefully planned—but I knew that if I let myself plan it, I would never do it. So I went.

'On arrival I booked myself into the Hilton at the airport, believing it was only ten minutes' taxi ride from my friends. Nobody warned me that Sunset Boulevard is thirty-five miles long. I visited Pet on the film-set, and although I worked with cameras myself, it was like wonderland. Big, Big, Big! That was the USA. When I arrived home, I regretted not taking my boss's advice and planning a trip of that kind— but it eventually paid off.

'Claude rang me one Sunday evening and asked: "How would you like to come to the States and produce a special for Pet for NBC?" Of course, there were going to be American producers for the show which was to guest-star Harry Belafonte. But as Claude explained, they wouldn't be able to be there until just before the first rehearsal and it needed someone who knew her to spend the first three weeks there while the show was being set up.'

Yvonne applied to the BBC for three months' leave of absence which was instantly granted. The show was to be recorded at NBC's Burbank studios in early 1968.

'Having been to LA so recently, I at least knew what it looked like,' she says. 'I wasn't frightened of facing it—or of entering the American world of movies. Hollywood was the hub of Variety, Music and TV at that time. Whatever it was that had prompted me to have that holiday in Los Angeles, it was a lucky coincidence.'

*   *   *

By the time Petula returned from filming *Finian's Rainbow* towards the end of 1967, she was determined to put down roots somewhere other than in France. Despite the fillip France had given to her career, she had never really settled there, hence the consideration she and Claude had given to emigrating to America. Although she had her beautiful home at Ciel St Cloud, she never felt really able to relax 'off-stage' in Paris. She was 'Petula Clark—Singer' not Madame Wolff, mother of Barra and Katy. She never had the opportunity to pop into a shop or walk with her husband and two little girls (and the family dog) in a park without being crowded by well-intentioned but privacy-intruding fans demanding an autograph or to shake her hand.

Whilst both she and Claude knew that this was the price one paid for fame, it was a price which she felt that she'd paid long enough. Since the age of ten she'd been expected, first by Leslie and later by her sensational rise to fame, to put a public face on even the most private and intimate parts of her life. She felt there had to be somewhere where she could call a halt to all that—and she thought she'd found it in Geneva.

'Geneva has some of the finest schools in the world,' she announced enthusiastically when her decison to move became known. 'The girls will attend the International School there which has a wonderful reputation.'

'I have to admit,' added Claude, always the businessman, 'Switzerland does offer certain tax advantages.'

They found a plot on a hillside overlooking Lac Leman with a picture-postcard view of the mountains and commissioned architects and designers to build them their dream home 'where,' Petula declared, 'I can have a quiet place to recharge my batteries and relax as Madame Wolff. I spent my life being all sorts of things to all kinds of people. I really need the chance to be myself for a while.'

Their new house, they decided, would incorporate the best ideas from all over the world. To satisfy Claude's Continental background, the six-bedroomed house was built in the style of a gracious French villa—the façade emphasised by the exquisite Swiss setting. There was an American style family room in the basement where the girls and Claude could play table-tennis and snooker.

The kitchen, too, was typically American with a split-level oven (hardly known to Continentals at that time), plenty of worktops, an Italian, brown-tiled, clay floor and a vast breakfast bay where up to eight adults or ten children could snack comfortably.

On the ground floor, the rooms were planned to interconnect with the lounge in the centre leading to a library through an elegant archway to the left and to the dining-room on the right. This opened into a glorious, plant-filled garden room, originally intended as a patio but glassed in when Petula realised its potential as a suntrap which could be enjoyed by the family all year round.

The garden, with its stunning outdoor pool, was to be as English as the rich, Swiss soil would allow—filled with heather and pansies and cotoneaster so that Petula could imagine herself back in a scented, English garden if she so desired.

This, then, would be her base. Her home. But, even while it was being constructed, her heavy schedule grew heavier. With shooting on *Finian's Rainbow* only just finished and 'Don't

Sleep in the Subway' barely out of the charts, her importance as an American star was burgeoning daily to undreamed of heights.

Las Vegas, the citadel of American show-biz, beckoned; the only city in the world where fortunes are won and lost seven days a week, fifty-two weeks a year, and where only the world's finest performers can lure the punters from the tables for a few hours' respite. Her name was again emblazoned over 'Caesar's Palace'—and now, despite all their former differences, she wanted her father to see her in the ultimate achievement of his dream.

But when first she invited him to visit Las Vegas, he refused. It took her some while to discover that the reason was not bitterness that she had achieved this success without his backing, but simply that he couldn't afford the fare. Petula, saddened at her oversight, immediately sent him the tickets for himself and Ann.

'I was astounded by the esteem in which she is held there,' he told friends on his return. 'When I met all these fantastic stars I'd only ever heard about, Sinatra, Astaire and the rest—and they themselves told me of the respect they have for my little girl—suddenly it was all too incredible to believe. I'm so happy and so very gratified.'

Petula was invited to appear on a plethora of the biggest and most popular TV shows in the States—among them, Dean Martin's Hollywood show. At first, she had to refuse. In the hectic Vegas schedule, there just wasn't time. But Martin's persistence is legendary.

'Dean Martin is a devil for having his guests rehearse until they're blue in the face—and then appearing without a single rehearsal himself,' she laughs. 'I told him when I accepted to do the show that I couldn't rehearse because I didn't have the time. So both of us went in and did the whole thing off the top of our heads. It was great. And although I've worked with Martin many times since, he's never asked me to rehearse a show again.'

Sinatra had by this time become one of Petula's greatest fans. And, he decided, it might be fun if he recorded her first great American hit 'Downtown'.

'To have Sinatra record one of your songs is a great compliment,' Tony Hatch explains. 'To add to that, he asked Petula to sit in the studio with him while he cut the disc. But no matter how hard he tried, he just couldn't seem to make it work. In the end, he made a joke of it, singing the chorus with an added "ooh aaah" in typical Sinatra style and where I certainly never put one.'

But the last laugh was on Petula and Tony. Sinatra had a huge hit with his version in Japan. To even the score, Petula recorded Sinatra's 'Strangers in the Night', sending it up in a way which, with her intrinsically dry British sense of humour, was all her own.

After her sensational success in America she came back to London in November 1967 to appear in a new *This is Petula Clark* series, again produced by Yvonne Littlewood, for which it was rumoured, she was to be paid a fabulous fee of £16,000.

'The fee doesn't interest me,' she told inquiring journalists at the time. 'I love my work and I would be happy to do it for nothing. I will never stop working until it becomes a drag.'

Her guests during the series included many old and well-loved friends—Tony Newley and Sacha Distel, Matt Monroe and Dudley Moore, and Don Francks who had been her 'boyfriend' in *Finian*. Continuity for the programmes was by Graham Chapman who later became famous himself as one of the Monty Python team. And again, the BBC's private survey on the programmes showed that the public were still mesmerised and enchanted by Petula.

Back in London, and within easy reach of the Pye studios and Tony Hatch, it seemed an opportune moment to record for the English-speaking market. There had been some minor hiccoughs in the Claude, Petula/Tony, Jackie relationship again. Says Tony:

'There was one occasion when Claude told me that my songs weren't improving because Jackie was now working with me on a full, partnership basis. It was the only thing he ever said that really disappointed me and I told him how wrong I thought he was.'

However, it seemed that both Jackie and Petula had decided to call a truce—and even socialise—a fact which delighted and amazed Tony considering, as he says, how 'rotten' the beginnings of their relationship had been.

'Jackie and I asked the Wolffs to come and spend a weekend with us at our home in Kent,' Tony explains. 'They arrived in the afternoon and we played them a new song we'd written.'

Petula said she was worried about the verses and while they ate the meal Jackie had painstakingly prepared, she reiterated her fears.

'When are you going to re-do the lyrics?' she asked.

'We can't do them now. We're entertaining you,' Tony laughed. 'Don't worry. You'll have them in the morning.'

The meal over, Claude and Tony disappeared to play darts and snooker while downstairs the girls chatted and watched a little TV. The four went for a walk in the glorious, three-acre grounds—beautiful even on a chill November evening, and it was quite clear to the Hatchs that their guests were enjoying themselves.

Finally Petula, never a night-bird, said she was tired and she and Claude went up to bed. Tony and Jackie cleared away the remains of the meal and then sat down to work.

'We rewrote the lyrics working almost until dawn,' Tony says. 'By the time Claude and Pet came down to breakfast they were ready and I played them through to her.'

'That's great,' Petula said. 'We've got another hit.'

That Sunday afternoon, Tony, Claude and Petula drove up to London. Jackie, still cautious, stayed at home. The session went as smoothly as ever and when the new song, 'The Other Man's Grass', was finished and released in December, it rose to number twenty in the British charts. Petula had not, however, forgotten her French public in all the excitement. In 1967, Vogue Records released no fewer than twenty-nine singles—of which thirteen titles, including 'La Derniere Valse' produced by American Ernie Freeman, were in French.

Yet, the depression which dogged her from time to time, always carefully hidden beneath the dazzling stage smile, was still lurking to rear its ugly head.

'In this business you are so busy projecting yourself that you miss those lovely quiet moments when there is absolutely nobody around. When you can lie on the grass and watch the ants. Things like that. I can't remember when I last did it. I'd like to do it again. After a while in Paris, Hollywood or London and all that rushing about, I want to get

273

down to looking at things again. Right now, that's very important to me,' she said longingly.

'I am not the star in our home,' she has often said in newspaper interviews. 'There is something more important than success and that is a man's love. Whether it's in a rented house in Belgravia or in our own home in Paris—that's where Claude is the star.'

Not that she wanted to revive the goody-two-shoes image she'd acquired as a child. 'Of course, we have our rows. When I've done a TV show I feel so good that I want to go out somewhere and dance. Just dance. But Claude doesn't like dancing. So we stay home...'

Claude was unabashed at his wife's chiding. He was equally determined to show that he still loved her as much as ever—and that even now, when she was worth a large fortune, it was still possible to surprise her.

Ever since she'd learnt to drive back in the fifties, she had had a passion for sleek cars—the faster, the better. She had never actually found time to take a French driving test but she had once had a whirl around the Brands Hatch circuit with Jackie Stewart. Now, she had set her heart on a white Rolls-Royce which she had spotted in a car showroom in London's Berkeley Square. She asked Claude to make inquiries about it and was bitterly disappointed when he told her:

'Sorry, darling. There's a year's wait for

delivery. I've put our names on the waiting list.'

As soon as work on her TV series ended, she flew from London to Geneva to spend a brief ski-ing holiday in Megève before travelling on to New York for a TV spot. As she stepped out of the airport at Geneva, she saw a car, identical to the one she had fallen in love with in London, waiting by the kerbside.

'There's your Rolls,' Claude laughed.

'You must be joking,' Petula gasped, tears of pleasure streaming down her cheeks.

'I'm not,' he said, handing her the key. 'I do love to tease you, Petula.'

CHAPTER TWENTY

ON THE PATHS OF GLORY

Before leaving London, Petula recorded a new single, 'Kiss Me Goodbye', penned by Les Reed. This time, Tony Hatch was not offended. He produced the record and said it gave him 'breathing space' to think of other new material himself. Although he approved of the song, he didn't feel it was the right one for Petula. 'Pet's successes always radiated sunshine and this one didn't,' he says. It crept into the charts at number fifty and sidled out again in a single week, her last entry in the British charts for three years.

After the seemingly endless round-the-world chase of '67, Petula was tired. But when she got the rest she'd so look forward to, it didn't come in quite the way she'd planned. Three days after arriving for her winter holiday, she was out skiing with Claude and the girls near their rented chalet when she fell and broke her right ankle.

'It won't make me give up my holiday,' she told reporters bravely, as she hobbled around on crutches with the prospect of staying plastered from knee to toe for four weeks stretching before her. 'I can still get the benefit of a long rest.'

Until the ankle healed, she was forced to remain at the chalet they had rented—and it was clear that the total unplanned rest did her good. But as soon as the plaster was removed, it was back to Los Angeles, to join Yvonne Littlewood who had already been there for three weeks helping to plan and produce her first American special to be called simply *Petula* and sponsored by the Plymouth Division of the Chrysler company.

'It was an enormous operation,' Yvonne Littlewood remembers. 'We had to film on the Queen Mary on the way over and we visited the El Rodeo Elementary School so that Petula could sing "Beautiful Butterfly" to their school orchestra's accompaniment.'

In the programme she was to sing many of her

best-loved favourites: 'Two Rivers', 'Who Am I', 'Better Times Coming' with the Dancers Concert Section and 'Gloccamorra' from *Rainbow* which had not yet been released. She was to sing 'Paths of Glory' in duet with Harry Belafonte, her special guest, and 'Downtown' as a grand finale. The Musical Director was Billy Goldenberg and Claude wore the proud title of Executive Producer.

'Petula was extremely excited at the prospect of working with Belafonte,' Claude says. 'Belafonte is something very special. When we arrived, we were introduced but I don't like to bother stars so at first, we kept our distance from him. Then the director of the programme told us that he was not very happy so we went over to talk to him and I found him a most charming man.'

Petula and Belafonte rehearsed together for a week. They were somewhat dismayed when an order came through from the programme's sponsors saying that there must be no physical contact between Little White Anglo-Saxon Petula and Big Black Belafonte during the filming as they wanted to network the show and felt that any physical contact between them would make it unpopular in the Deep South. Despite the laws against racial discrimination, there was still deep-rooted racism. So instead of sitting side by side for their song, Petula was to sit slightly forward and to one side of Harry as together they sang 'Paths of Glory'.

The show was recorded on 2 March and all went well until they came to the duet. They did three takes but each time there seemed to be something missing. When they got to the fourth, Petula forgot the 'touch-me-not' ban and instinctively brushed his arm with her hand as they sang. So slight was the gesture that she hardly realised what she'd done.

'Stop. Cut cameras. That's not acceptable,' screamed Doyle Lott, Plymouth Chrysler's advertising manager and their representative at the recording.

Cameramen, directors, producers, sound engineers and the stage-hands froze in amazement.

'What's wrong?' someone demanded impatiently. 'The song was great.'

'She touched him,' bawled Lott. 'Touching is forbidden.'

Claude was instantly alert. 'I knew what was going to happen next,' he says. 'My lawyer and I quickly slipped down to the basement where I knew the other takes were and together we erased them.'

'Now we're safe,' he told Yvonne and the lawyer. 'They have no choice about which take they use. The sponsor can't fool us because that's all we have left.'

Back in the studio, the argument was still raging. Belafonte was screaming, justifiably,

278

that this was the worst case of racism he'd ever encountered in his career. Petula was upset that a spontaneous action on her part, which she had felt put the missing 'something' into the song, could be misconstrued in such a way.

'After the furore began to die down a bit the director ordered a break,' Claude says. 'He told Lott not to worry because they still had the other takes. I told them that I was afraid they didn't,' Claude laughs. 'I told them that the others had gone and that Petula would not record the song again. I told them that was all they had and that if they didn't use it, they didn't have a show.

'Belafonte was astounded. He could not believe I'd done it. I was like the big brother to America. But I didn't do it for political reasons but only because, artistically, it was so much better.'

Within hours of the incident, Lott found himself fired. The Chrysler Corporation issued placatory statements insisting that they were delighted with both Petula Clark and Harry Belafonte's performances in the show and claiming that 'the incident resulted from the reaction of a single individual and did not reflect the policy of the company'.

Steve Binder, co-producer and director of the show for NBC with Binder Howe, announced that it would be screened as planned the following month. He could do nothing else.

There was nothing in America's National Association of Broadcasters' code to support Lott's action; it merely called on producers to uphold the moral standards of American life and at that time even mixed-marriages were becoming acceptable in America as racial prejudices crumbled.

The show which caused such a stir in the States caused some speculation in Britain, too, although for quite different reasons. It was naturally assumed that as Yvonne Littlewood had been granted three months' leave of absence from the BBC to help produce it, the show would be screened on that channel in Britain. But Tito Burns, the former band-leader, a great personal friend of Petula's French agent, Claude Deffe, and at this time Head of Variety at London Weekend Television, put in a massive bid for it the very day after it was screened coast-to-coast in America. It failed.

'I had worked on it so it had to go to the BBC,' says Yvonne. Its first British screening was on 5 August 1968 on BBC 1 and it was repeated three months later on BBC 2. 'Entirely inoffensive,' was how the British press saw the storm-making touch of hands.

*   *   *

While she was working on *Finian's Rainbow*, news of Petula's incredible performance as

Sharon spread like wildfire through Hollywood. So much so that MGM asked Warner Brothers for an unprecedented preview showing.

Within days, producer Arthur P. Jacobs (known fondly as 'Apjack' in the studio) was offering her the part of Mrs Chips in an updated version of James Hilton's 1939 tear-jerking classic *Goodbye Mr Chips*—a role played with such sympathy and *gentillesse* by Greer Garson in the original, in which Robert Donat had taken the title role.

If the idea sounded attractive, so did the estimated fee of £75,000. The only thing which dismayed Petula about the whole project was the press's insistence, once again, on comparing her with Julie Andrews. Rumour at the time had it that Julie had originally been offered the part and had declined it because the studio was unwilling to pay the fabulous fee she demanded.

Julie was not the only other person named as a possible new Mrs Chips. It was a plum role and the inevitable grape-vine resounded with names who were 'guaranteed' to land the part, ranging from Samantha Eggar to Lee Remick (who later sued MGM for £416,000 claiming that they had signed her first to play opposite Rex Harrison and had broken the contract).

But it was the outright comparison with Julie which disturbed Petula most. 'All these comparisons are so foolish,' she says. 'We grew up together but we have never been rivals.' And in an interview with the *Daily Express*, she said: 'If she sang "Downtown" and I sang "The Sound of Music" you'd soon notice the difference. She's so much more ladylike. Not that I'm not a nice lady too,' she added impishly.

After the controversial Belafonte incident in New York, Petula returned to Paris in April 1968 to begin preliminary rehearsals for *Goodbye Mr Chips*.

'When I read the script, I thought it was beautiful,' she says. 'Terence Rattigan (who had been working on the screenplay for MGM for the past six years) was a lovely, lovely man and I suppose I imagined it finished, as one does. We started rehearsing in Paris, but then things started to go terribly wrong.'

Paris was not a happy place to be that spring. Student riots raged around the Sorbonne and on the Left Bank. For the first time since the German occupation, a time Claude remembered all too vividly, gunshots rang out in the Parisian streets, filling the peace-loving population with dread. Shops were closed and boarded. Petrol was scarce.

'The film company decided that we should move out of the city as quickly as possible, lock, stock and barrel,' Petula explains. 'We had to pack up everything and as the house in Geneva was far from ready, it meant moving the children into a hotel there. They had to stay in that hotel for a very long time.'

Rattigan had altered the screenplay, originally set in the Edwardian era, by updating it twenty years to the thirties and early forties. Greer Garson's sad death in childbirth had been changed so that Petula would be killed off in more dramatic style by a stray doodle-bug. The new Mrs Chips, far from being the gracious lady of the quadrangle, was supposedly a seedy, West End night-club singer recovering from a sordid love-affair at the time she first meets Mr Chipping of Brookfield school.

Petula saw Mrs Chips as a character part. She wanted to play her as a fiery woman for whom taking stands on such issues as civil rights is a matter of principle rather than mere pride. Such a woman she personally found it easy to relate to. But this was not the interpretation Herbert Ross, directing his first film, saw for her.

'Little by little, I had to change the way I felt the role should be played until I eventually fell between two stools,' she says. 'The trouble was that right from the beginning, it was never made clear to us where we were going and the director wasn't strong enough to lead us.'

There was also a problem with the music, composed by Leslie Bricusse after some sixteen song-writers had first submitted scores. It was no secret that Petula was never entirely happy with it.

There were, as Leslie Bricusse says, too many

people involved over too short a period with too many ideas on how the film should be handled. Production and direction became disjointed. There were times when the management weren't even sure that they wanted it to be a musical. In the end, nobody was decisive enough to pull it through with a single thread.

Rattigan claimed that if all the screenplays he had written for the new *Mr Chips* during the six years he had been working on it were added together, they would represent double his lifetime's published works. So many scores were written by different composers that, when the film was finished, Leslie Bricusse, Petula and Peter O'Toole made a private double album called 'Fifty-one Forgettable Songs' representing all the songs written for the film which hadn't been used!

Although Petula often described working on *Mr Chips* as 'one of the most anguished times in my career', she admits in retrospect that despite the professional and personal problems she was facing at the time, parts of making the film were a great deal of fun. Best of all was working with Peter O'Toole.

'We were just about to start shooting in London when Peter invited me to his home in Hampstead,' she says. 'We went to a local restaurant for dinner and a fair amount of alcohol was consumed, particularly on Peter's part. When you go out with him, you automatically consume a fair amount of wine. It got rather late and he decided he wanted to sing. He sings well when he really lets go with the real Irish kind of thing. Eventually, we were asked to leave and he decided he would carry me down Heath Street. So he picked me up and there we were, roaring songs together through Hampstead.

'Then the film company decided that it would be funny to dress Claude up as one of the guards in the London scene and put him in a sentry-box. Of course, I didn't know anything about it and somewhere there is a picture of me discovering him. He looked very French under his busby. It was the second time he almost joined the British Army!'

Much of the shooting took place at Sherborne School in Dorset where five hundred pupils had been paid six pounds a day to stay on through the summer holidays and act as extras. Whenever possible, Petula would hire a twin-engined Beechcraft channel-hopper stationed at the RAF station at nearby Yeovilton and fly home to see the girls, still billeted with their nanny in the hotel in Geneva to which they had fled earlier in the year. By August, she was physically and mentally exhausted and took a short break in Deauville with Claude and the girls before flying to Italy to complete the filming in Pompeii.

The new house in Geneva had been

completed in October but Claude and the children refused to move in until Petula could be there to share the excitement.

For the first time since the late fifties—and for very different reasons—Petula was beginning to talk again of retirement. She was longing for the chance to relax in the house which she and Claude had built, designed and furnished with exquisite antiques collected from every part of the world and with such loving care. But, as always when the thought of throwing in the towel entered her head, she was more in demand than ever.

When *Finian's Rainbow* was premiered in New York and London within twenty-four hours in October 1968, Petula was there for both opening nights. As a child, at the premiere of *Vice-Versa*, she had remarked that one of her ambitions was to grow fat and that the other was to own a fur coat. While she knew now that she would never achieve the former, the latter had, it was clear, become a reality. She arrived at the Odeon, Marble Arch, on a chill autumn evening, wearing a magnificent, full-length white mink over her bejewelled evening gown. And how she'd worked for it!

In November, she was requested to appear at Britain's show of the year—the Royal Command Performance in front of their Royal Highnesses the Queen Mother and Princess Margaret. It was not the first time she had entertained them.

As a teenager she had gone to Windsor Castle with the Beverley Sisters, Cecil Madden's other pet protégées, to entertain the late King George VI, Queen Elizabeth and the two little Princesses, Elizabeth and Margaret Rose.

'I remember that at the time, Petula and I laughed because we thought our gowns very grand and that the Royal Family's were rather shabby by comparison,' Teddy Beverley says. 'I can remember her remarking that even Royalty had to be thrifty with their clothing coupons.'

But this was no post-war occasion but a glittering night in the swinging sixties. Petula's gown was a Dior creation; white satin encrusted with gold-leaf embroidery and weighing a massive 40lbs—'My suit of armour,' she called it.

She shared the billing that night with many old friends; Arthur Askey, with whom she'd first shared the stage as a ten-year-old at the famous BBC birthday party in 1942; George Mitchell—who'd held her on his lap and worked the pedals of his mother's old harmonium so that she could play it in the 'Cabin in the Cotton' days—and his Black and White Minstrels. Claude's friend, Sacha Distel added a familiar French flavour to the evening while Diana Ross provided the American taste.

At the Royal presentations after the performance, Petula did not mind, for once, being reminded of her childhood stardom when an onlooker heard the Queen Mother remark as she was presented to her:

'My dear, I so enjoyed your performance tonight. You gave us such pleasure as a child, I've watched you grow up!' Her reaction was a shy, gracious smile.

But despite international stardom there was one small incident which occurred at this time which showed how little she had been spoiled by success. Earlier that year, her old friend Alan Freeman had gone to Australia on a three-year contract. Petula knew that while he was there, he would celebrate his fiftieth birthday.

'Sharp on the stroke of midnight Australian-time on 27 September, the day itself, the phone rang,' he says. 'Much to my amazement, it was Petula in Geneva. She sang "Happy Birthday to You" down the phone. That call meant so much to me. We had shared a great deal together over the years and I knew just how busy she was. The mere fact that she could think of me at all showed a great deal about her character. She didn't forget her old friends.'

In early 1969, she returned to Los Angeles for her second American special—*Portrait of Petula*—this time with Andy Williams as the special guest star and with Sacha and her compatriot, Ron Moody, too. The co-producers for this show, again sponsored by Chrysler, were Alan Handley and Bob Wynn for NBC and—of course—her favourite English producer

Yvonne Littlewood.

During her spell in London, she had recorded a new song 'Happy Heart' which she planned to plug on the new American show. When she met Andy in the studio for the first rehearsal, she naturally asked him what he was going to do.

'I'm going to sing my new single—"Happy Heart",' he said.

'How does it go?' Petula asked.

Andy, quite unaware of the situation, hummed it through to her.

'Have you recorded it yet?' she inquired nonchalantly.

'Actually, I did last night,' he replied.

Petula swallowed hard but said nothing. She secretly rearranged her own repertoire and Andy Williams sang the song on her special. It was a huge hit. And it wasn't until years later that he learned the saga of how Petula's generosity had allowed him to have a hit that might so easily have been hers.

'She's a real pro,' he said when he discovered the truth. 'A fine musician as well as a great singer. I always had a kind of crush on her. I think that made it kind of nice working with her which we've done several times since then. When we sing together, something kind of special happens between us.'

The feeling was reciprocal. 'When singing with Andy, we take off. It's a beautiful experience,' Petula says.

Petula's altered repertoire included such old favourites as 'This Girl's In Love With You' and what she considered the best arrangement ever of 'My Funny Valentine'. She sang 'When I Was a Child' against a film of herself playing with Barra and Katy and her old hit 'Two Rivers', cleverly rewritten to 'Three Rivers' to include the Hudson, symbolising her acceptance in America as much as in both England and France. Then, as though to emphasise her British roots, she sang 'Maybe It's Because I'm a Londoner'.

The musical direction for this show was in the hands of a brilliant young French arranger, Michel Colombier, especially imported from Paris with his wife and two small children. Suddenly Michel's two-year-old son was taken very ill. He was rushed to hospital where, it was discovered, he had a tumour on the brain. He needed immediate surgery if he was to stand any chance at all.

'Petula was wonderful,' Michel says. 'She and Claude became my family. We were in a strange country among strangers yet they became mother, father, brother and sister to us all. They told us not to worry about anything. They would help us with whatever they could. During my son's operation, they stayed with us, comforting us and holding our hands.

'My son recovered but it became clear that he would be partially paralysed for the rest of his life and that we would have to stay in America for some time. The medical bills were huge. And in America, no one knew me. Petula arranged a meeting for me with Herb Alpert and Herb put a lot of work my way. As if that wasn't enough, she introduced me to the film company. It was only through her kindness and Claude's that I was able to support us in the States during that difficult time. It also got me known there—so much so, that that is where my life now is.'

CHAPTER TWENTY-ONE

THE SONG OF
MY LIFE

Petula had appeared in concert all over the world—but with one notable omission. Since her appearance at the Albert Hall as a child of twelve in 1944, she had never given a live concert in her homeland. It was an omission which the BBC and Yvonne Littlewood decided to rectify.

The concert, in April 1969, was called *Just Pet* and it was made all the more alluring when Yvonne told her that the show would be screened in November as the very first programme to launch BBC1's regular colour transmission service.

'We chose Pet because there just couldn't be a better person to launch colour TV on 1,' said a BBC spokesman. He had obviously done his homework and must have known the significance of choosing the woman who had helped relaunch television after the war by appearing in the test film—and who had made an appearance at every BBC landmark since, including the *Goodbye Ally Pally* programme and Cecil Madden's controversial thirty-pound tea-party.

On the only previous occasion she had appeared at the Albert Hall, she had read comics until the final second before appearing and then, without any apparent trace of nerves, had performed like a trouper before rushing back to her paper. Coming home to 6,500 expectant faces with the reputation of a world-famous star was quite a different proposition.

'I was more terrified than I've ever been in my life. They literally had to push me up the ramp on to the stage and when I got there, my knees turned to jelly as I looked at all those faces. But, when Peter Knight's orchestra struck up the first notes, I forgot everything and concentrated on my job—entertaining people to the best of my ability. Their response made it a wonderful, beautiful evening.'

The critics agreed. 'She sang like a star who has lived,' wrote the *Daily Express*. There was no doubt that Petula had 'lived' since her first appearance on that very same stage.

At one second after midnight on 15 November 1969, BBC1 launched their first regular colour transmission service with their own protégée, Petula Clark, and pipped Independent Television Service to the post by several hours. It was a sensational show. By the time she sang 'Downtown' as her finale, the audience were on their feet, screaming and cheering just as they did in every other country in the world.

Johnny Harris conducted the orchestra for her that night. And again, this upset Tony Hatch. 'I used to do all her cabaret stuff, all her Las Vegas stuff,' he says. 'I had done all the scores for her appearances at the Coppa Cabana in New York and I thought that on her return to London with all these hits and all that triumph behind her, I would be called up to conduct. I'm a damned good conductor. Not an idiot when it comes to facing a big orchestra. And I was very disappointed when she and Claude decided to use Johnny Harris. I told them so, but Claude's answer was: "You are a song-writer and arranger, not a conductor."

'It was one of my two great disappointments with Petula and Claude.'

At the end of 1969, Yvonne Littlewood was told that she had been recommended for a SEFTA award (the forerunner of BAFTA) for two Petula

Clark programmes—the Andy Williams special *Portrait of Petula* and *Just Pet*. She was asked to decide which of the two she would prefer the SEFTA jury to consider.

'I chose the Albert Hall,' she says. 'I thought that if I was going to win anything, I wanted it to be home-brewed. I was over the moon when the Albert Hall concert won.'

The award was presented to Yvonne by the late Lord Louis Mountbatten at the London Palladium and Pet and Claude were there to share the glory. Says Yvonne: 'Afterwards, we went on to the Grosvenor House Hotel for the reception. It was the first time I had ever been introduced to a member of the Royal Family and it was the greatest thrill of my life.'

Petula's daughter Katy has vivid memories of watching the screening of that particular concert—but for quite different reasons to those of Yvonne Littlewood and Petula herself.

'We all sat down to watch it together. I was sitting next to Mummy cuddling her and suddenly, I saw her on the screen. I couldn't understand it. I knew, of course, that she travelled to places like Las Vegas and New York and all over the Continent. But having her sitting next to me and seeing her on the screen at the same time foxed me. I was only about seven I suppose.'

Soon after recording the Albert Hall concert, Petula and Claude travelled to Montreal to fulfil some engagements and visit Expo '69. It was not her usual, happy, Canadian tour.

'I was performing at the Place des Arts and I found myself in a ridiculous situation,' she says. 'When I had first sung in Montreal, it had been as a French-speaking singer at Les Comedies Canadiennes. In fact, wherever I had performed in the province of Quebec, it was as a French-speaking star. I had been in Quebec when "Downtown" broke. As the Canadians get all the TV from the States and the records, too, and are very influenced by America—I decided that when I went back to play at the Place des Arts, which is much bigger and more of a bilingual venue, I would introduce my English repertoire as well as the French one.'

She also decided that rather than splitting the programme into two distinct halves, she would make one announcement in English and one in French and that the linguistics of the two songs would be intermingled in an easy, relaxed fashion.

But, as Petula soon found, there were troublemakers in the audience. When she sang in English, they chanted 'en française, en française'. When she switched to French, the catcalls were 'Sing in English'. She couldn't win.

While she was facing these hostile and unpleasant audiences, John Lennon and his wife Yoko Ono were staging a 'bed-in' at the nearby

Queen Elizabeth Hotel.

'Late one night,' says Petula, 'I decided that I would go and see him. It was open house; a very odd kind of atmosphere. Anyway, I went in and there they were. Just sitting in bed. There was nothing saucy going on. It was really a very nice thing. I sat on the edge of the bed and talked, more with him than with her, and we talked about lots of things. He told me that I should do what I liked and what I could and that it was too bad if people didn't understand. I guess I knew that—but I think it helped just being able to talk about it with someone who was completely out of my circle and perhaps hearing his views on it.'

They discussed another subject too—one very close to John Lennon's heart. Buddhism. 'He told me how it had offered him so much inner peace. How he lived not from day to day but from minute to minute and how it teaches that if you give out energy, it comes back to you. Relatively, it wasn't a heavy conversation at all.'

Petula and John met on two or three occasions after that. There was, she says, a bond between them which grew out of mutual understanding. 'When John was killed, I was absolutely devastated and I called my ex-guitar player who had been playing with John on all his sessions, including the last one. Jim McCraken is a New Yorker and he played for me for about three years before he left me to join Paul McCartney at the beginning of Wings but he didn't get on too well with Paul for some reason so he went back to New York where he was very well-known. He was playing for John and Yoko on that last album. I told Jim that I had to speak to somebody who had been close to John and we talked for about an hour. It was very hard, that one.'

Contrary to rumour, Petula herself didn't take up Buddhism although she admires and respects many of its teachings.

'I have,' she says, 'had several adventures in religion in my life. The way I see things now is sort of very vague. I just want to do my best and give as much of myself as I can and that's about it. If I boil it all down, I guess that's what it should be.'

She spent that summer in Las Vegas, performing at the Plaza and as popular as ever with the American public, returning to London in the autumn. *Goodbye Mr Chips* had been chosen for the Royal Variety performance, at which Petula looked as stunning as ever in a gown of white chiffon smothered with pearls and silver beads with a matching headband, flower-girl style, across her forehead. But the film itself did little to impress the critics.

Leslie Bricusse's music came in for some criticism too, especially from another song-writer much involved in Petula's career, Tony Hatch. 'I had heard the score well before the film went into production and I was very disappointed with it,' he says. 'Apart from one song called "You and I", which is beautiful, there was nothing outstanding about it at all. I felt the one thing badly missing was a song called "Goodbye Mr Chips". Such a song is necessary to promote the musical—and to promote Pet Clark in relation to the musical.

'Twenty four hours after hearing the score for the first time, Jackie and I came up with a great title song. We sent it to America for inclusion in the film. I have to say now that my main aim was to so impress the producers that they would say: "Hold everything. Let's give the whole script to Tony Hatch and see what the Hatchs can come up with". I was totally disappointed that they didn't.'

But if that upset Tony, there was more to come: 'They not only turned it down for the film but they said that I'd infringed their copyright because they owned the copyright in the title "Goodbye Mr Chips".'

The American Passing Off Law meant that Tony could not write a song and say that it had been inspired by the book. It was quite obvious the Hatchs had written it because they had seen the script of the film. MGM did not sue, but the Hatchs had to hand over the publishing copyright. Even so, it was never used although Petula later recorded it on an album.

'I felt that as her number one songwriter at

that time, the man who had given her "Downtown", "I Know a Place", "I Couldn't Live Without Your Love"—all the songs which Jackie and I had written for her—I had a right to feel disappointed. Disappointed that, in the first place, I hadn't been asked to write the score for *Goodbye Mr Chips* and in the second place because I hadn't hustled and Claude hadn't used his muscle power to help me.'

Petula herself was still trying desperately to take a break from work and spend some time at her lovely Geneva home. But in the spring of 1970, her name was at the centre of a controversial deal between the BBC and Lew Grade's ATV. In a £6m deal, it was announced that Grade had bought exclusive rights to both Petula and another popular British export, Marty Feldman, and sold shows in which they both starred to American TV.

Once the annual season in Las Vegas was over, the Wolffs took off to a secret hideaway on the secluded island of Cavalo, south of Corsica. There, at a private resort owned by Michael Castell, where guests are strictly by invitation only, she had one of the all-too-rare chances to relax and let her hair down amongst friends.

'It was a very primitive place with just a single telephone which lived on top of the ice-cream machine,' Claude explains. 'I remember getting phone calls from America while the machine was working. It was crazy. The Americans thought we were nuts to go somewhere like that but we adored it.'

Petula's private life was becoming increasingly precious to her. So much of it had been on parade for so long that perhaps she felt the necessity to guard it more closely and jealously than ever. Her daughters were growing up and she wanted them to be themselves—not a star's offspring.

'I have told them so many times, then and since, that they are the Mesdemoiselles Wolff not Little Petula Clarks,' she says. 'I never pushed them towards a stage career and although at one time Katy wanted to be a dancer, she started training too late.'

She felt the need for one thing more—she longed to have another child—and she prayed that, if she did, she would have a son. Her heavy commitments had made any thoughts of increasing her family an impossible dream until this time. When she discovered that, at the age of thirty-eight, she was pregnant again, she was delighted, but her joy was premature.

'Almost as soon as I discovered I was pregnant, I lost it. It wasn't really a miscarriage. It just didn't hold,' she says. 'I was in London, doing a BBC at the time, and they had to rush me to hospital from the studio.'

The public invitations continued to roll in with the same velocity as ever. Cuba's Fidel Castro heard that she had performed for the

Queen of England and the President of the United States and sent her an invitation to appear for him too at Havana's music festival. As Ed Leffler, her American agent, explained: 'It's obvious that Fidel is a fan of hers and that he likes blondes.' It was one invitation, from a Head of State, that she refused.

In early December, Petula was invited back to Paris to receive a special citation. She was awarded the Grand Medal of the Council of Paris—an honour bestowed only on those who have brought great honour to Paris and increased its fame. When M. Midier Delfour, President of the Council of Paris, made the presentation at a ceremony at the Hotel de Ville, he told Epsom-born Petula:

'You are still young and you have already had a whole career as a beloved artist. You have succeeded in pleasing the Parisiennes, the most difficult public in the world. To us, you are the living illustration of the warm-hearted and sensitive English. Thank you for bringing us the sweetness of the Epsom nightingale.'

Petula's reaction was to burst into tears, but with Britain's affiliation to the Common Market imminent, it was a particularly pertinent and diplomatic speech.

She filmed her Christmas special that year in June with Peggy Lee and David Frost and it was, as usual, a great success. 'I had been a Peggy Lee fan for some time,' she explains. 'She

301

is definitely my favourite singer. We had a relationship before we ever met.' The friendship had indeed begun when Peggy had read of Petula's admiration for her in a newspaper and had promptly sent her some flowers. Petula wrote to thank her and they finally met in Vegas in the summer of '68.

'Our friendship was instant. Singing with Peggy was something new,' Petula recalls. 'We made a funny sound together. Like four voices rather than two.'

Petula had recently terminated her contract with Pye after being associated first with Polygon and then with Pye, when Alan Freeman amalgamated with Nixie to form the new company, for more than thirty years. It was three years since she'd had a hit record in the charts—and she felt it was time to get one going again. Since the 'Mr Chips' affair, she had had very little to do with Tony Hatch so, for the new song, she turned to an even older friend, Jack Fishman.

'Ian Ralfini, who had been Joe Henderson's office boy and who used to run errands for Pet and Joe, had worked his way up, first as a song-plugger and later to become chief of Warner Brothers Records in this country,' Jack says. 'When Pet split with Pye after all those years, Ian Ralfini began to produce her records for Warner Brothers.'

In late 1970, Jack went to Tokyo with his wife

302

for a musical festival. One evening, he received an urgent call from Ralfini in his hotel bedroom.

'Thank heavens I've got hold of you at last,' Ralfini breathed with obvious relief. 'I've got an urgent job for you. Pet has got a new melody from France and she has already recorded the tracks in French. Now she wants an English lyric immediately. I've got to record it for her.'

'Why are you ringing?' Jack asked, puzzled. It was many years since he'd written a Petula Clark lyric.

'Because she feels this song should be about her life and she thinks that you are the person who can best put it into words,' Ralfini replied. 'You've known her so long.'

'When do you need it?' Jack inquired. 'I'm going on to the States from here and I won't be back in England for quite a while.'

'We're hoping,' said Ralfini, 'to record in two days' time.'

'Typical,' sighed Jack.

'I had a reputation for being very quick,' he says. 'I'd written "Help Yourself", the Tom Jones record, and phoned it through within an hour. First, I insisted on hearing the melody because if I didn't like a melody, I wouldn't do a lyric for it. Ralfini played it to me down the phone and then repeated it so that I got it into my head. I told him to ring back at the same time the following afternoon.'

Jack worked through the night writing 'The

303

Song of My Life'. Petula's sister Barbara, who was Ian Ralfini's secretary at that time, rang him back next day and he dictated the words down the telephone. Twenty-four hours later, Petula had recorded it. 'The Song of My Life' was not a chart-topper. But it stayed in the British top-fifty for twelve weeks. She was back in the chart-scene again.

CHAPTER TWENTY-TWO

MOTHER OF US ALL

Britain was on the verge of entering the Common Market after a decade of wrangling. But as the political arguments with France still raged on, the woman who had married a Frenchman and been transformed by him from 'Our Pet' into a top-flight international star, was the obvious choice for comment on the marriage between little island England and the vast European Continent.

'England is a wonderful country and so is France—or should I say that France is a marvellous country and so is England,' said the woman with a foot in both camps who knew her diplomacy as well as her show-biz. 'I think there would be tremendous advantage if the two countries really got together. I don't think it

304

would be easy but I'm sure it's possible.'

All her life, humour had been vitally important to her. One of the things she had missed most when she had first gone to live in France was the British sense of humour, the special English ability to laugh at themselves in a way no other nation can. As far as she could see, it was this difference in humour that might prove the biggest bone of contention in the proposed merger.

'British humour is unique and has, in the past, seen us through all sorts of problems,' she says. 'The French don't always realise that we are being funny. When they do catch on they fall over themselves laughing—but sometimes it takes them rather a long time to see the joke.'

Whilst the more mundane aspects of the deal such as food subsidies and a Common Agricultural Policy were clearly of little interest to her, she had acquired a palate for delicious seasoned foods and plenty of excellent wine. Fun, fashion and food. These were her priorities, then—most importantly the former. But total peace of mind was the one quality of life which, however hard she searched, still seemed to evade her.

Even at this time, she possessed a 'little girl lost' quality which seemed to have remained with her as a hangover from the hard years. Those closest to her, like Alan Freeman, Jack Fishman and Tony Hatch, agreed that it was as though the vitality and depth that she gave her songs—that 'gut' feeling which enraptured audiences across the world—emanated from her deepest emotions. Whenever she performed, and whether it was the 'pop' sound of 'Downtown' or the soul-reaching ballads, it came from her heart. She had searched through religions and found her own. As she says, it is based on 'giving of herself'.

All her life, she had performed at charity concerts and appeared to lend her name to good causes. She had for many years been associated with Geneva-based UNICEF. It was not a side of her life that she has ever cared to capitalise on. In June 1971, she gave another Albert Hall concert in aid of the Royal Philharmonic Trust and the Gurkha Welfare Appeal Fund. Lord Louis Mountbatten and Lord and Lady Harding of Petherton were the Guests of Honour at that 'Night of One Hundred Pipes'.

It was a glittering occasion. The Royal Philharmonic Orchestra conducted by Sir Vivian Dunn gave a spectacular performance of Tchaikovsky's 1812 Overture with special effects by the Army in the arena, dressed in French and Russian uniforms of the period. The Pipes and Drums of The Black Watch, the Brigade of Gurkhas and the London Scottish Orchestra all took part and—as always when she appeared there—Petula delighted her audience, her tiny figure dominating the immense hall.

She was conducted by Johnny Harris.

There followed further American and Continental tours and then she returned to London briefly to record *Stars on Christmas Sunday* before flying to Megève to spend Christmas with Sacha and Françoise Distel and their children. The Wolffs had now decided to build themselves a chalet in this idyll where Petula could walk around unnoticed among a plethora of famous faces and where she had become known simply as 'Germaine'. Then in January, she left for Miami to combine an engagement in cabaret at the Diplomat Hotel with a recording session and a rest.

They arrived on a Saturday afternoon—and the dramatic change in climate had an immediate effect on Petula. On the Sunday morning, with a recording session booked for the afternoon, she awoke feeling distinctly unwell.

As Claude explains, finding a doctor on a Sunday morning in a strange American city is not always easy.

'Eventually, I managed to contact someone at ICM, who were our agents for that particular tour,' Claude remembers. 'They knew a good doctor whose wife was a dancer. He came at once and he turned out to be very funny and very nice. He gave her a shot but all day long she complained of feeling shaky.

'We all got on very well together so we asked

the doctor, whose name is Claudio Patcheko, and his wife to come out to dinner with us. We had a very good evening. The next morning, Petula was feeling much better but she was still wobbly on her feet. By this time, we had become good friends with Claudio and he had told us he was Cassius Clay's medical adviser. I asked him why Pet still felt the way she did and whether it was a side-effect of the drugs he had given her. He thought for a while and then he told me: "I know what I did. I gave her the right drug but the wrong dose. I gave her what I usually give my boxers".

'Petula is very strong but she is very petite and doesn't have the physique of a boxer to withstand a dose like that. We are still very close friends with the Patchekos. The injection has become a standing joke.'

*   *   *

Soon after the booking in Miami ended, Petula suspected that she was pregnant again. There were rumours that she went home to Switzerland to consult Professor Gelsendor, who had successfully seen Sophia Loren through two difficult pregnancies, but these she vehemently denies.

'Naturally, I was a little worried. I was forty years old after all—no youngster to start a new family. But I wanted another child and secretly cherished a wish for this one to be a boy. However, there was absolutely no question of cancelling engagements. I went on working, just as always, under careful medical supervision of course.'

As whenever she had babies, there had to be a hit song to croon over the new arrival's cradle. In Miami, she had recorded 'I Don't Know How to Love Him' from the smash-hit musical *Jesus Christ, Superstar*. As she announced the expected baby, it hit number forty-seven in the British charts. It stayed there for a mere two weeks and it was her last appearance there until 1981 when she opened in *The Sound of Music*.

She conceded to cut down her usual heavy schedule just a little, which meant cancelling a new BBC show in Britain, but in America there was one engagement in particular she was immensely keen to fulfil—as a guest on Lucille Ball's show *I Love Lucy*.

'I rang Lucille to tell her I was pregnant and she told me that she would build the show around that,' Petula says. 'Her idea was that she would be working in an employment office and that I would ask her to find someone to keep an eye on me. She decides it sounded a glamorous job and takes it herself. She wanted Claude to play himself.'

To Claude, who had never had aspirations to appear before the footlights, this was a disaster. According to Petula he pleaded first that there were thousands of out-of-work French actors who badly needed such a role. But Lucille was having none of that.

'It was hilarious,' Petula says. 'She cajoled and pleaded with him. But he kept saying that he wasn't an actor and didn't want to act.'

'Aw, come on, Claude. Do it for *me*,' she begged.

'No, not even for you, Lucille,' he insisted.

Lucille Ball was just too much for him and in the end he capitulated. Everything went well during rehearsals. As Claude had only a single-line part, he wasn't required. But, as Petula explains, when it came to the actual shooting things really became impossible:

'Every time we got to a take, the engineers would look at their watches and say: "OK fellows. Let's take half an hour's break. Claude's going to rehearse his line." When we finally got round to shooting and Claude was needed to say his single line "Where is my wife ..." he was on the phone! He's always on the phone. At that point, Lucille screamed the place down. It was hysterical.'

The show, of course, ended up as perfectly as Lucille Ball's shows always did.

'We've been together several times since and we always laugh about it,' Petula says. 'That was her last series. She's a brilliant woman and a brilliant comedienne and she knows what she's doing. But I don't think she ever had to work

310

with anyone quite as difficult as Claude.'

★   ★   ★

Petula worked right through the pregnancy. She was put on a no-salt diet during the last three months when she began to gain too much weight and it was diagnosed that the cause was excessive retention of water. In her eighth month, she flew to London to record a new album with Don Costa which, by pure coincidence, included that beautiful refrain 'Mother of Us All'. Then she went home to Geneva to await the birth.

Patrick, her longed-for son, arrived on 7 September 1972 weighing 6lbs 8ozs. Like Katy, he was born quite naturally without the help of any of the drugs which had caused her so many horrors when Barra was born eleven years previously. And again, it wasn't long before she was back at work with a vengeance. Christmas that year saw her on the British TV screen in *Sounds of Petula* with Tony Newley, the Wandsworth Boys' School Choir and the City of London Brass Band, who accompanied her in singing Beatles favourites such as 'When I'm Sixty-Four' and 'With a Little Help From My Friends'. Under Peter Knight's direction, she ended the show appropriately with her new favourite 'Mother of Us All'.

She stayed in London long enough to film a

six-part series for Yvonne Littlewood on the *Sounds of Petula* theme before bouncing back to Las Vegas for a season with all three children in tow.

Barra and Katy were at an age when a new baby in the family is at first a novelty and then a nuisance. 'I didn't think it was particularly exciting to have a baby brother around,' Katy explains, 'but Barra felt it more than I did. One day, when he was about six months old she got fed up with all the noise he made and put him in a drawer. Luckily, Mummy heard him screaming in time and rescued him before any damage was done.'

Naturally, the family had to have a nanny to cope while their mother and father were working—the 'nanny syndrome' as Petula calls it. 'From the time the children were born we must have had about sixteen nannies in all,' she laughs. 'Some were quite unsuitable and lasted only a couple of hours. Others stayed years. There has to be a kind of chemistry between the nanny and the family and it either happens or it doesn't. With some girls, it was very traumatic. Others stayed and became very dear friends. When they left, the children had to comfort me. Nannying is not a glamorous job and it has to be a very special, devoted lady to take on other people's children and to fit into a household and be able to care for them without becoming a replacement mother.'

Whoever cared for their children day-to-day, Petula and Claude insisted on playing as large a part in their lives as was possible. She tried to make time to talk to them about the things she considered were important as well as their daily lives.

'I believe in always telling my children the truth,' she adds. 'When the girls were about seven or eight, I told them about drugs and sex. When they began to ask me questions, I thought I may as well explain it all.'

★   ★   ★

On 1 January 1973, after all the years of wrangling, Britain finally took her place among the eight other member nations of the Common Market and it was Petula who compèred for Britain during the Eurovision celebrations which ensued. In the spring of that same year, 50,000 British sweetshop owners voted her their 'Mother of the Year'. When the presentation of a huge box of chocolates, tied with an outsize pink ribbon, was made at a London hotel, she couldn't receive their accolade personally because of her only real weakness—a sore throat. She sent Claude along instead to accept the gift for her—much to the amusement of the British press who dubbed him 'Claude—mother of the year'.

'Pet knows how it feels when you've just had a

baby,' said the new father proudly, 'so she asked me to ask you if you would send these chocolates to St Thomas' Hospital Maternity Unit so she can share her happiness with some other new mums.'

That summer, the Las Vegas season was followed by a world tour which was to embrace visits to South Africa and the Ivory Coast, a concert to celebrate the opening of the new Opera House in Sydney, Australia, and entertaining GIs in Japan.

'We were booked to do a TV show in Japan, and then a concert for the American Navy Base there,' Claude explains. 'With her memories of the kindness of the GIs during the war in Britain it was something she was really looking forward to—but it did not have a very happy ending.

'She did the concert as planned and the Admiral sent his own American car with a driver to pick us up afterwards and take us back to the hotel. We were going far too fast and Petula, who hates bad drivers being such a good one herself, was clinging to me, petrified. Suddenly, there was a tremendous collision. We found ourselves flung from the back seat to the front and we didn't know how we got there. We managed to get out. We could see that the people in the other car were bleeding badly. But the Japanese are a charming nation. The man in the other car was not worried for himself although he was dripping blood all over the road. He was worried for us. Neither of us was physically hurt but we were shaking all over. We had never been involved in a crash like that before.'

From Japan, Petula and Claude flew, via Moscow, to Germany—popping home to Geneva for a single night to see the children before fulfilling engagements in Paris, Brussels and Milan. Then they returned to London for an ITV *Sunday Night at the London Palladium*, where she co-starred with Rudolph Nureyev and Jim Dale compèred.

It was no wonder if she was again feeling exhausted and less than pleased with herself by the end of it all. 'I don't know if I'm a happy person,' she said at that time. 'I seek perfection but I feel I never get anywhere near it. It's very frustrating. I have contrasting moods which make it more difficult for people around me. I'm so lucky to have someone like Claude who is up and coming. The stage can be a great help to me. Singing is a safety valve and I suppose that's better than having a fight with your husband.'

The pressures and general malcontent which had dogged her for most of her thirty-year career were beginning to surface again. True, she had now entirely healed the once-shattered relationship with her father. But she had tired of the beautiful mansion in Geneva, built with such love and enthusiasm only six years before, and talked of selling it and buying a flat—

315

'because the grand life-style no longer interests me.'

In the event, Claude decided it was more propitious to rent it than to sell it but they bought the flat anyway. The house in Valiteneuse—the place that Petula had always considered 'my only real home'—was sold too as the Wolffs had now built a magnificent chalet at Megève, with an indoor swimming-pool and a sauna, where they had spent so many wonderful holidays among friends like the Distels and Andre Délon.

In February 1974, she came back to London to appear on a Jimmy Savile chat show and for her fourth appearance at the Albert Hall on Valentine's Night. She spoke about settling in England but had to admit that 'the tax position worries us a little'. Eventually, however, she agreed to return to Los Angeles where the Americans were now begging to see her live again.

CHAPTER TWENTY-THREE

SENTIMENTAL JOURNEY

Once before, Claude and Petula had considered making their home in the USA but at that time neither had felt that they could settle easily into the Hollywood way of life. But now they decided after much soul-searching that they had to give it at least one more try.

They rented Hope Lange's magnificent Westwood mansion. She rented it out regularly and its last occupant had been Dustin Hoffman. As both Barra and Katy were now firmly established at the International School in Geneva, it was apparent that they would need to continue in the same style of education so they were enrolled at the Lycée Française in Los Angeles. As Petula explains, this proved a big mistake.

'It would have been tough on them to send them to an American school,' she explains. 'But I soon discovered that in Beverley Hills there is a whole snob thing about speaking French. They found themselves among all the film stars' kids with miles of limousines outside the school waiting to take them and collect them. They didn't get on with it at all—and although I was hoping that they would settle, I was rather proud of the way they felt about it.'

Petula was nevertheless enjoying the American showbiz lifestyle. 'It's a whole different ball game,' she explains. 'Once you get into the swing, your outlook on life changes completely.' But it wasn't all fun.

On one occasion, Barra was taken sick while Petula and Claude were touring in Nevada. She was rushed to hospital for an emergency appendix operation. Luckily, money was no object.

'Pet was in the middle of a show when we got the news,' Claude says. 'When she finished the show, a private limousine was waiting to take us to the airport where a private plane stood by to rush us back to Los Angeles. Barra was happy when Mummy was there as she woke up. But she knew that her mother couldn't stay even though she was ill. As always, there was still a show to do. She knew that we'd fly back to complete the contract and come and see her again as soon as we could. The girls were used to our lifestyle of private limousines and planes and luxury hotels. They knew no other and it meant nothing at all to them.'

As always, she tried to keep her diverse worlds of show-business and motherhood in two separate compartments. But even when the two took her hundreds of miles apart in the USA, it wasn't always possible to be totally schizophrenic about them.

'Towards the end of our time in Los Angeles, I went to Nashville, the home of Country and Western, to finish off an album. Claude had stayed in LA with the children and their nanny,' she explains. 'Nashville is a very relaxed place to work in. Our studio was a beautiful converted old house where they had kept the lounge and dining-room intact with all the lovely old American antiques. There was a kitchen too where the guy who did the engineering also did the cooking. In the middle of a session, he would say "Hang on a minute. I've got to see if the ham's OK" or "I've got to do the beans".'

But suddenly, one day, nobody came in. Much to her amazement, Petula noticed that all the doors were locked. There was a tension about the old house that she had never noticed before. She was too polite to comment on this strange turn of events, thinking perhaps that it had something to do with finishing the work they were engaged on.

'I had heard that that evening there was a big Country and Western Association celebration being held in a huge local hall and that all the big stars were going to be there,' she says. 'I thought it would be fun to go along after such an odd day and the producer, "Chips" Mollen, said that he was sure he could get me in. First, we went to a small, intimate dinner-party attended by just a handful of people. Then we went on to the show. I'm not really into Country and Western but this was the real thing in Nashville and no fooling. It was like a huge party with thousands and thousands of people.'

Across the crowded hall, Petula saw an old friend from Warner Brothers Records, her American company. They waved to each other and then she made her way across the packed hall to chat to him. 'Chips' Mollen called after her, 'Come back, come back, Pet.' But she couldn't see why she should.

'He kissed me and then above the noise I could only catch snatches of what he was saying to me—"Isn't it awful?... Petoola whaddy'a think ... assassination..." I kept saying "What? I can't hear you." And all the time these alarming snippets were coming at me.'

At this point, 'Chips' Mollen found her. 'Cum on, honey,' he said firmly, leading her by the arm. 'You don't want to hear about all that.' He led her outside where it was teeming with rain. Now she was getting increasingly anxious.

'What's happening? What's going on?' she pleaded pathetically.

'Calm down. Everything will be just fine,' 'Chips' soothed. 'We got a call from Claude this morning. He made us promise that we weren't to tell you and you were not to worry. We vowed to him that we wouldn't let you read a newspaper or listen to the radio or TV today. Or meet anybody. That's why we locked the doors.'

Somebody had threatened to kill everybody in Hope Lange's Westwood house. Whoever had made the threat thought that the star of *The Ghost and Mrs Muir* was herself in residence. The police had taken the threat seriously. Somehow, the news had leaked out on the radio and now it was common knowledge that the occupants of the house were Petula Clark and her family.

'I arranged to fly back the following

morning,' Petula says, 'and by the time I arrived there were only a few policemen left. Little by little, they told us that they couldn't carry on the personal protection. If we wanted cover, we would have to pay for it. We agreed to pay for an armed guard and for a few days, he lived in the house with us. We got really fed up with that. It was really sinister. Eventually, we dispensed with his services but that's the way it is in Los Angeles.'

Living in the States did have its compensations, among them the chance to spend time with friends like the former doctor Claudio Patcheko and his wife, and racing-driver Jackie Stewart—always one of Petula's idols:

'Jackie and I lived close by in Geneva but we never had time to get together there. I have always loved car-racing and it was Jackie who took me round Brands Hatch many years before—but we never seemed to be in Geneva at the same time. He's always travelling.'

Jackie was one of the leading racing commentators for NBC. Patcheko, the former doctor, was their chief boxing commentator. They knew one another through work and one evening both were invited to dinner at the Westwood mansion. 'Claudio Patcheko said afterwards that he thought it was the most extraordinary evening,' Petula recalls. 'Jackie and I run a mutual admiration society. All I wanted to talk about was music and singing. The others just sat at the table dumb, listening to our conversation. They couldn't get a word in edgeways.'

In America she also met up with Tony Newley again, for the first time in several years. As always when they were together, she left a lasting impression on him.

'We had both grown-up, married and had children,' he says. 'We had a great respect and regard for one another. Yet I found myself still treating her with that same deference I did the first day we were introduced on the set of *Vice-Versa* all those years before. I always felt there were times when we could have been closer. I suppose I was romantic about her because I didn't know any of her faults. I knew that my feelings for her were very one-sided. Nevertheless, there was a preciousness in the fact that they were never expressed.

'When I work with her and even when she sings happy songs, I always get the feeling of the Piaf thing—of great sadness beneath it all. It is the tragedy in her life that one hears in her music.'

Her Hollywood friends were, of course, delighted to have her near. Leslie Bricusse and his wife Evie decided to throw a party in her honour: 'The idea was to invite Fred Astaire—who I was longing to meet anyway—as a special surprise for Petula. I also invited Sammy Davis

Jr. who I knew was a great Astaire fan although they had never met. When Sammy walked in and saw Astaire, he literally fell on his knees in front of him which greatly embarrassed Astaire who is basically a desperately shy and unassuming man despite his reputation, and hugely amused Petula.'

But the enjoyment had gone out of the American scene. Petula and Claude both realised that their daughters would never settle and—despite her gigantic earning capacity—the sacrifice was too great. Her family came first.

'I had got to a pitch where I was convinced I couldn't perform unless I had a forty-piece orchestra and a change of clothes for every number,' Petula smiles. 'I realised that it was not a way of life that any of us could truly be happy living permanently.'

She came to London to make a new Yvonne Littlewood series, *Sounds of Petula*, featuring such greats as Peter Ustinov and Telly Savalas. Then there was a *Roaring Forties* programme, a *His 'n Hers* with Jack Jones and, on her forty-second birthday, a *Tale of Scorpio* where she was joined by other famous Scorpios including Diana Dors and Georgia Brown. In *Off to the Movies* her guests were Michael York and David Essex; *All That Jazz* featured one of Petula's especial favourites, Oscar Petersen; a *One Man Band* show had Gilbert O'Sullivan who wrote both lyrics and music for the songs he performed. The very last was a Christmas show with Frankie Howerd, with whom she'd last worked in *The Runaway Bus* days, and the fantastic Norman Maen dancers.

In the spring of 1975, Petula was nominated for one of the TV Times' Top Ten awards for the best performing artistes of the year. As she stood in line to receive her trophy from TV Times Editor Peter Jackson (now Editor of the *Sunday Times* Colour Supplement) another familiar figure approached. To her mixed horror and delight it was Eamonn Andrews, red book again in hand. She was only the fifth person, and the first-ever woman, to have been a *This is Your Life* victim twice.

The entire family were of course in on the secret. Katy in particular has vivid memories of that second time around. 'Mummy had been at home with us in Geneva before coming to London to receive the award,' she explains. 'Barra and I were both very worried about what we would wear on the programme.

'We couldn't tell Mummy the reason we decided that we both needed new dresses so we made up a story about being invited to a special party while she was away. Of course, she told us that we had plenty of clothes to choose from. We would have to make do with what we had.'

Petula set off to receive her prize. But at home, Barra and Katy were frantic. 'We decided in the end that the only thing we could do was ransack her wardrobe. I found one of her dresses which was far too big for me—I was only twelve at the time—and a pair of her high-heeled shoes. Barra did the same. We felt absolutely wonderful in them although of course we looked dreadful. That's how we appeared on British TV.'

Little Patrick, just two years old, was overwhelmed by the situation. When he was led on to the stage by his sisters he burst into tears!

Eamonn's surprise package included an amazing conglomeration from her past. Cecil Madden, now retired from the BBC, was one of her first homage-payers. He was followed by Alan Freeman and Peter Ustinov, Jimmy Young, Charles Aznavour, Sacha Distel, Harry Secombe, Val Doonican, Andy Williams and Jack Warner and Kathleen Harrison from the 'Huggetts' days. Mai Zetterling, whom Petula hadn't seen since they had worked together on *The Romantic Age* in 1948, was there, as were more recent friends like Tony Hatch and Jackie Trent—and to her especial delight, her father and Ann.

Being home among her family and friends again made her realise just how much she had missed England, the warmth of its people and the humour she held in such reverence.

That summer she travelled back to Wales to film a Christmas special for Harlech TV with Sir Geraint Evans in her mother's homeland. Her grandparents had died some years previously and it was at least twenty years since she had last seen Emma Rose, her mother's sister. Now she decided to pay a sentimental journey.

'We talked for a very long time,' says Mrs Rose, now in her late seventies. 'She wanted to know all about her family. I felt rather sorry for her. Despite all the wealth and fame, I detected a loneliness as though she was searching for something and couldn't quite find it.'

While she was in Pontlottyn, a retired miner of over ninety who remembered her impromptu childish concerts in the *Colliers Arms* sent her a message asking if she could possibly find time to see him for old times' sake. She went into the tiny miner's cottage, almost identical to the home in David's Square where she had spent so many happy hours, and gently held the old man's hand. Tears rose in the almost blind eyes as she sang for him. It was, claimed neighbours who heard it, a performance as perfect as though she was singing to an audience of thousands in the world's grandest concert hall. The old pit-man's face glistened with pleasure.

Her family as a whole became more and more important as the years went by. Now she came back to England frequently. Often, she combined the visits with engagements—but the real purpose behind them was to maintain close links with her father and Ann. The pull of her roots became stronger as she continued on the seemingly never-ending round of cabaret and one-woman concerts during 1975 and 1976. In December '76, she talked of buying a home in England again so that she could be close to her friends and family. But the real reason was that she knew that her father was suffering from a fatal illness.

'My father had never been ill in his life,' she explains. 'He was a very handsome, physical man with a wonderful figure which didn't change from the time he was eighteen until he was sixty. When he became ill, it was a terrible thing to him. At first, he simply wouldn't accept it. But as I wasn't with him all the time, I could see the change that was taking place in him on every visit. I knew it was more than serious.'

Petula's concern at what she was witnessing ran deep. If there was any cure that money could buy, then she was determined that her beloved father would have it. She gleaned as much information on his condition as she could from doctors in London and Paris.

She was warned that, little by little, he would seize up until a vital organ was affected. Eventually, it was. He died on 5 October 1977, thirty-five years after he had launched his daughter on the road to what might then have been considered an impossible dream.

Petula was in Geneva when the end finally came. 'The last time I had been with him a few weeks before I had had a premonition that I might never see him again,' she says. 'Paddy had had a bad night and I was in his room when Claude came to break the news. He just touched me on the shoulder and before he'd said anything, I knew what he was going to tell me.'

She came home to Chichester for the funeral to comfort Ann and spend time with her family.

CHAPTER TWENTY-FOUR

COME TO MY PLACE

Petula had never been involved in the commercial side of advertising. It was an area of show-biz which she had avoided—but in late 1977 she agreed to make an ad for Sunbeam Chrysler, the British division of the company which had sponsored the controversial Harry Belafonte show in the States, for an allegedly not inconsiderable fee of £100,000. In return, all she had to do was sing the catchy jingle 'Put a little Sunbeam in Your Life'. But it wasn't long before the tune was at the centre of almost as a big a row as the Belafonte incident.

The tune was so pretty and so popular that Petula decided to extend it into a full-length single for commercial release on the Polydor label. But, within days of its release, both the BBC and the Independent Broadcasting

Authority were refusing to promote a record which they believed would undoubtedly be seen as free advertising plug for private enterprise. The record was withdrawn and reissued with the word 'sunshine' replacing the offensive 'sunbeam'. It never made the charts—but that was not the end of the Chrysler saga.

Datsun, the rival Japanese firm, engaged Petula to entertain some nine-hundred of their dealers and their families at a dinner at London's Hilton Hotel. She was, it was rumoured, paid £10,000 for the single night's work, but when Chrysler, now estimated to be paying her around £50,000 a year to promote their cars, heard about it they were furious, even though publicity on the performance was banned in her contract with Datsun.

The promotions manager, Norman Wild, who had organised the evening, tried to cool the situation by explaining that while she was under contract to Chrysler, Datsun had merely paid her to entertain at a private party.

If there were hiccoughs in her professional life, her private life was not escaping its own traumas. For the eighteen years since Barra's birth, she had fought the emotional conflict of motherhood and stardom. Each time she had considered giving up her career and settling down with her family, the unconquerable magnetism of the stage had pulled her back. However hard she tried to protect her daughters from the influence that her fame inevitably had on them, they were and will always be 'Petula Clark's children'. Finally, it all proved too much for Barra.

To her parents' distress, she dropped out of school. 'She seemed pretty miserable,' Petula says. 'I felt that at that time, my place was to be around in case she needed me. She seemed to feel that she was just an appendage and although I had tried all her life to impress on her that she was only herself and a person in her own right, she couldn't feel it like that. I kept telling her that she must do what she felt was right for her and not what she thought would please us.'

This time, Petula was determined to stay out of the limelight for a while, trying to make up to her precious eldest daughter for all the time when her career had taken her away. She cancelled engagements in the USA and London and a French tour which was to have been her first for some years.

'There is nothing—absolutely nothing—in either of our lives more important to Claude and me than our children,' Petula says sincerely. 'They come first every single time.'

For a short while, Barra took a job in a local boutique. When she agreed to return to her studies, her parents believed that they were winning.

In late 1977, during this troubled period, Claude introduced Petula to a young man who had had his share of trying to keep his own public and private lives apart—Princess Margaret's close friend Roddy Llewellyn.

Roddy had had several careers including his well-published venture into communal market gardening, and was now about to try his luck in the world of show-business.

'He has a terrific voice with a distinctly romantic quality about it,' Petula declared at the time. 'He cannot fail.'

The couple invited him to their home in Megève where he signed a contract appointing Claude as his agent. Petula, who had just accepted a booking to do a new TV special in France, asked him to join her on the show. It seemed an ideal opportunity to launch him on his career in a country where he might at least get the chance to be judged on his merits rather than on his royal connections.

He recorded a song with the slightly suggestive title of 'Venez Donc Chez Moi'— 'Come to My Place'—and then, dressed in a silk-bound dinner jacket and velvet bow-tie, sat nervously in his dressing-room at RTF in Rue Cognac-Jay cuddling a bottle of Moët et Chandon at ten o'clock one morning, waiting to mime the voicetrack of the newly-recorded song in front of his first real audience.

'It's an experience I will never forget,' Roddy says. 'To begin with, I had dressed in a dinner jacket but had forgotten to change my socks. As green socks and a dinner jacket don't go together, somebody in the studio had to lend me a pair of black ones.

'Then, when we started filming, Petula had to appear from behind a screen as I launched into my song. She was wearing a nylon dress which kept catching on the screen and flying into the air. But by the third take we got it right. It was amusing to see the reaction of the audience when they realised that I actually could sing.'

With his first public appearance satisfactorily concluded, he disappeared for a much-needed holiday on the island of Mustique with Princess Margaret but on arrival he developed a severe stomach infection and was flown to a hospital in Barbados for intensive care. Yet, all the while, both Claude and Petula were determined to keep his name in the public eye in France. And to launch him seriously in Britain.

The three discussed Roddy's future when, after touring in New York and Italy on engagements Claude had booked for him, he went to spend a few weeks with the Wolffs at their St. Tropez house. Princess Margaret was taking the sun just a little further along the Mediterranean coast at Amalfi at the time, at the home of banker Mario D'Urso.

'They were extremely hospitable and gave me a really wonderful holiday,' Roddy explains. 'We decided that we would try to get a live stage booking in England.'

But fate often works in mysterious ways and Roddy's opportunity came, not in a paid concert but in a charity fund-raising affair.

The secretary of the Margate branch of Petula's fan-club, Terry Young, wrote to her begging for her help. His five-year old son, Matthew, was dying from a brain-tumour and British doctors had told him that there was no hope for the child. But, he said, he had heard that American doctors could almost perform miracles. As a council official he stood no chance of raising the £20,000 necessary for the journey and medical treatment but now neighbours had began a massive drive to find the money for the last-hope trip.

The appeal went straight to her heart. Little Matthew was only two years younger than Paddy. She agreed to appear as the star performer in a concert to be held at the local Winter Gardens and travelled down early to see the sick child, bringing with her a surprise guest in the form of Roddy.

'He was a dear little boy,' she says sadly. 'But as I sat there with him on my lap that day, I knew there could be no hope. As a parent, one hoped beyond reason that miracles were possible. But I knew in my heart, even before the concert began, that it was too late.'

That night, with Roddy Llewellyn's help, she raised £4000 towards the mercy-visit. Roddy even raffled his tie to raise extra money. But, as

Petula had feared as soon as she had seen Matthew, it was already too late.

She had been in England on a dual-purpose visit. Filming had begun on *Second to the Right and On Till Morning*, a low-budget British film in which she played aunt to two children of a broken marriage. The film has not yet been released but at its press showing the *Daily Telegraph* commented: 'Mr Anett's handling of these young players is very good indeed though the adults, led by Petula Clark, are a regrettably dull lot.'

Petula took the part because she said it 'interested her' and agreed that she had been known to give better performances. She was not greatly disappointed when its release was withheld. However, her second professional reason for coming to England in 1979 was a rather more successful venture into drama.

Independent Television had invited her to star in their £100,000 musical spectacular, *Traces of Love* in April 1979 with David Kernan and pop-star Paul Jones. It was a chance not only to demonstrate her extraordinary musical versatility but also to prove her talent for straight acting in the part of Polly Curtis.

'I am getting tired of standing before an audience, dressed in lovely gowns singing beautiful songs,' she said at the time. And no wonder. Her performance demonstrated to the British public that she bore no trace of the sweet little girl whom they wanted to keep 'Our Pet'. But the press were now intent on showing that she had something in common with Polly Curtis other than her initials. They were looking for proof that her marriage too was on the rocks.

It was not the first time that Petula and Claude had encountered such rumours. Years before, Katy had once come home from school sobbing bitterly that someone's mother had read in the papers that her parents no longer shared a bed and demanding to know what that meant. Petula had managed to laugh it off as a joke but when, in late 1978, they resurfaced, fuelled like a forest fire by the apparent 'proof' that she had accepted several engagements in Britain whilst he spent most of his time in Paris and Geneva, she was furious.

'After nineteen years together working in our world there are often times when business takes us apart for weeks or even months at a time,' she explains. 'Our children have always been our most important concern and we had long ago decided that if one of us had to travel, the other would always be available should they need us.'

'In every marriage which lasts as long as ours has done,' Claude interjects, 'there are ups and downs and it would be foolish to deny that we have had ours. The difference between us and ordinary people is that if we have a row in a hotel bedroom and a waiter knocks on the door, it is immediately public and rumours fly that we are about to split up.

'After being married for twenty-one years, everything changes. You don't behave in the same way as you do after twenty-one weeks. When you are first together, you want to share every moment. Later, you have to stay apart at times to freshen up the relationship.'

Petula's anger at these stories which lingered through the late seventies and early eighties knew no bounds.

'There are many occasions when I am in London and Claude is in Geneva or Megève or Los Angeles. If I am asked to dine by a male friend or a record producer, the gossip writers immediately have me leaving Claude for him. And vice-versa. It happened quite recently when I was making an album with Tony Ayres and had dinner with him. These rumours are malicious, salacious, ridiculous and stupid. Claude and I are still in love.'

In the summer of 1979, the whole Wolff family rented a house at St Tropez for their annual holiday. But the peaceful vacation she had so looked forward to turned into a nightmare that none of them will ever forget.

'We were all so happy,' she says. 'That day in August, we had been joined at the house by a whole crowd of Barra and Katy's friends and we had decided it would be fun to go to the Fifty-Five Club for lunch. Barra, Claude and some of the other kids had motor-bikes so we decided that they would go ahead and that I would follow in the Range-Rover with all the others.

'The last thing I remember about Barra that day was that as I was waiting for her friends to get themselves together, I suddenly noticed two beautiful legs coming down the stairs towards me. It's an image that's ingrained in my memory. I'm not the sort of woman to notice other women's legs, but this pair just struck me as so beautiful. As the rest of their owner appeared, I suddenly realised that these gorgeous legs belonged to my daughter.'

The others set off and Petula piled the remainder into the car and followed on. At the beach, she dropped them off and then went to park the car.

'It was terribly hot,' she says. 'An intense sort of tropical heat. I was sticky and bothered by the time I joined the others and the first thing I noticed was that neither Claude nor Barra had arrived. And everyone seemed to be terribly quiet.

'"Where are they?" I asked.' There was an almost unbearable silence. Then, quietly, one of the youngsters told her: 'There's been an accident. Barra's been hurt.'

'Impossible,' she cried. 'Ridiculous. It can't be.'

It ran through her mind that perhaps these were reckless teenagers playing a cruel, practical joke. But then she saw that their expressions

337

were serious. In a blind panic, she ran back to the car she had parked so happily moments before.

'I drove back along the road to the house like a wild thing,' she says, tears filling her eyes at the memory. 'I was going so fast that I passed the spot where it had happened without realising it and missed seeing Claude who was standing, waving frantically at the roadside for me to stop. I suppose I had expected to see the police or an ambulance. But by the time I drove back, it had all been cleared up and Barra had been taken away.'

From the villa, she phoned the local hospital. Then Claude arrived—and together they set off.

'No one can imagine how primitive that hospital in St Tropez is until they've seen it. Barra was on the bed in the emergency room, in shock. They had given her an injection in the ambulance. And they had to find a surgeon.'

Summer in St Tropez! There were only a few nurses manning the casualty department. The surgeon was sunning himself on the beach during his lunch hour.

'There just didn't seem to be anyone there. No one,' she says.

All her life, Petula had abhorred using her name to gain privilege for herself:

'If I ever entered a shop and heard someone whispering, "Look. That's Petula Clark," and was then given better service than I deserved, I would run out again, as fast as my legs would take me. But this time, I didn't care. This was for Barra, not for me.' All her instincts told her that her daughter's life was at stake.

'For the first time I remember, I let them know exactly who I was. Yes! I told them. It's *my* daughter. Now do something. Quick.'

After what seemed like an eternity, the surgeon was located and set to work. Barra, wearing only a mini-skirt and sandals over her bathing costume, had been turning right on the right-hand side of the road. A motorist had been turning at the same time. The car had caught her and almost ripped her right leg off entirely.

'The surgeon had to remove bits of the road from her leg and then work on the small amount of muscle that was left,' Petula says. 'The operation took more than three and a half hours. Claude and I sat in a waiting-room unable to say very much. We watched other accidents coming in. There was one poor man who had got his leg caught in the propeller of his boat and he had to have it amputated. They told us afterwards that Barra had been very, very lucky not to have to have hers amputated as well. But, even watching all that, all we could think of was our daughter.'

The worst cases from the village hospital at St Tropez are usually transferred to the large general hospital at Marseilles where every modern facility is available. But Barra had lost too much blood and was too ill to be moved. For the first three days and nights, her parents sat at her bedside turn by turn.

'Everybody was great,' Petula says. 'Gradually she improved and her friends came in to see her. I used to take her food in every day and it became a great part of the central play to see me arriving with Barra's meals. There was no security at the hospital at all and her chums used to climb in through the windows. The whole thing turned into a huge party. I think it was partly that that pulled her through.'

Barra's leg was plastered from thigh to toe. As soon as it was medically safe, both parents were naturally anxious to take her home to Geneva and the best medical care that money could buy. But going home was not as easy or as delightful as it sounded.

'She suffered from terrible insecurity at first,' Petula explains. 'I sat with her night after night. She couldn't sleep, partly from pain and partly from the dawning realisation of what had happened to her—and what might have happened. We had long conversations. Conversations which I am not prepared to talk about and of a kind we hadn't been able to have for many years.

'You can talk to your children all their lives and think you understand them. And still have problems. What's good for one child is not necessarily good for another. Both our daughters had had ·the same upbringing and shared the same experiences. But it wasn't until Barra and I talked at this time that I fully understood the different effect it had had on them both.'

It was clear to Petula that Barra's mental and physical road to recovery would be long and arduous. Once again, she made up her mind that her daughter came before her career. There was no question of going on any long tours or undertaking any large projects in the foreseeable future. Or so she thought.

CHAPTER TWENTY-FIVE

THE SOUND OF MUSIC

In the autumn of 1979, Petula was settling down to a life of semi-retirement in Geneva, helping Barra to recover from her traumatic accident. In London, *The King and I* starring Yul Brynner and Virginia McKenna was drawing to a close after a hugely successful second stage run—and impresario Ross Taylor was debating how he could follow it.

'The executors of the Rodgers and Hammerstein estate had been absolutely thrilled by the reception of *The King and I* and asked me what I would like as a gift from the estate,' he says. 'I told them jokingly that I would like *The Sound of Music*. I didn't give it much more thought but about a month later, I received a letter asking me to go to New York to discuss any proposals I had for restaging the show. I told them I wanted to present it in a way in which it had never been presented before. Then they asked me who I thought would play "Maria". There was only one name in my mind. Petula Clark.'

The executors thought it was a wonderful idea but Ross's next problem was to secure the proposed leading lady.

'I approached her agent saying that I wanted to stage a show at London's Apollo Victoria Theatre, which had been used as a variety show-house in recent years. Believing that I wanted her to star in a variety show, Petula agreed to see me.

'By this time it was November. When I went to see her in her London flat, I took her two dozen red roses. She had a filthy cold; her eyes were red and her nose was streaming. She was huddled up in jeans and a great thick jumper. I knew that things had not been going too well for her in her personal life and she wasn't in a very good mood. She knew that I was going to ask her to do something.'

Ross Taylor is an impresario in the grand sense of the word, an imposing, tall, grey-haired man with a mission in life—to alter and improve the opportunities of the great stars who surround him.

'When I first mooted the idea of *The King and I*, Yul Brynner was waiting for people to bring him to England. I felt the same way about Petula. But when I said to her, "How about *The Sound of Music?*", her first reaction was a very firm "No".

'I found out later that she has a tendency to say no before she says yes,' he says laughing. 'I took her out for lunches and for dinners. Eventually, she agreed that she would give me an audition—it was she who insisted on it, not I. Kenny Plane was her accompanist and I was enchanted by her but still she wouldn't give me an answer.'

Gradually, curiosity overcame her reluctance. She wanted to know who would co-star with her should she accept the part. When Ross told her he wanted June Bronhill, Honor Blackman and Michael Jayston, she didn't believe they would agree.

'Eventually,' he says, 'I took her out with Claude and after a meal I asked her straight—"Are you going to play Maria or not? It's getting near Christmas and I've got to open the box-office. Even though it wasn't scheduled to open until the following August, I like to do a big advance thing." This time, she looked straight at me and said: "OK. For you."'

It was twenty-four years since Mary Martin

343

had first opened as Maria in *The Sound of Music* on the London stage and almost twenty years since Julie Andrews had cocked an ear a'top a Swiss mountain to hear if the hills were alive. Petula's initial reaction to the offer was, no doubt, swayed by the hated comparisons with Julie which were inevitable in the circumstances, as well as the fact that she was now forty-eight years old and had never played in a stage musical. She was unsure of herself; of where she was going and what she was doing. She had recently formed a small group with four young Frenchmen and had declared that she intended to set off on the road again. She had one unfulfilled ambition left and that was to star in a stage musical—but a new one, written tailor-made for her.

Her agreement to step into Maria's part met with the predictable reaction from the critics that she was (a) too old and (b) following in Julie Andrew's footsteps. She determined that, no matter what, if she took the part she would do it in a way which would make the role entirely her own.

When the announcement was made in January 1981, again the rumours of a marriage rift flared, this time sparked off by—of all things—the attentions of an over-ardent fan.

In late 1980, Claude explains, one persistent male began showering her with bouquets of red roses—and for some inexplicable reason, it was more than he could bear: 'I should have known better but I made such a scene that Petula ran out of our flat in Geneva, slamming the door. She flew to London. When she cooled off, she came back to Megève and the family spent a quiet Christmas together before she flew back to London to begin rehearsals. But a journalist caught a whisper of what had happened. A report appeared in an American magazine claiming that she had run from the apartment screaming, "We're divorcing."'

'Nothing could have been further from the truth,' Petula contends hotly. 'All the years Claude and I have been together our private lives have been free of any hint of scandal. We are proud of our record. We *are* something of a record in show-business and, come to think of it, any marriage which lasts twenty years is a bit of a record these days. Claude and I are an institution.'

The couple had already worked out a formula for keeping their relationship close while she spent an initial eight months rehearsing and promoting the new version of *The Sound of Music* in England and Austria and then fulfilled her nine-month contract until May 1982, with a three-month renewal option.

Claude would continue with his business as usual, commuting between their flat in Geneva, the chalet in Megève and the tiny flat he shares with daughter Katy on Avenue de la

Bourdonaisse in Paris, while Petula would remain during the week at the rented Knightsbridge flat. Whenever possible, he would come to London for weekends so that together they could visit young Paddy at his prep school in Chichester and Ann at her home in nearby Middleton-on-Sea or bring Paddy up to the London flat.

One of Ross Taylor's most brilliant innovations was to introduce the real Baroness Von Trapp, on whose life-story the musical is based, into the picture for the first time. The old lady who, coincidentally, as one of the 'Von Trapp Family Singers' had worked for the BBC and Petula's mentor Cecil Madden back in 1937, loved Petula from the moment they met.

'Petula studied the real Maria to the tiniest detail,' says Ross Taylor proudly. 'She watched the way she walked and the way she moved and spoke. Maria Von Trapp came with us to Nonnberg Abbey in Austria where it all began. She and Petula became very close.

'Maria had only ever been back to the Abbey a couple of times since she left to marry the Baron. The Mother Abbess of what is a very closed order would not let any photographers inside. While we were taking pictures, Maria started tugging Petula's hand saying that she had something she wanted to show her. She took her to see the corridor and the passageway through which she had walked on her wedding day back to the outside world as the Baroness Von Trapp.

'I asked if we could take pictures inside but the answer was a firm "No". No man had ever been allowed inside the cloisters and all our photographers were men. But then Maria took pity on me and went to speak to the Mother Abbess. When she came back, she said that the Mother Abbess had agreed to just one photograph of Petula and Maria Von Trapp.'

The rehearsals were extremely hard work, especially since the same laws which had once posed so many problems for Leslie Clark regarding the use of children in live performances governed the children in the show in which Petula was now working. There had to be changes every eight weeks—and rehearsals had to begin all over again with each set.

Aside from the rehearsals, the prepublicity demanded by the restaging of such an show was enormous. Mary Martin, the original Broadway and London Maria, flew in from the States to appear with Petula and Leslie Bricusse on *Parkinson* and the two girls sang a duet together on the show. Afterwards, Mary was quoted as saying that she believed Petula would be the best Maria yet.

Despite the view of the press that she was too old for the part—and all the dreaded comparisons with Julie Andrews—Petula opened to enormous acclaim on 18 August 1981.

It was, without doubt, a vibrant and youthful interpretation—as vivacious and charismatic as any performance she had given anywhere in the world. True to his word, Ross Taylor's presentation was remarkably different from any that had gone before. The sombre tone of the period had been cleverly preserved amid the joyful, tuneful and sometimes soulful music. There had been no attempt to gloss over the horrors of the Jewish predicament or the Nazi takeover of Austria.

Among the audience on the opening night sat the elderly Baroness Maria Augusta Von Trapp. To Petula, the old lady's appraisal of her portrayal of the novice nun who can't stop singing and marries into aristocracy was more important than the comments of any critic.

'If I never see *The Sound of Music* again, this is the way I want to remember it—and I want to remember Petula's performance as the greatest performance of Maria,' she told Ross Taylor.

That same night, Petula stood in the centre of the stage—as tiny and frail-looking as ever—to receive a standing ovation and no fewer than twenty curtain calls. Press and public alike greeted her début in the stage-musical world with an enthusiasm and delight even she had not thought possible.

'When she woke up next morning, she was the toast of the West End stage,' Ross Taylor says proudly. 'I had known she would be, of course. That woman can do absolutely anything.'

As with everything she had undertaken during her forty-year-plus career, co-stars and directors and producers alike could not fail to be impressed by Petula's total professionalism, even in the face of problems. At Christmastime, she had gone shopping with her son Paddy in a London store. Since living in America, she had always been in fear of personal attacks on herself and her family and when, as she stopped to examine some purchases she was about to make, Paddy apparently disappeared, she was panic-stricken.

Without thinking twice, she ran out of the store screaming his name at the top of her voice. Suddenly, she experienced every shopper's dread—the hand of a store detective on her shoulder. She found herself accused of shop-lifting. Moments later, as she tried to explain, Paddy reappeared. He had simply wandered to another counter to examine something that had caught his eye. But the news of the 'arrest' was splashed across the headlines that evening.

'It was horrible,' Petula says. 'I believe I reacted as any mother would have done in the same situation. But because I was who I was, it made headline news. It left a very nasty taste.'

She flew home to Geneva with Paddy on Christmas Eve to spend the holiday with her family, but on Boxing Day she was back for her performance as bright as ever but with another of her vicious colds.

'Claude rang me to say that she had laryngitis and the doctor had said she couldn't sing,' Ross Taylor remembers. She came into the office that Friday morning and croaked that there was no way that she could go on. 'I asked her if she had the courage to speak all her lines, including the songs, if I announced the reason and she said she would. We made the announcement and by some incredible miracle she talked her way through the entire performance.'

The following day was Saturday and a double house. Her voice was no better. Ross met Petula who was having lunch with Katy in Overtons, the nearby fish restaurant, and Katy told him that Petula was worried. She didn't know if she could repeat the exercise twice in a single day.

'I told her we were sold out for both performances and that I had to leave the final decision to her. She went ahead—and she sang. We didn't have to give any money back. That is what Petula Clark is all about. She is truly one of the great people of the theatre. People laugh at the word magic but it's a word I use all the time. It's a word I'd use to describe Petula. Magic. Total, professional magic.

'You never hear her complain. She possesses a rare commodity which few artistes possess. She radiates happiness. And despite that illness, and apart from a much needed two-week break in

May, she has never missed a single performance during the entire thirteen-month run of the show.'

On the night of 11 July, Ross Taylor sat in the stalls to watch his show for the umpteenth time. The following morning, he wrote her a letter summing up how he felt:

'Sitting in the stalls last night I was once again carried away by your utter magic and professionalism and total commitment to a world I introduced you to only a short time ago. In years to come, when people talk about one of the great performances of this decade, they will remember your stunningly memorable performance as Maria and all the love and beauty you brought to the role.

'When the show closes on 18 September, it will not be the end but the beginning of another road we shall take together.'

Not the end—not the beginning of the end—but to quote Winston Churchill, Britain's Prime Minister at the time her career began, 'the end of the beginning...'

While Petula was in London for *The Sound of Music*, Britain had been fighting another war, in the Falkland Islands. This time, she took no part in entertaining troops. But it is telling of her character that when the twelve-week battle was over and she was asked to perform at two fund-raising concerts for the war's victims and their families on the same July night, she chose not the prestigious, star-studded London Coliseum show but to appear at a smaller presentation at her 'local' Chichester Festival Theatre.

Now she is planning a long rest. After that—'Perhaps another musical but this time one written especially for me. Or perhaps a straight play. I haven't any definite plans at the moment. We'll have to see.'

Watching the lithe figure in baggy, khaki jeans and battle-jacket slipping out of the stage-door hand in hand with her tall, curly-haired husband after a performance, it was almost impossible to believe that this was a fifty-year-old woman with more than forty years' experience in show-business and twenty-two years of marriage behind her—and not a young girl on her very first date.

It's just the fourth verse in the song of three separate careers which have brought her all the way from England's little 'Pet', through France's 'Petulante Petula', to become the toast of the USA and a grand international star.

The lyrics and music for the rest remain to be composed in the years ahead—as Petula's song flows along in its own, melodious way.

Photoset, printed and bound in Great Britain by REDWOOD BURN LIMITED, Trowbridge, Wiltshire